TICO ROMAO

ACTION SCENARIOS

THE ESSENTIAL GUIDE TO ACTION IN FILM

Superchamp Books SB

New York

Editor, Amir Said

DESIGNED BY AMIR SAID

Cover, Design, and Layout by Amir Said

Print History:
September 2023: First printing.

Action Scenarios: Volume 1
/ by Tico Romao
Author Tico Romao
1. Romao, Tico 2. Film Criticism 4. Movie Criticism
5. Television Criticism
I. Romao, Tico II. Title

ISBN 978-1-64404-004-1 (Paperback)
Library of Congress Control Number: 2023941566

CONTENTS

Introduction

As we enter 2021, one of the outstanding facts about cinema-going during the past three decades is the staggering and enduring popularity of the action film. Amongst the top thirty films that have earned the most worldwide lifetime grosses through theatrical release, twenty are frequently classified as action films or, minimally, films in which action prominently features and is marketed on that basis: *Avatar* (James Cameron, 2009), *Avengers: Endgame* (Anthony Russo and Joe Russo, 2019), *Star Wars: Episode VII - The Force Awakens* (J.J. Abrams, 2015), *Avengers: Infinity War* (Anthony Russo and Joe Russo, 2018), *The Avengers* (Joss Whedon, 2012), *Furious 7* (James Wan, 2015), *Avengers: Age of Ultron* (Joss Whedon, 2015), *Black Panther* (Ryan Coogler, 2018), *Star Wars: Episode VIII - The Last Jedi* (Rian Johnson, 2017), *The Fate of the Furious* (F. Gary Gray, 2017), *Iron Man Three* (Shane Black, 2013), *Captain America: Civil War* (Anthony Russo and Joe Russo, 2016), *Aquaman* (James Wan, 2018), *The Lord of the Rings: The Return of the King* (Peter Jackson, 2003), *Spider-Man: Far from Home* (Jon Watts, 2019), *Captain Marvel* (Anna Boden and Ryan Fleck, 2019), *Transformers: Dark of the Moon* (Michael Bay 2011), *Skyfall* (Sam Mendes, 2012), and *Transformers: Age of Extinction* (Michael Bay, 2014) (from Box Office Mojo).

While many factors have contributed to their box office success, it would be bizarre to claim that the anticipation of action scenes, often showcased through their marketing in the forms of trailers, posters and TV spots, played no role in attracting audiences. A significant component of the popularity of these films likely derives from their extended action sequences. Considering the vital role that they play in contemporary cinema and throughout film history, one would expect a sustained effort within film studies to identify, describe, and theorize such action scenes.

However, when reading the literature on the action film, a lack of clarity about what precisely constitutes action in film is immediately apparent. One of the reasons that this situation has come about is that analytical attention amongst film scholars and critics has been primarily directed at other aspects of action films. One popular approach has been to study action films under the critical framework of gender and masculinity, particularly concerning action stars. Susan Jeffords (1994), for example, examines the masculine traits exhibited by action stars Sylvester Stallone and Clint Eastwood in the *Rambo* (1982-2019) and *Dirty Harry* (1971-1988) franchises. She situates their particular expressions of masculinity within their American political context during the Ronald Regan presidency, viewing them as representative of the politics of the New Right. Yvonne Tasker (1993) has also critically analyzed action films but in relation to the ways in which action heroines and black masculinity are frequently expressed through different forms of gendered and racial identity that do not necessarily advance a New Right agenda in a clear-cut manner that Jeffords presents.

Other approaches to action films have directed attention towards production trends, genre, and spectacle. *In Action Speaks Louder: Violence*, Spectacle, and the American Action Movie (2007), Eric Lichtenfeld presents the action film as a production cycle deriving initially from a combination of the western's plot structure and values with the darker urban milieu manifested in the crime thriller, with *Dirty Harry* (Don Siegel, 1971) proposed as the original progenitor of the contemporary action film. Steve Neale (2000, 55), in contrast, sees the advent of the action film well before the 1970s by observing that the use of the term 'action-adventure' as a generic label was employed as early as the 1920s to describe *The Gaucho* (F. Richard Jones, 1927) in a contemporaneous review published in *Film Daily*. Neale (2000, 57) additionally notes that the casting of women as action stars also arose during the silent era through the popularity of adventure serials that starred female protagonists, such as Pearl White in the lead role in *The Perils of Pauline* (1914).

Another influential approach to understanding action films is within the framework of the 'spectacle' that adopts Tom Gunning's influential account of the cinema of attractions (1986). According to Gunning, the first decade of cinema primarily consisted of films that presented visual attractions instead of offering a narratively constructed world, such as Birt Acres's *Rough Sea at Dover* (1895) that exclusively consists of the sheer spectacle of huge waves crashing into a seawall. Richard Maltby, amongst other film theorists, has attempted to apply Gunning's concept of the attraction to action sequences in films by characterizing them as 'spectacles of movement' that are non-narrative, emphasize visceral thrills over character and story, and temporarily suspend the advancement of the film's plot. As an example of non-narrative spectacle, Maltby cites the celebrated car chase sequence in *Bullitt* (Peter Yates, 1968) and states that "the sequence as a whole emphasizes the general impression of speed for its own sake, rather than developing the narrational possibilities of the scene" (1995, 239). However, this extreme view of considering action sequences as exclusively as non-narrative spectacles is over-stated and has been challenged. I have argued elsewhere that pursuit sequences are narratively constructed, and progress narrative development (Romao 2004), and Geoff King (2002, 185-193) contends that spectacles are typically narratively integrated within a broader story structure of an action film, a logic of narrative integration that Warren Buckland (1998) demonstrates is manifested by the story structure of *Raiders of the Lost Ark* (Steven Spielberg, 1981).

These different perspectives have their value in developing a broader understanding of the action film in its manifold historical and generic forms. However, these perspectives have not made much headway in establishing what precisely constitutes 'action' in the films that these authors discuss. One of this book's main assertions is that the identification of action is an investigation that lies *logically prior* to investigating other types of issues that have been previously pursued in the scholarship on action films. The question of whether action scenes are more spectacle orientated than narrative-driven cannot be adequately answered if what counts as an action scene has yet to be established. Similarly, if the aim is to demonstrate how action scenes integrate with a film's broader narrative structure, then the ability to identify the action scenes in a film before examining how they have been integrated should, arguably, come first.

In a parallel manner, adequately charting the development of the action film either as a genre or as a production trend is difficult if the aspects to be historically tracked are not specified at the outset. Lichtenfeld (2007, 190-191), for instance, points to the disaster film trend of the late 1990s that includes *Dante's Peak* (Roger Donaldson, 1997), *Volcano* (Mick Jackson, 1997) and *Armageddon* (Michael Bay, 1998) as indicative of a mutation in contemporary action film development, but does not identify any features that these films share with previous action films to warrant their inclusion within the broader production trend. Even with respect to questions regarding the main action protagonists' social identity, the issue of what constitutes action is of paramount importance. If the main and privileged loci of agency in action films occur in moments of manifest action, as opposed to situations in a film that are more mundane and are of lesser significance, then the identification of these moments will play a critical role in determining the narrative agency of characters who are female or possess ethnic or racial identities that differ from the standard identity of the white male action hero. To paraphrase Gregory Bateson (1972, 271-272), it is a difference that makes the difference.

The main aim of this book, then, is to establish what action scenes are. In the following chapters, I will show that the most appropriate way to understand them is in terms of the concept of *action scenarios*. In doing so, this book will take a scenario approach that other authors have applied initially to the study of silent-era films but has not been applied comprehensively to understanding action in films. Lea Jacobs and Ben Brewster applied a scenario approach to explain the transition from theatre to early melodrama, where the construction of early silent melodramas relied upon stock situations, situations that resemble what is described here as scenarios. Jacobs and Brewster contend that during this period there was a view that plot in melodramatic theatre and films should be constructed "as a series of discrete moments called 'situations'"

(1997,15). A number of manuals existed at the time that recommended how melodramatic plots were to be constructed, be they employed for theatre or film, with Georges Polti's *The Thirty-Six Dramatic Situations* (1916) one of the more notable guides. Although written in the early 20th century, Polti identifies situations that are frequently manifest in contemporary action scenes. These include 'Deliverance' that entails a rescue, 'Abduction' often involving the capture of women, 'Daring Enterprise' that includes war and combat, and 'Pursuit' entailing both the pursuit of fugitives and their escape from justice. Scott Higgins (2008) more recently highlights the significance of melodramatic situations and applies Polti's scheme to contemporary action films to illuminate their story structure but does not go on to generalize what situations tend to define action as a whole.

Building upon the work of these previous authors, I propose that action scenarios possess the following defining traits: they are event schemas from which action scenes are generated in films; such event schemas additionally have narrative dimensions; action scenarios assume different forms and are historical recurrent throughout the history of film; they entail physical risks to the characters situated in these scenarios; their manifestation is normally found at the local level of a scene or a sequence as opposed to being located at the global level as a type of plot that structures an entire film, or at the even higher level of genre. Since the concept of an action scenario is fundamental to the approach that I am advocating and which is further developed throughout this book, it is necessary to expand upon these traits.

Event Schemas

At the most fundamental level, an action scenario is constructed from an event schema, a term that cognitive psychologist Jean Mandler (1984, 13-15) introduced that describes the knowledge a person possesses concerning the sequence of a particular event. As an example, consider the scenario of purchasing a coffee at a coffee shop. In this scenario a person will have a set of expectations concerning how the event will transpire and knowledge of the likely sequence of events through which the transaction takes place. Such expectations derive from an event schema, a type of mental concept that is held in long-term memory, based upon one's previous experiences of going to coffee shops. This schema will retain the most salient aspects of the event in sketch, such as first entering into a shop, standing in a queue waiting to be served, putting in an order and making payment, and finally being provided with the purchased coffee. Event schemas are also open-ended to accommodate variation based upon novel instances. An event schema therefore can be more broadly understood as a type of concept that is based upon knowledge derived from previous experiences of events and activities, which is subsequently applied to categorize events in the world, whether they are real or fictionally depicted.

Event schemas similarly govern an understanding and categorization of action scenarios, with each type of action scenario defined by the event schema that underpins it. Consider a pursuit sequence as a type of action scenario. When a filmmaker designs a pursuit sequence, they will draw upon its underlying event schema, which itself originates from previously viewed pursuit sequences, and in many cases, from the filmmaker's own experiences creating them for films from script to realization. In a parallel manner, a viewer will apply a similar event schema when watching a chase scene in a film to understand and better follow the action depicted. Such an event schema would most likely represent in sketch a scenario where character A flees from a scene with character B in pursuit with the intent to capture or kill character A. The scenario normally ends with the success or failure of that pursuit. Since an event schema is 'formulaic' in nature (i.e., follows a standard pattern or schema), it can admit creative variations, be it with respect to whether the pursued is a protagonist or an antagonist, or with respect to the means of locomotion, be it on foot, horseback, or some form of vehicle.

Narrative Dimensions

Talk of action scenarios as a sequence of events suggests that they inherently possess narrative dimensions. Film theorists David Bordwell and Kristin Thompson have defined narrative as "a chain of events in a cause-effect relationship occurring in space and time" (2003, 69). If narrative can be considered as a cause-effect chain of events, then it is reasonable to consider action scenarios as proto-narratives that, although they are not full-fledged detailed stories, still manifest story elements and serve broader narrative functions. In addition, action scenes often end with what I describe as an 'aftermath' shot, or set of shots, which depict the consequences of an act of violence, such as a large-scale battle, and usually comes at the end as a form of punctuation that marks closure to the action element of a particular scene. For instance, in *X-Men Origins: Wolverine* (Gavin Hood, 2009), the final shot of its climactic fight sequence, and the film itself, between Logan and his brother Victor against Weapon XI is an overhead shot that registers the destruction that stemmed from their battle that lays waste to much of Three Mile Island [*Figure* 1.1].

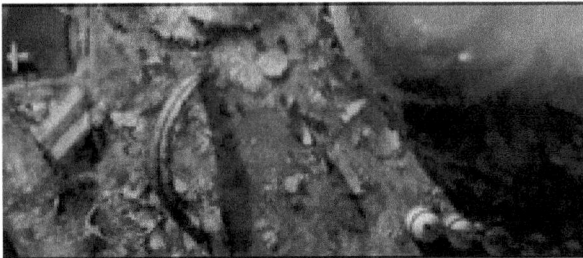

Figure 1.1 Overhead aftermath shot at end of final fight sequence in *X-Men Origins: Wolverine* (2009).

By putting forward the claim that action scenarios possess inherent narrative structure, I want to distance the action scenario approach that I advance in this book from those accounts of action that attempt to understand it in terms of non-narrative notions of spectacle, as was the case with Maltby's description of the car chase in *Bullitt*. The action scenario approach should also be

7

distinguished from those accounts that seek to contrast action as a filmmaking style with the related term 'adventure' that is assumed to possess narrative traits. Film historian Brian Taves (1993, 5), for instance, takes this stance toward action when he describes it as a "style of storytelling that runs through many genres, a male-orientated approach dependent on physical movement, violence, and suspense, with often perfunctory motivation and romance." Taves presents adventure, on the other hand, as a robust genre that possesses more aesthetic value than action and has distinct plot structures that express specific themes and values.

What the style and spectacle perspectives on action fail to acknowledge are the narrative dimensions of action scenarios. Film theorist Murray Smith correctly observes that in action films "the plot advances through *spectacle*; the spectacular elements are, generally speaking, as 'narrativized' as are the less ostentatious spaces of other genres" (1998, 13). In the following chapters, I will show that these narrative dimensions assume five forms that often work in combination and manifest traits that are routinely associated with narrative. These five dimensions consist of: characters that populate action scenarios; the goal-orientated behaviour of such characters; the moral valences of the scenarios themselves; their local narrative structure; and the narrative implications of the scenarios on the rest of a film's story.

The best way to illustrate these points is to refer to a specific example of an action scenario, in this case, one of the crucial fight scenes in *Black Panther*. The kingship ceremony is set atop a giant waterfall that adds additional physical risk to the hazards of the fight. It is a ceremony that also entails proving the candidate's worthiness to assume the throne of the kingdom of Wakanda through physical combat. King T'Challa is challenged by Erik Killmonger, the film's antagonist, who claims the right to the throne by announcing his given name N'Jadaka to prove his birthright as the son of T'Challa's uncle, Prince N'Jobu. As this basic outline already indicates, this fight scene manifests one fundamental aspect of a narrative, namely the centrality of characters to a story. Remove T'Challa and Killmonger from this scene, and there would be no action expressed through physical combat. In fact, if characters are removed from fight scenes, then they cease to function as action scenarios since a fight minimally requires combatants. As I will demonstrate in this book, characters are consequently ineliminable in all types of action scenarios.

In addition to the centrality of characters is their goal-orientated behaviour through which action scenarios gain their narrative meaning. Killmonger instigates the ritual challenge as a result of his plans to assume the throne of Wakanda, and through its vibranium riches and superior weaponry, he plans to a liberate the oppressed black diaspora around the world. T'Challa, in contrast, not only seeks to retain his right to the throne but wants to additionally protect Wakanda from the likely ravages of war it would experience if Killmonger's plans were put into effect. This leads us to the next point. This central fight scene does not solely present the spectacle of action but also manifests a moral valence that metaphorically expresses the main thematic oppositions of the film. Within the moral framework of the film, T'Challa's paternalistic vision of Wakanda's place in the world is presented as the morally correct stance as compared to Killmonger's aggressive aims to foment revolution through war. This moral framework is additionally expressed through their behaviour when T'Challa gallantly offers Killmonger the opportunity for alternative means of resolution prior to the fight, but which Killmonger rebuffs by exhibiting his baser motives for revenge.

As an instance of an action scenario, this fight scene also manifests an internal sequence of events based upon an underlying event schema that lends its dramatic structure. This dramatic structure consists of an orchestration of events through which the ascendency of a combatant is depicted in a fight that eventually reaches a decisive turning point where one combatant normally emerges victorious. Like other action scenarios, the event structure of a fight scene admits variation, including the timing of the central turning point within the scene, which may come at the outset or at the end of a fight scene. Variation is also manifested in terms of outcome as to whether the protagonist or antagonist

9

is victorious, or whether the fight ends with a stalemate with the fight taken up again later in the film or as a rematch appearing in a future installment of a film series. Variation can also arise whether the fight sequence consists of a one-on-one contest between two combatants, such as the fight scene in *Black Panther*, or assumes a larger cast of combatants, such as depicted in the Omaha beach landing sequence in *Saving Private Ryan* (Steven Spielberg, 1998). Further variation can also be introduced with respect to whether the combatants are equal in skill and combative power and can also vary in the selection of weapons, from fists to common utensils to highly futuristic instruments of destruction, all of which have been manifested throughout the history of film.

The fight scene in *Black Panther* again can illustrate these points. To make the combat even, T'Challa is first stripped of his Black Panther superpowers that derive from consuming a heart-shaped shrub local to Wakanda that feeds upon vibranium. With the opponents bearing swords and spears, the challenge commences in a trade of blows with T'Challa becoming initially ascendant by tripping Killmonger into the water and by slicing his cheek with his sword [*Figure* 1.2]. But this cause-and-effect chain of micro-events is reciprocated when it is Killmonger's turn to kick T'Challa into the water and slash his leg [*Figure* 1.3]. This balance is eventually broken when Killmonger ascends by slitting T'Challa's abdomen, and the central turning point of the fight arrives when Killmonger critically wounds T'Challa with his spear [*Figure* 1.4]. With Killmonger now fully ascendant, he beats T'Challa senseless and, when he is on the verge of administering a lethal blow, Zuri, the tribal elder officiating the challenge, intervenes. Zuri confesses to Killmonger that he was the cause of his father's death and that he should take his life instead. Killmonger obliges by lethally killing Zuri with his spear, an act that arouses T'Challa from his vanquished state to attempt one last assault, but he is too weakened, and Killmonger handily responds with a series of punishing blows and tosses T'Challa over the falls to his presumed death.

Figure 1.2 Initial ascendancy as T'Challa trips Killmonger. *Black Panther* (2018).

Figure 1.3 Restoring balance as Killmonger reciprocates by kicking T'Challa down. *Black Panther* (2018).

Figure 1.4 Turning point of fight with Killmonger critically wounding T'Challa. *Black Panther* (2018).

In addition to possessing local narrative structure, action scenarios are additionally narratively significant given the consequences that follow from them. In contrast to the extreme view of the action as spectacle account where action scenes are considered hermetically sealed from the rest of the story in which they are inserted, the narrative consequences of those action scenes are easily ascertained when action scenarios are examined more closely. With respect to Killmonger's victory over T'Challa, narratively significant consequences ensue. Killmonger assumes the throne and sets his plan in motion to deliver Wakanda's advanced weaponry around the globe to foment armed revolutions. Later in the film, T'Challa's supporters discover T'Challa is miraculously still alive but in a comatose state, narratively indicating he had survived his ordeal. When revived through the consumption of the heart-shaped shrub, T'Challa returns to Wakanda and informs Killmonger that the ritual challenge is not yet over. A larger-scale battle commences, this time with T'Challa emerging victorious. In such ways, the fight scene in *Black Panther* illustrates an action scenario instead of representing the antithesis of narrative. The scene patently manifests narrative not only through its goal-orientated characters, moral valence, local narrative structure and causal linkage with the remainder of the film, but most significantly, by also constituting one of the main turning points of the film's plot.

Action Scenario Forms

One of the most glaring omissions in the existing action cinema literature is the lack of a sustained effort to specify action forms in their historical variety. Yvonne Tasker's discussion in T*he Hollywood Action and Adventure Film* (2015) is illustrative. She states that the essential elements of action consist of "physical conflict, chase and challenge" (p. 2) that manifest themselves at the level of action sequences as a "particular kind of scene or spectacle (explosions, chases, combat)" (p. 12). Lichtenfeld's summary also exhibits the same degree of brevity and limited number of scenarios when stating that the "foundation for defining the action movie must be that the films showcase scenes of physical action, be they fistfights, gunfights, swordfights, fights against nature, or other derring-do" (2007, 5). For Tasker, the essential elements of action only consist of physical conflict, challenge, explosions, chases and combat. Lichtenfeld only acknowledges action scenes that offer variations on fighting despite the fact that he goes on to acknowledge other action types in *Action Speaks Louder*, such as the captivity/rescue scenario that he sees as a recurrent feature of the action genre (2007, 89). These summaries list elements, such as physical conflict and challenge, which are either too abstract and broad to be analytically helpful, or so narrow in focus that action is restricted to just one type of action – in Lichtenfeld's case, fights. Most notably, action film scholar Lisa Purse expresses overt reticence to provide "an exhaustive taxonomy" of the variety of types of action forms in her book *Contemporary Action Cinema* (2011), focusing instead on their stylistic traits and sources of pleasure (p. 43).

One of the main aims of this book then is to precisely provide an exhaustive taxonomy of action forms. This book proposes that there are seven major action scenarios that have manifested themselves over the course of the history of film and throughout world cinema. These are: rescue, escape, capture, heist, fight, pursuit, and speed scenarios. This list derives from the analysis of an initial sample of sixty films produced between 1938 to 2019, with films selected from a range of genres, with an eye toward identifying historically recurrent action scenarios. This list is also more representative than the standard and limited reference points of pursuit sequences and fight scenes that action film scholars have standardly identified by capturing the varied narrative situations in which action scenarios manifest themselves in film. This is not to say that action film scholars have not acknowledged other types of scenarios. For instance, in his analysis of *Raiders of the Lost Ark*, Warren Buckland identifies the film's action scenes to include last-minute rescues and escape scenarios (1998, 174-175). But these types of acknowledgements do not go further to situate these instances within a broader set of action scenarios to establish their shared and contrasting traits.

It is also important to recognize that the seven action scenarios identified do not exhaust all the manifestations of action in film. Consider the transfer scene in *The Hunt for Red October* (John McTiernan 1990). Jack Ryan, a CIA analyst, requests to be on board the *USS Dallas*, an attack submarine patrolling the North Atlantic Ocean. But to do so involves flying a helicopter with limited fuel supply to an agreed destination point in stormy weather to lower Ryan via a cable to the submarine. The transfer is fraught with a number of dangers, the hallmark of an action scene, and arguably constitutes a distinct action form. Nor is this scene an isolated instance. Transfers of this ilk can be found in *Airport 1975* (Jack Smight,1974) when a pilot is transferred to a 747 airliner while in flight, as well as *Unstoppable* (Tony Scott, 2010) when a rail employee attempts to board the control cab of a runaway train via a helicopter. Yet beyond a few scattered instances these transfers do not appear as frequently as the seven action scenarios listed above that are the most recurrent action forms and are consequently the most analytically significant where initial focus should be directed.

One significant benefit of comprehending a particular action scene as a manifestation of a distinct type of action scenario is that it better enables one to see the wider class of instances of that action scenario. To better understand this point it is necessary to introduce a set of terms derived from the psychology of categorization, namely *prototypes*, *typicality gradients*, and *exemplars*, features of categorization that were first identified by cognitive psychologist Eleanor Rosch through her pioneering investigations on how colours are universally categorized (1973). A key feature of a category is that instead of all its members being considered equal, they vary considerably with how good an example they are with respect to representing the category in which they are a member. For example, a robin is more representative of the category of birds than penguins or ostriches since the latter cases are unable to fly, a trait considered central to being a bird. Such cases that best represent a category are called prototypes in that they are more recurrent and possess a greater number of defining features of that category, and are consequently more experience near than other members in the same category.

The same considerations apply to action scenarios in that each type of action scenario will manifest its own distinct prototypes. The car chase in *Bullitt* can be said to be more representative of the pursuit scenario and hence more prototypical than the bobsled pursuit sequence in *On Her Majesty's Secret Service* (Peter R. Hunt, 1969), given the novelty of the mode of locomotion in the latter case. Equally, the final shootout in *The Wild Bunch* (Sam Peckinpah, 1969) is arguably more prototypical of the fight scenario given its dynamic nature than the ritualized showdown that ends *The Good, the Bad and the Ugly* (Sergio Leone, 1966) that emphasizes instead stillness and a sudden burst of speed when weapons are drawn. Given the immense variety of action scenes it makes sense then to conceptualize the category that defines a particular action scenario as a typicality gradient that consists of a spectrum in which instances are ranked from those examples that exhibit the greatest degree of typicality to those instances that manifest the least degree of typicality.

In this context, typicality should be understood as the possession of a high degree of the defining attributes of a particular action scenario. Some of these traits derive from event schemas that underpin action scenarios but also include traits that are historically variable. Consider the *Bullitt* example again. During the 1960s and 1970s there was a cycle of films that were influenced by the car chase in *Bullitt*, whose major set pieces consisted of automotive pursuits such as *The French Connection* (William Friedkin, 1971), *Vanishing Point* (Richard C. Sarafian, 1971), *The Seven-Ups* (Philip D'Antoni, 1973), *Dirty Mary Crazy Larry* (John Hough, 1974), *McQ* (John Sturges, 1974), *Smokey and the Bandit* (Hal Needham, 1977), and *The Driver* (Walter Hill, 1978) (Romao 2003, 2004). In this period automotive chases were consequently prototypical of the pursuit scenario and determined its typicality gradient. But the same cannot be said for the period before when westerns, swashbucklers, and samurai films were amongst the dominant modes in which action was expressed and when horseback chases were prominent including, *The Adventures of Robin Hood* (Michael Curtiz, 1938), *Stagecoach* (John Ford, 1939), *Virginia City* (Michael Curtiz, 1940), *At Sword's Point* (Lewis Allen, 1952), *Wichita* (Jacques Tourneur 1955), and *The Hidden Fortress* (Akira Kurosawa, 1958). During this period, horseback chases were as prototypical, if not more so, than automotive pursuits. One of the aims of this book, therefore, is to spell out in greater detail the identifying traits of action scenarios that determine their prototypes, their typicality gradients, and their historical variation. Although this study does not engage in an empirical analysis of what viewers perceive to be prototypical action, the conceptual analyses of action scenarios that follows can serve as a starting point for such an investigation.

Along with prototypes and typicality gradients that underpin categorization, exemplars are specific examples of a particular category that are stored in long-term memory (Murphy 2016). Just as one remembers specific encounters when seeing a robin, filmmakers and viewers both recall memorable action scenes in films that are correlated with specific action scenarios. Such exemplars may not be prototypical and can be memorable for being precisely atypical in certain respects. One reason why the car chase in *Bullitt* attracted attention upon its release was with respect to how it differed from previous car chases. Atypically, it avoided the use of rear-screen projection, the dominant practice at the time, to instead film characters in vehicles that were moving at speed (Romao 2004, 133-134). Such exemplars constitute the basis for filmmaking innovation.

Discussing the production context for the pursuit sequence in *The French Connection*, director William Friedkin refers to the car chase in *Bullitt* as "perhaps the best I've ever seen" and that it "stands forever as a kind of yardstick to shoot at…a challenge for other filmmakers" (1977, 392-393). As such, the car chase in *Bullitt* acted as an exemplar for Friedkin, a concrete memory, on the basis of which he innovated the pursuit sequence in *The French Connection* by depicting the protagonist pursuing by car an assailant who commandeered an elevated subway train instead of the previous standard scenario in which both the pursued and the pursuee are situated in cars. This invocation of previous exemplars as yardsticks that directors use to innovate action scenarios are not unusual in the film and television industries as attested by Miguel Sapochnik's comments about how the Battle of Helm's Deep in *The Lord of the Rings: The Two Towers* (Peter Jackson, 2002) was used as a reference point to create an even longer battle sequence for the 'Battle of the Bastards' episode of *Game of Thrones* (James Hibberd, 2019). In this capacity, exemplars have been significant drivers of the diversification of instances within action scenario forms.

Speaking of action scenarios as distinct categories may give the erroneous impression that they manifest themselves in films in a similar pure and individuated way. But the reality is that more often than not, action sequences in films are combinations of action scenarios. Although the car chase in *The Seven-Ups* primarily derives from the pursuit scenario, the gunplay and vehicular ramming towards the end of the chase is more akin to a fight scenario. The climactic action sequence in *Lethal Weapon* (Richard Donner, 1987) exhibits even greater levels of combination that warrants closer examination as a means to illustrate the ways action scenarios arise and merge with one another.

Martin Riggs and Roger Murtaugh are a biracial cop team who work together to bring down a drug-smuggling operation headed by General Peter McAllister, who leads a group of special forces operatives. In a failed attempt to retrieve Murtaugh's kidnapped daughter, Riggs and Murtaugh are captured. They are then taken to the backrooms of McAllister's hideaway, a Los Angeles club, with Riggs and Murtaugh temporarily separated, with the sequence initially intercutting between both lines of story development. The action sequence commences as Joshua and Endo, two of McAllister's operatives, begin to administer electro-shock treatment to Riggs, who is suspended on ropes, as a means to get him to divulge what he knows about the upcoming heroin shipment [Figure 1.5]. Such an instance of violence realizes the fight scenario but in an atypical way since the fighting is unidirectional with the use of an electro-shock device itself an unusual type of weapon. The action then cuts to Murtaugh, who is tied to a chair and punched by another operative, as McAllister attempts to extract the same information from Murtaugh. When Murtaugh refuses to divulge any information, McAllister orders one of his operatives to apply salt to a bullet wound in his shoulder, thereby mirroring the unidirectional use of violence applied to Riggs [*Figure* 1.6].

Figure 1.5 Unidirectional torturing of Riggs.
Lethal Weapon (1987).

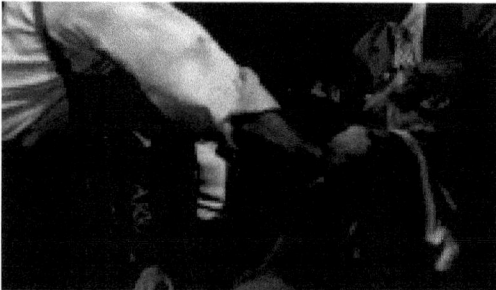

Figure 1.6 Mirroring of action.
Lethal Weapon (1987).

As Endo is about to administer a last and presumably lethal shock, Riggs head-butts him and breaks his neck using his unconstrained legs, with the soundtrack music becoming percussive, signalling ascendancy and the start of an escape scenario. The film cuts back to McAllister, who threatens sexual violence against Murtaugh's daughter. Heroically Riggs bursts into the room at that moment bearing Endo's body on his shoulders, and hurls it at McAllister's operatives [Figure 1.7]. Riggs then proceeds to disable them through bodily force and gunfire, thereby simultaneously enacting the fight and rescue scenarios. With his operatives killed, McAllister flees, instantiating the escape scenario again, while Riggs frees Murtaugh and his daughter. Since the hideaway is still teaming with remaining operatives, they make their way through the club exchanging gunfire with McAllister's men, now combining both the escape and fight scenarios [Figure 1.8].

Figure 1.7 Enacting the rescue scenario.
Lethal Weapon (1987).

Figure 1.8 Combining the escape and fight scenarios.
Lethal Weapon (1987).

As the gunfight rages in the club, Joshua and Riggs trade gunfire with each other until Joshua takes to the street to commandeer a vehicle as a means of escape, with Riggs following in pursuit, with both firing at each other as Joshua speeds away. Riggs gives chase on foot while Murtaugh waits for McAllister to show himself, causing the storylines to split again. As Riggs continues his foot pursuit and Joshua speeds towards the freeway, the action illustrates how the pursuit scenario can decompose to more basic scenarios, namely escape and speed, and in this instance, Riggs' aim to intercept with the intent to kill, an instance of the fight scenario [Figure 1.9 and Figure 1.10]. Riggs eventually catches up with Joshua at an overpass and fires at his vehicle, causing it to burst into flames, combining the fight with the pursuit scenario. Joshua abandons the vehicle after crashing into a pole and exchanges fire with Riggs once again while both are on foot until Joshua commandeers another vehicle [Figure 1.11]. Riggs,

19

however, is accidentally knocked down by a taxi driver, causing Joshua to successfully escape, which ends that plotline of action.

Figure 1.9 Decomposing the pursuit scenario – speed and escape. *Lethal Weapon* (1987).

Figure 1.10 Decomposing the pursuit scenario - pursuing at speed with the intent to kill. *Lethal Weapon* (1987).

Figure 1.11 Merging the fight and pursuit scenarios. *Lethal Weapon* (1987).

The film cuts to the other plotline as McAllister, and his driver, enter their vehicle loaded with heroin and hand-grenades to escape. Murtaugh awaits at the end of the alley with an appropriated pistol, with the intent to kill McAllister, enacting the fight scenario basic to the police thriller. McAllister orders his driver to run him down but Murtaugh responds by firing at the driver, killing him at the wheel, with the action manifesting an atypical fight scenario where a handgun and a speeding vehicle are used as weapons. McAllister attempts to steer the vehicle from the passenger seat but when reaching the intersection collides with a bus that overturns his vehicle, thus bringing an end to his planned escape [Figure 1.12]. Murtaugh approaches the burning vehicle with a gun in hand, still with the aim to kill McAllister, yet the flames set off the grenades, causing the vehicle to explode in a fiery ball of fire, illustrating the destruction scenario, a subcategory of the fight scenario that I will go onto discuss in Chapter 5 [Figure 1.13]. Thus, within a ten-minute-plus-action sequence the escape, rescue, fight, pursuit, and the destruction variant manifest themselves in ways that combine and merge action scenario forms, that are all ultimately based upon character goals.

Figure 1.12 McAllister's escape foiled.
Lethal Weapon (1987).

Figure 1.13 Enacting the destruction scenario.
Lethal Weapon (1987).

This analysis of the climactic action sequence in *Lethal Weapon* also illustrates two notable ways in which action forms combine that warrant their own terms to highlight their differences. Horizontal combination refers to the ways action forms link up sequentially as an action sequence unfolds over time. Vertical combination, in contrast, refers to the means by which action forms combine concurrently. With respect to the *Lethal Weapon* sequence, horizontal combination manifested itself consecutively first as an escape, then rescue, followed by another escape, then segued to a pursuit, to end with a fight and destruction. Horizontal combination alternatively was first manifested when Riggs' escape was combined with a fight scenario, an action form that continued to piggyback onto the remaining scenarios throughout the sequence. In addition, during those moments when Riggs fired upon Joshua, his respective antagonist was at the same time equally determined to escape, thereby vertically combining the fight and escape forms as well. Horizontal and vertical combinations, therefore, are important concepts that assist in the analysis of actions sequences and will be employed in the chapters that follow.

Physical Risk

Although action scenarios vary considerably in terms of their instances over the course of film history, there is one defining property that they all share – the threat of physical risk to the characters situated in those particular scenarios. The analysis of risk in film has itself been for the most part overlooked in film studies and is critical to the understanding of action scenarios, although has become a focus of recent investigation. As Paisley Livingston has correctly observed, the threat of "physical injury and death is the staple of the horror, crime, war, and action genres" with risk a defining feature of these genres (2012, 73). Rikke Shubart, in addition, invokes the sociological concept of edgework, the study of risk-taking as leisure activity, and applies it to television series narrative as well as a mode of spectatorship in relation to depicted action (2019, 421-422). This threat of physical risk can be an element that characters experience directly or is inherently potential in the action scenario.

Consider the heist scenario. In some instances, the risk of physical harm and death is palpably present such as in the central bank robbery sequence in *Heat* (Michael Mann, 1995) in which the bank guards are bludgeoned into submission by the robbers, a bank employee is slugged to release the key to the vault, and the robbers exchange automatic gunfire with police officers that results in fatalities to both parties, gunfire that additionally poses a broader danger to bystanders. In contrast, compare the heist scene in *Mission: Impossible* (Brian De Palma, 1996) in which Ethan Hunt, an agent for the Impossible Missions Force, and his team infiltrate CIA headquarters to steal a list of its agents from a terminal in a secured vault. The physical risk derives not from the danger of merely being caught but that the CIA guards are armed with the implication that the threat of capture could turn lethal, a point illustrated when Hunt neutralizes one of the armed guards prior to entry into the vaulted room.

Another important aspect of physical risk is that its depiction in film is a significant driver of innovating action scenarios. Filmmakers have constantly added novel ways to add risk to existing action scenarios. Fight scenes offer endless variation by heightening risk, normally in relation to their setting. In *Lust for Gold* (S. Sylvan Simon, 1949), the climactic confrontation between Barry Storm and Deputy Ray Covin, who are both searching for a lost gold mine, engage in a brutal fistfight atop mountainous cliffs that pose the additional danger of falling to one's death. In *True Lies* (James Cameron, 1994), the fight scene takes place on a Harrier Jump Jet as Harry Tasker, a government agent, is in the cockpit and fights off a terrorist, with Tasker's daughter hanging onto the plane all the while. *The Wolverine* (James Mangold, 2013) places the action in one crucial scene of an extended fight sequence on top of a speeding commuter train as Logan, a genetic mutant, fights off yakuza gang members. Obi-Wan Kenobi and Anakin Skywalker duel it out with their lightsabres in *Star Wars: Revenge of the Sith* (George Lucas, 2005) on an erupting planet, first in a facility that collapses into a volcano with the fight then continuing as they ride its fragments down a lava flow. One setting of the action in *Pirates of the Caribbean: Dead Man's Chest* (Gore Verbinski, 2006) is particularly extravagant as a three-way sword fight for possession of a key extends onto a giant water wheel that detaches from its mill and rolls down the island, making their fight even more precarious for the three participants as they continue with the swordplay. In such ways, scenes can become exemplars of risk enhancement for other filmmakers to attempt raise the bar even further.

Local vs Global Level of Manifestation

As my discussion has indicated, I have not attempted to define action either at the level of the entire narrative of a film, as an action film, or at the broader level of genre, as an action film genre. I have done so since one of the main aims of this book is to make the case that action is primarily manifested at the local level of the scene or sequence. One reason for this focus is that while different action scenarios can arise over the course of a film, the entirety of a feature film, as opposed to a short film, rarely if ever consists of one elongated action sequence. It would be exceptional for an action scenario to be played out over the entirety of a feature-length film, given the difficulty of maintaining spectator engagement. There are films whose titles suggest that are structured as such, but closer inspection indicates that they are not. The title for *The Great*

Escape (John Sturges, 1963) suggests that the entire film entails an escape scenario, but a considerable amount of time entails digging the tunnels rather than actually escaping. War films focused on a particular battle like T*ora! Tora! Tora!* (Richard Fleischer, Toshio Masuda, Kinji Fukasaku, 1970) similarly portray events leading up to an attack. In addition, although action sequences have become longer over time, most of the extended ones tend to be restricted to the final act of a film, such as the epic battle sequence in *13 Assassins* (Takashi Miike, 2010) that runs close to 45 minutes, as opposed to covering the entire duration of the film in which it is situated. Since the types of narratives in which actions scenarios appear can vary considerably, as well as the extent of their appearances, it makes more sense to restrict the analysis of action scenarios to their local manifestations than to attempt to study action at the level of a film's story.

Since one of the main ways film genres are identified are by their recurrent types of narratives, the same problems arise with attempts to define action at the level of genre. Action scenarios can arise within romantic comedies, such as the concluding pursuit sequence in *What's Up, Doc?* (Peter Bogdanovich, 1972) or within horror films such as the final battle with the vampire creatures in *From Dusk till Dawn* (Robert Rodriguez, 1996). Indeed, acknowledgements of the different type of genres in which action appears are routine. James Kendrick, for instance, states that the action film becomes a "recognizable genre" (2019, 36) in the latter half of the twentieth century and charts its evolution through 1960s westerns, vigilant films, car chase films, blaxploitation, martial arts films, disaster films, science fiction, buddy cop films nostalgic adventure, and superhero films. However, Kendrick never establishes what these genres have in common to categorize them as action films.

What these film cycles share is a reliance upon certain action scenarios but in a manner that does not supersede the genres through which they have been primarily classified. What is labelled a car chase film can be better understood as a road movie or crime/police thriller that contains automotive pursuit sequences amongst other generic traits. In Kendrick's list, only the martial arts film can be said to be specifically characterized by a type of action scenario, namely a fight scenario that showcases martial arts. Yet martial arts scenes do not exhaust what defines martial art films since there are other defining elements such as reluctant heroes, training sequences, apprentice and master relationships, and often period setting. Consequently, it is better to understand martial arts scenarios as just one element of the martial arts film, albeit an essential trait. The same can be said for those other genres that are routinely identified with the action film. As this book will demonstrate, certain types of action scenarios do tend to be affiliated with certain genres, such as the western and its recurrent horseback pursuit sequences, stampedes, barroom brawls, and showdowns. By identifying action scenarios with greater precision one can gain a better understanding as to what makes these varied genres distinct.

The chapters that follow are dedicated to outlining a specific action scenario to better detail its defining traits and variations, with reference to illustrative examples. Chapter 1 examines the rescue scenario where the agency of the rescuer is compared to that of the captive. In Chapter 2, I turn to the escape scenario that is primarily differentiated from the rescue scenario on the basis of the agency exhibited by the escapee. Chapter 3 looks at the capture scenario that often accompanies the escape scenario but can be manifested on its own as an action form and possesses its own distinctive features that are highlighted. In Chapter 4, I discuss the heist scenario in its prototypical form and outline its spectrum from petty theft to major robbery set pieces. Chapter 5 turns to the fight scenario from its one-on-one instances to cases that involve countless combatants. The chapter also investigates how the fight scenario manifests itself within the sports film. In Chapter 6, I examine the pursuit scenario to show how it can be decomposed to more basic action elements as well as describe its various modes. Chapter 7 outlines the speed scenario, one of the purest action forms, and in addition to detailing its variations in film, the chapter examines its manifestation in the racing film. In

Chapter 8 I turn to the issue of narrative complexity and how it is manifested in extended action sequences that are normally found in the last act of a film.

Chapter 1: The Rescue Scenario

"Another definition of a hero is someone who is concerned about other people's well-being and will go out of his or her way to help them, even if there is no chance of a reward. That person who helps others simply because it should or must be done, and because it is the right thing to do, is indeed without a doubt a real superhero."

—Stan Lee[1]

Arguably, no other action form expresses the moral trait of the hero as well as the rescue scenario. After all, as Marvel Comics legend Stan Lee highlights, the defining feature of a hero is to undertake actions that protect the welfare of others. As an action scenario, the rescue narrative has been traced to films as early as *Attack on a China Mission* (James Williamson, 1900) and *Fire!* (James Williamson, 1901) (Grey 2019, 221-234). How this heroism is filmically expressed, though, is best understood through the lens of the rescue scenario prototype.

The Rescue Scenario Prototype

Edwin S. Porter's Life of an American Fireman (1903) is an important film concerning the early development of film narrative, but it is also significant in that it portrays the rescue scenario in an almost pure form. Around six minutes in length, the film commences with a fire chief, seated asleep on a chair, who appears to be dreaming. He has a vision of a mother and child, who the viewer infers are in peril by his agitated pacing when he wakes up. The film cuts to the hand of someone pulling a fire alarm on a street, causing the firemen to dress hastily, slide down a pole, and race off to the fire in their horse-drawn engines, invoking the

---

[1] Quoted in O'Connor, Tom. 2018. 'Stan Lee Quotes: Legendary Comic Book Creator Dies at 95', *Newsweek*. 12th November.

speed scenario in the process. The firemen arrive at the burning building with the film cutting to the same room depicted in the vision but this time billowing with smoke. A fireman bursts through the door and breaks the window. He then carries the mother and child, one at a time, down a ladder to return with another fireman to extinguish the flames using a water hose. The film ends with an exterior shot of the building and the mother and child embracing in relief.

In many ways, Life of an American Fireman manifests the traits of an action scenario as outlined in the Introduction. But it is the rescue scenario, in particular, that is played out in this short narrative. As film historian Charles Musser points out, the fireman rescue scenario was prevalent in popular culture at the time of the film's release, appearing in lantern shows, songs and even in previous films (1991, 218). As a result, most spectators had a fairly well-formed event schema of the rescue scenario and the type of events that it entailed. Indeed, given the fragmentary nature of film narratives during this period of film history, spectators required prior knowledge of the kinds of events depicted to facilitate their understanding of these filmic stories.

Most critical to this understanding was the knowledge of the characters' roles in the rescue scenario. These can be principally categorized as the *captive* and the *rescuer*, and in some cases, captors who additionally keep the captive confined. Typically, the captive is unable to extricate themselves out of the situation they are in by their own means, whereas the rescuer is routinely presented as agential if not heroic. This dichotomy is visibly evident in *Life of an American Fireman*, where the mother is presented as helpless, collapsing on the bed and lacking the agency to free herself and her child from the burning building, no doubt a helplessness also consistent with prevalent notions of gender and femininity [Figure 2.1]. By contrast, the fireman is actively agential as he bursts into the room and breaks open the window to create a means of escape [Figure 2.2]. As a proto-narrative, the rescue scenario also entails goal-oriented behaviour of the principal characters that propels the scenario's cause and effect structure. In the case of *Life of an*

American Fireman, the firemen are the sole figures that manifest goal-oriented behaviour by rescuing the woman and child and putting out the fire, given their occupational function. However, while one can presume that the captive woman desires to free herself and her child from their predicament, she does not engage in any action, leaving the actions of the firemen to drive forward the narrative exclusively. In this context, agency refers to the ability of a character to not only exhibit free will but also to possess the skills and knowledge to pursue their goals.

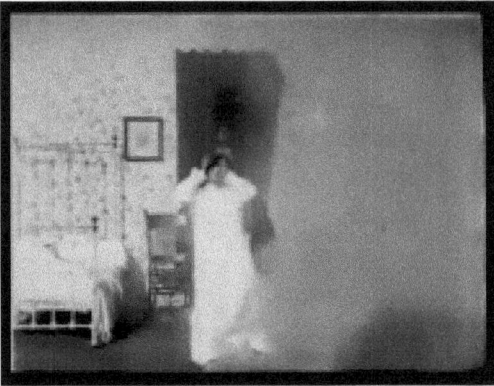

Figure 2.1 The helpless female captive. Life of an American Fireman (1903).

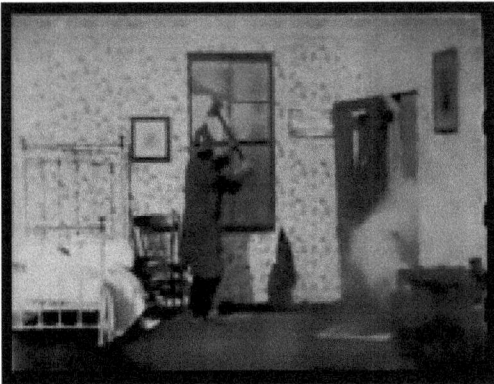

Figure 2.2 The agential male rescuer. Life of an American Fireman (1903).

As noted in the Stan Lee quote, one of the outstanding features of the rescue scenario is its inherent moral valence. The rescue of people in physical danger is normally considered heroic and held in high moral regard, especially if this involves the sacrifice of oneself to save another. In relation to *Life of an American Fireman*, Musser observes, at that time, "the urban firefighter was a working-class hero par excellence, an individual who risked his life to save others" (1991, 222). This moral framework is an enduring feature of the rescue scenario that is later manifest in race-to-the-rescue shorts, silent action serials, western captivity tales, Vietnam POW rescue films, and superhero tales where rescuing amounts to a superhero job description.

Consider the rescue scene in *Pulp Fiction* (Quentin Tarantino, 1994) where Butch Coolidge, a boxer, and Marsellus Wallace, a mobster, are captured by Maynard, a pawnshop owner, and are taken to the basement of the store. Previous to their capture Marsellus had paid Butch to throw a fight, a deal in which he had reneged by winning the match, resulting in them trying to kill each other afterward. In the basement, Marsellus and Butch are secured to chairs with their arms tied behind their backs and are gagged. Maynard invites Zed, a security guard, and brings out 'The Gimp' in bondage costume, making their plans clear to sexually assault Marsellus and Butch. Marsellus is then taken into a backroom where he is raped while the Gimp is ordered to keep watch on Butch. Wriggling his hands loose, Butch is able to free himself and knocks out the Gimp with one punch. He then heads upstairs with the initial intention to escape but pauses at the door. He then searches through the pawnshop for an appropriate weapon and selects a samurai sword. Butch then proceeds stealthily downstairs and kills Maynard with the sword, and dares Zed to pick up his gun. Marsellus gets up, grabs Maynard's shotgun, and shoots Zed in the groin. Butch then asks Marsellus if things are cool between them, to which he agrees upon conditions. Despite the film's broader narrative context of criminality, Butch's decision to return to rescue Marsellus is a moral act in the sense that he could have simply left Marsellus with the rapists, and quite possibly a fate that may have resulted in his death. Butch's actions are additionally heroic given the dangers he took returning to a basement with armed rapists.

This moral framework, of course, can be flipped upside down in those instances in which it is the villain who is imprisoned, and it is their gang that comes to rescue, normally combatting a legal force that is securing the captive's confinement. A good example of the moral inversion of the rescue scenario occurs in *Mission: Impossible III* (J.J. Abrams, 2006), where Owen Davian, an arms dealer and the film's nemesis, is imprisoned in a secured armoured vehicle, travelling in a convoy across the Chesapeake Bay Bridge. Foreign mercenaries hired by Davian use an unmanned aerial drone to attack the convoy, and the mercenaries are able to extract Davian from the vehicle and cut the chains constraining him. Beyond arranging the extraction, Davian demonstrates no ability on his own to escape from the secured vehicle and must rely upon the mercenaries to rescue him.

Rescue sequences, like other action forms, possess a dramatic structure through which ascendency is arranged. The fundamental dramatic question that the rescue scenario poses is whether the rescuer will be successful in their attempt to rescue the captive. Dramatic turning points, therefore, consist of the narrative obstacles that impede the rescue progress, with the decisive threshold moment consisting of either the rescuer successfully extracting the captive from their captivity, or the rescue proving unsuccessful, with the rescuers instead captured or killed in the rescue attempt. In continuous rescue sequences, ascendency increases with every obstacle surmounted to the threshold moment, with the chance of a reversal of fortune if any obstacle poses too much of a challenge to overcome. In *Life of an American Fireman*, these obstacles are the door to the room that impedes entry and the window that impedes escape from the fire and smoke.

Like all action scenarios, the rescue scenario is defined by physical risk. Physical risk can arise either with respect to the captive or to the rescuer, or both. In those cases, in which the rescue situation also involves captors, they also often run the risk of danger by encountering rescuers who are willing to use physical force in their rescue attempt. In *Life of an American Fireman*, the helpless mother and child are at risk of being engulfed by the flames, and if they were not at risk, there would be little motivation for their rescue by the firemen or rationale for the film's story itself. Equally, the fireman takes physical risks while attempting the rescue through exposure to fire and smoke, factors that underscore his heroic status in the film. Heroism in the rescue scenario, then, is primarily expressed as the trait of a character who undertakes physical risks with the laudable aim of rescuing others. If physical risks are taken out of the equation with respect to the rescuer, then the less likely that heroism will be attributed to that character by the viewer. Risk is, therefore, an indelible feature of the rescue scenario and its moral valence.

Rescue Combinations

Just as other action scenarios can combine different action forms, so to can the rescue scenario. Its most inherent and frequent combination is with the fight scenario where the rescue effort is met on many occasions with resistance from adversaries who want to keep the captive imprisoned. Such resistance is motivated not just to simply introduce a greater degree of physical risk to the sequence by having the rescuers and the captors engage in battle but to also add suspense by placing obstacles to the rescuers' goal of freeing the captive. If the rescuers do not meet with resistance, and there is no jeopardy to their enterprise, then the viewer will likely take less interest in the outcome of their actions.

The rescue sequence in *Star Wars* (1977) can illustrate these points. While on route to Alderaan onboard the Millennium Falcon to deliver information to the Rebel Alliance, Obi-Wan Kenobi and his team are pulled into the Death Star by a tractor beam. After hiding in the smuggling compartments of the Millennium Falcon, they overpower the scanning crew and two stormtroopers. Luke Skywalker and Han Solo then disguise themselves as stormtroopers to sneak into a security room and neutralize the guards stationed there. Obi-Wan separates from the group to disable the tractor beam, a mission that leads to his fateful rendezvous with Darth Vader, thus creating an additional storyline that the film cuts to as the sequence unfolds. Meanwhile, R2-D2 discovers while hooked up to Death Star's computer mainframe that Princess Leia is on board and held captive in a detention cell to be eventually executed. Luke Skywalker, taking on the mantle of the hero, recognizes that Leia is at risk and convinces a reluctant Solo and Chewbacca, through the possibility of financial gain, to attempt a rescue. In so doing, the film lays out the implicit physical risks of the enterprise: ultimate bodily harm awaits Princess Leia through her scheduled execution with Solo's reticence signalling the risks of possible death or imprisonment by trying to rescue Leia from her detention cell.

It is at this point the rescue sequence starts in earnest, embedded within the broader objective to escape from the Death Star in order to save their own lives and to deliver the information stored within R2-D2 to the Rebel Alliance. Skywalker and Solo disguise themselves as stormtroopers under the ruse that Chewbacca, placed in unlocked handcuffs, is their prisoner, who they are transporting to the detention center. They reach a set of prison guards who are suspicious of the transfer leading to a shoot-out in which the guards are presumably killed or at least rendered immobile. The rescue sequence thus segues seamlessly into a fight scene, in an instance of vertical combination, as a result of the rescue scenario's underlying event schema in which rescue attempts normally encounter some form of resistance, often in the form of armed captors [Figure 2.3]. Skywalker locates Leia's cell and announces that he is here to rescue her and that Obi-Wan and R2-D2 are with him. Freed from her cell and now with her rescuers, the sequence shifts into an escape scenario, a horizontal combination that is also vertically combined with fight scenes, as they battle their way back to the Millennium Falcon. In such ways, the sequence exhibits multiple action forms as a rescue scenario combined with multiple fight scenes while also embedding an escape within the sequence.

Figure 2.3 Obstacle and vertical combination of rescue with fight scenario. *Star Wars* (1977).

Rescue Scenario Variations

In discussing the rescue scenario in relation to a captive whose agency is restricted by some sort of physical confinement, I have been outlining the scenario's prototypical form. However, rescue scenes have manifested themselves in ways where a rescuer is present, but the rescuee is not captive in this strict sense. Since the rescuer as character type is a constant in the rescue scenario, the more fundamental variation in the scenario's typicality gradient is to be found in the ways in which the restrictions on the captive's agency are expressed in different rescue situations. One major variant of the prototype is that the captive is not literally confined but does not possess the ability or resources to escape out of the endangering situation and is, so to speak, 'trapped' in the situation.

Superman Rescue Variants

The final action sequence in *Superman* (Richard Donner, 1978) offers ten specific instances of rescue that can illustrate divergences from the prototypical rescue scenario [see Table 1]. Lex Luthor, Superman's arch-enemy, has purchased worthless desert land east of the San Andreas Fault with the aim of transforming it into prime real estate. To do so, Luthor diverts two nuclear missiles during a joint US Army and Navy exercise with one missile headed toward a random target to act as a diversion and the other missile headed toward a particular point of the San Andreas Fault with the aim of splitting California's landmass and causing any land west of the fault to sink into the Pacific Ocean. Superman is lured into Luthor's underground hideout where the villain proudly reveals his plans, exposes Superman to a piece of kryptonite that is affixed to a heavy chain necklace, and then hangs it around Superman's neck, thus rendering him powerless. Luthor then shoves Superman into a deep pool of water to presumably drown.

Eve Teschmacher, Luthor's girlfriend and accomplice, learns that the target of the diversionary missile is Hackensack, New Jersey, the town in which her mother lives. Superman persuades her to save him from drowning, but Teschmacher first extracts a promise from him to save her mother first from the impending missile impact. Superman assents, triggering the sequence's first rescue. Weakened by the Kryptonite, Superman does not possess the strength to remove the chain necklace from his body and even struggles to remain afloat. It is at this point, then, that Luthor is at peak ascendency by temporarily vanquishing Superman, allowing his nefarious plans to proceed unimpeded.

Table 1: Superman (1978) Rescue Sequence Breakdown*

Rescues	Section 1	Section 2	Section 3	Section 4
1 Superman drowing	(2) Luthor shoves Superman into the pool	(3) Eve removes Kryptonite necklace		
2 Hackensack missile	(1) Luthor diverts missile	(4) Superman redirects missile		
3. Lois Lane	(5) travelling in desert	(8) falling powerlines	(18) Lane's car sinks	(20) Superman reverses time
4. Jimmy Olsen	(6) Hoover Dam	(15) dam collapsing	(17) Superman carries Olsen to safety	
5. Californian citizens	(7) fault line	(12) Superman lifting up the plate		

Rescues	Section 1	Section 2	Section 3	Section 4
6. school bus	(9) Golden Gate bridge	(11) bus hanging off the bridge	(13) Superman shoves bus to safety	
7. speeding train	(10) falling debris	(14) Superman acts railway track		
8. and 9. power plant workers	(16) Superman shuts off power; workers carry an injured colleague (19) Superman blocks water's path			
10. dam burst				

*The ten rescues in the sequence are listed in the first column. Sections of the ten different rescue situations are numbered in chronological order of appearance in sequence.

While not technically in captivity, Superman's reduced agency deprives him of the ability to save himself, but crucially he has not lost his powers to persuade, thereby illustrating that the loss of agency can be graduated. In a reversal of the convention of the helpless maiden manifest in many rescue scenes, Teschmacher dives into the pool and frees Superman by removing the chain necklace and tosses it away to a safe distance causing Superman's superpowers to return. Superman then hurtles into the sky to pursue the eastbound missile through a desert landscape, once again illustrating how action scenarios can vertically combine. Superman eventually catches up to the missile and redirects its trajectory to explode in the Earth's upper atmosphere, thereby saving the townsfolk of Hackensack from nuclear annihilation. In the process, Superman starts to gain ascendency as Luthor's schemes are thwarted.

Captivity in this particular situation takes on a different non-literal and non-prototypical form. The citizens of Hackensack are not literally captive inside an enclosed space but are captives nonetheless of the impending strike by being unaware that they are at risk. First and foremost, to possess the agency to escape, one first must possess an awareness of the *need to escape*. Even if the townsfolk were aware of their situation, there is nothing implied within the film's story that would indicate that they could escape in time before the nuclear blast. Even the military personnel tracking the flight of the missiles, who are aware of the impending destruction, lack the means to regain control of their flight or the ability to shoot the missiles down, leaving Superman the sole figure to save the day. In addition, unlike the prototypical captivity scenario, this rescue is *preemptive*. Superman's efforts are directed at preventing a catastrophic situation from occurring in the future as opposed to the prototypical rescue scenario where the captive is already under threat.

Through parallel editing, the film then cuts to the imminent impact of the westbound missile and reveals Lois Lane, *Daily Planet* reporter and Superman's love interest, out in the desert proximate to the San Andreas Fault. Superman sees the nuclear blast from the Earth's outer atmosphere, with its impact registered next by the military personnel who are portrayed as passive, helpless spectators, and then by Jimmy Olsen, the *Daily Planet's* photographer, who both hears and sees the explosion while at the Hoover Dam.

From this point, the second part of the rescue sequence commences and is more complex than the first, with the rescues enacted at the collective and individual character level. The film depicts the fault widening with Superman going deep into the Earth's crust in an attempt to stop the landmasses from further separating and, it is implied, to save the affected citizens of California from sliding into the ocean. The film then cuts to Lane to reveal the danger she is in as she drives away from an exploding gas station and navigates through powerlines that have collapsed onto the road. We hear over her car radio an emergency announcement detailing the missile's impact and the resulting earthquake, although the film does not make it clear if other threatened Californians hear this message, nor does the film present this additional knowledge as assisting the ability of Californian citizens to escape from the ravages of the earthquake.

The film cuts to the Golden Gate Bridge as it begins to shake and break apart, with the narration focusing specifically on the fate of a school bus filled with high school students as its driver tries to maintain control of the vehicle. The scene shifts again, this time to a speeding passenger train whose passengers are aware of the earthquake through the train's sway and the danger posed by the falling debris. The film cuts back again to the school bus that, as a result of an impact with another vehicle, hangs precariously on the edge of the bridge.

All of these different plotlines function to set up future rescue situations for Superman to resolve. Superman first attends to the fault line, in effect solving the crisis at its source by lifting the collapsed plate deep within the Earth's crust through a colossal act of strength, thereby stopping the plate's downward slide and shifting ascendency to his advantage. Superman thus rescues the affected Californian citizens from the dangers of the earthquake through a superhuman feat that they themselves could not have accomplished, a contrast in agency that repeats itself as a pattern throughout the remainder of the rescue sequence.

The film returns to the Golden Gate Bridge that reveals that the bus is on the verge of falling off the bridge with its occupants unable to exit the vehicle, a deficit of agency to extricate themselves out of their precarious situation. Superman flies into view and shoves the bus away from danger with ease, and then flies off to rescue the occupants in the speeding commuter train. Through the continued aftershocks, the ground begins to separate, causing the tracks above to break, a danger that would cause the train's derailment. The train's engineer spots the danger and immediately applies the breaks in an act of desperation. The engineer does take action but not early enough to prevent the train from derailing, requiring Superman to once again come to the rescue, which he does by bending one of the tracks back into place while using his body as a track that bears the weight of the train as it speeds by.

The film then cuts to the Hoover Dam that has been structurally damaged as a result of the earthquake and begins to collapse, introducing a new set of situations that repeats the narrative pattern of set-up and rescue. The first entails Olsen, who is at the top of the dam as it collapses, and hangs onto a remaining wall, in imminent danger of falling to his presumed death. Next, the dam's power plant begins to explode, causing a high voltage cable to disconnect and whip dangerously through the air. Superman flies into the complex and shuts down its power by switching off the main breaker, an act that rescues the workers but did not require superhuman strength to do so. In this instance, captivity takes on a different complexion from the other rescue situations in the sequence since the power plant workers are aware of the danger, attempt to escape, and even assist in carrying an injured colleague to safety, itself a heroic rescue act. They thereby exhibit some degree of agency. However, none of them seem able to resolve the situation at a more effective level by switching off the main breaker. The state of being captive, in this case, consequently derives from a lack of cognitive wherewithal to redirect attention from the immediate crisis and a panicked escape towards effecting a broader and more level-headed solution, attributes of the heroic if not the superhuman.

The film returns to Olsen, whose grip at the top of the dam is weakening and who is on the verge of plummeting, but Superman arrives just in time and carries him to safety. In other films, action leads are often portrayed in similar situations but able to climb to safety through their own physical ability, as the opening scene in *Mission Impossible II* (John Woo, 2000) attests when Ethan Hunt handily free climbs up a cliff face. Olsen, however, does not show such action lead prowess, and so his 'captivity' within this situation derives from the limits of his own physical strength and dexterity [Figure 2.4]. As the dam bursts, the film cuts to a town downstream that is in danger of being washed away by the onslaught of water. The townsfolk flee from their homes, aware of the disaster to come and evidence agency through their ability to escape by foot or vehicle. It is unclear, though, whether it is sufficient to take them all out of harm's way, and therefore they require Superman's intervention.

Figure 2.4 Jimmy Olsen and the physical limits of his agency. *Superman* (1978).

It is at this point that the final rescue scene of the sequence is introduced when Lane's car stalls while debris perilously tumble-down an adjacent cliff. To make matters worse, the road splits, causing her vehicle to sink into the crevice that has opened up, burying her alive. Preoccupied with the dam burst, Superman speeds past the rushing water and proceeds to create rock slides on both sides of the canyon, creating an improvised stone dam that forestalls the water's advance on the town. When satisfied with his rescue efforts, Superman finally hears in the distance the sounds of Lane in jeopardy and speeds to rescue her. The film cross-cuts between Lane being buried by debris and Superman flying at speed in a style reminiscent of the parallel editing associated with the rescue sequences of D. W. Griffith. This technique generates suspense by posing the question of whether or not Superman will arrive in time. When he does, he pulls the car from the crevice only to find that Lane has died from suffocation, in his first seemingly unsuccessful rescue effort. Unable to accept her death, Superman flies into space and circumnavigates the Earth at such an incredible velocity that he reverses the direction of the Earth's spin, thereby reversing time to the precise moment when Lane's car stalled, just before the crevice appeared. Safely out of danger, Lane's miraculous rescue brings to an end a twenty-four-minute action sequence that commenced with the missiles' launch and establishes Superman as the ascendant power, as reinforced in the film's final scene when he delivers the now vanquished Luthor and Otis to prison.

The Transport Variant

An important variation on the rescue scenario prototype entails not merely that the rescuer frees the captive from a trapped situation but also is required to transport the captive to a point of safety. This variation is present in an incipient form in my original example, *Life of an American Fireman* when the fireman had to carry the mother and child down the ladder since they were unable to leave the room through their own agency. This was also the case in the *Superman* rescue sequence when the plant workers carried an injured colleague out of a building with the aim of taking him out of danger. However, in both cases, the transportation is more inferred than depicted.

An example of the transport variant in its fuller manifestation can be found in Rambo: First Blood Part II (George P. Cosmatos, 1985), when John Rambo, a former Vietnam War soldier, is sent back to Vietnam to confirm reports of American prisoners of war still in custody. After Rambo is captured by Vietnamese forces and escapes from Soviet operatives, he commandeers a Russian helicopter and lays waste to the enemy camp. He then frees the POWs from their bamboo pen and ushers them into the helicopter to then fly them to safety to a nearby American base in Thailand. Significantly, the POWs are too emaciated to attempt escape from the compound through their own agency and, with the exception of one prisoner, the rest are too feeble to assist Rambo as he evades destruction from the pursuing and far superior Soviet helicopter, a pursuit that additionally enacts the pursuit-rescue variant discussed in Chapter 6 [Figure 2.5]. Once again, a contrast is made, this time between the rescuing agency of Rambo and the POWs who lack the ability to breakout of their bamboo prison, let alone outmanoeuvre and outsmart a Soviet helicopter pilot. The sequence additionally illustrates that the rescue extends beyond their mere release from prison to the journey to safety at the American base camp. Their captivity not only derives from the prison but also encompasses the enemy territory in which they are situated and which puts them in jeopardy if caught. Had the POWs, through their own agency, made their way through the enemy territory to the camp, then that journey would be better categorized as an escape. But since they are entirely reliant on Rambo's combat and flying abilities to take them to safety, the sequence exhibits the classic features of the rescue scenario instead.

Figure 2.5 The transport variant and the pursuit-rescue variant exhibiting Rambo's superior agency. *Rambo: First Blood Part II* (1985).

The Embedded Rescue Variant

Another variation on the rescue scenario prototype that reoccurs frequently and warrants further discussion is the embedded rescue scenario. Its embedded nature derives from the fact that the rescue normally occurs within another action form, typically a battle, and which is not long in duration, acting primarily as a component of the larger sequence. The scenario consists of a combatant who is on the verge of being killed by an opponent, but at the last moment, an ally arrives and vanquishes the enemy, thereby saving the life of the combatant. An instance of this variation can be found in the early battle sequence in *Thor: The Dark World* (Alan Taylor, 2013) when Thor, along with his fellow Asgardian warriors Fandral, Volstagg, and Sif, face marauders on the planet Vanaheim that is home to an ally of Asgard. At one

44

point in the battle, a marauder fires a spear from his gun aimed at Thor that is intercepted by Sif with her shield, thereby saving Thor from serious injury if not his life [Figure 2.6]. Critically, Thor had his back turned toward the marauder, unaware that he was in danger, again underscoring the importance of awareness in relation to agency. To possess the ability to defend oneself, one first needs to be aware that one is under attack. Upon hearing the impact of the spear onto the shield, Thor then turns and gazes blankly at Sif, who ironically says "you're welcome" to underscore her rescuer status. What is of interest in this rescue situation is how the notion of captivity is manifested in the scene. Had Thor first seen the marauder, it is likely he would have easily defended himself from the attack. Consequently, his captivity does not derive from a lack of physical fighting ability but from being in a mental state, albeit transient in duration, that lacked awareness of impending danger.

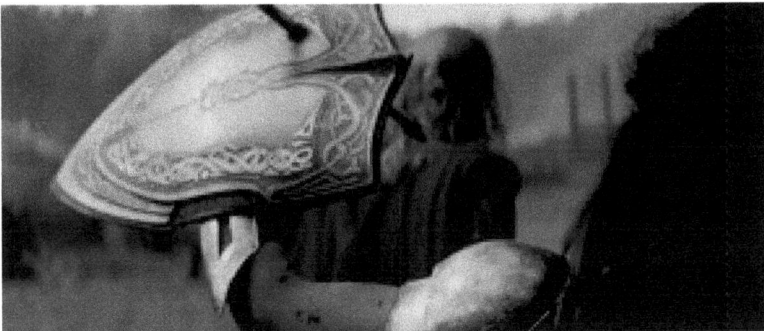

Figure 2.6 The embedded rescue variant as Sif saves Thor. *Thor: The Dark World* (2013).

In discussing these variations on the rescue scenario and by illustrating how they diverge from the prototype, it should not be taken that the examples cited exhaust the manifold ways in which rescue scenes have appeared in film. Innovation is an inherent part of the filmmaking process, and that innovation also applies to rethinking how rescue scenarios have been envisaged for the screen, as the different rescue situations in the Superman sequence attest. However, based upon the examples of rescues discussed in this chapter, some initial observations on the general nature of captivity can be drawn that can help identify the manifestations of rescue scenes in film. First and foremost, the depiction of captivity in rescue scenes is connected to the underlying notion of boundaries. These boundaries can be physical in nature, such as the apartment walls in *Life of an American Fireman* and the cell that imprisons Princess Leia in *Star Wars*. Or the boundaries can arise as a result of the mental or physical limits of a character that makes them captive to a risky situation. As indicated in the *Superman* rescue sequence, Jimmy Olsen lacked the physical ability to pull himself up to the top of the dam, whereas the plant workers lacked the mental ability to focus their attention upon the main breaker switch to turn the plant's power off. Second, what makes boundaries notable despite their varied form is that they restrict the agency of the captive. However, as the previously discussed rescue situations have shown that agency can vary in degree from the helpless mother in *Life of an American Fireman* to Thor, a superhero with superhuman abilities, but who was temporality inattentive to his battle environment. Most critically, agency itself has limits within the rescue scenario since if a captive is fully capable of extricating him or herself from a dangerous situation, then they would be better understood as an escapee, a point that will be developed in the next chapter.

Exemplar: *The Birth of a Nation* (1915)

At this point, it will be useful to take a closer look at two exemplars that played a pivotal role in influencing the development of action sequences to take note of their construction and to examine further how they instantiate the aspects of the rescue scenario discussed in this chapter. On that score, no thorough account of the development of the rescue sequence can leave out reference to silent film director D. W. Griffith. Over the course of his early narrative shorts, Griffith developed the race-to-the-rescue format that would find its most advanced, and notorious manifestation, in the climactic rescue sequence in *The Birth of a*

Nation (1915). The film is both heralded as a major advancement in storytelling in film and, at the same time, decried for its appalling racism (Stokes, 2007). As film historian Tom Gunning (1991, 133, 195) has noted, race-to-the-rescue films that predate *The Birth of a Nation* include *The Guerrilla* (1908), *The Drive for a Life* (1909), *The Lonely Villa* (1909), *The Lonedale Operator* (1911), *The Girl and Her Trust* (1912), *The Lesser Evil* (1912), and *An Unseen Enemy* (1912).

What is also notable about the race-to-the-rescue format is that it introduced three features that have become fundamental not only to the rescue scenario but also to action sequences more generally. The first feature that Griffith developed was parallel editing between two or more storylines, a style of storytelling that, although not restricted to action sequences, is closely associated with them. This editing technique allows filmmakers to follow the actions of multiple characters who are in different locations in the story, as demonstrated by the extended rescue sequence in *Superman*. The persistent use of parallel editing in contemporary action sequences, especially in pursuit sequences, is a point that will be further explored in Chapter 8, where its role in the creation of narrative complexity will be highlighted.

The second feature of the race-to-the-rescue format that Griffith developed was the narrative device of a deadline in which characters must undertake an endeavour within a prescribed period of time, such as arrive at a set appointment. David Bordwell has observed that the use of a deadline is a major convention in classical Hollywood cinema that has been used for a broad range of story purposes, and is also manifested in the action film (1985, 44-46; 2007). Particularly with respect to Griffith's work, deadlines tend to be associated with last-minute rescues. All of the instances of rescues discussed in this chapter have either implicit or explicit deadlines. In *Life of an American Fireman*, the fireman has a time limit to rescue the mother and child before they are engulfed in smoke and flames. Princess Leia in *Star Wars* has been ordered to be executed; consequently, Skywalker's rescue cannot be postponed for another day. Superman must catch up with the missile headed toward Hackensack before it impacts upon the city. Fundamental to the deadline device is its ability to create suspense. As film theorist Noël Carroll has argued, suspense is generated in a film by making the film spectator care for a character where their goals, or their very life, are in jeopardy (1996). Last-minute rescues consequently motivate the viewer to pose the question of whether or not the hero will rescue the captive in time, as was the case in the final rescue attempt in *Superman* in which Lois Lane is shown struggling to breathe while cutting to Superman desperately searching for her.

The third feature that Griffith refined in his race-to-the-rescue sequences was the insertion of delays, be it story events that retard the progress of the rescue or by the narration itself presenting scenes that are not directly connected to the rescue effort. As Gunning argues, Griffith's films were unique at their time through their introduction of such "suspenseful delays" (1991, 191). Along with the deadline device, the insertion of delays in a rescue sequence assists in the creation of suspense by either throwing up obstacles to the rescue effort, placing the success of that effort in greater jeopardy, or by redirecting the attention of the spectator to some other story element that delays the relay of information about the rescue itself.

Such strategies of building suspense continue to this day and can be found in the examples already cited. The rescue of Princess Leia in *Star Wars* does not proceed unimpeded. Luke Skywalker and his team encounter an obstacle in the form of prison guards who are dubious of their masquerade and engage in a shoot-out, thereby delaying the rescue of the Princess. Had there been no obstacles faced by Leia's rescuers, then no suspense would have been created, running the risk that the spectator would be less engaged with the sequence. In the *Superman* rescue sequence, other delay tactics are used, principally in the form of dialogue. From the point at which the missiles are launched to Superman vaulting into the sky to intercept the eastbound missile, nine minutes elapse in which the narration provides the viewer: greater clarification about Lex Luthor's nefarious plans; an explanation about the San Andreas Fault and its relation to earthquakes in California; an abbreviated comedic moment between Luthor and Otis, his accomplice; views of Lane and Olsen who are shown to be proximate to the San Andreas Fault and are consequently in jeopardy; and a return to the missiles now in their redirected trajectory, reminding the viewer of the danger that they pose. One would think that these delays would be sufficient to generate increased suspense, but the interruptions continue to lastly include Luthor's ploy to trick Superman into being exposed to kryptonite, leading to the greatest obstacle of all in the sequence: Superman himself in need of rescue. These delays serve a double narrative purpose. Not only do they function to augment suspense, but they also provide clarifications about character aims and story events, narrative developments, and comedic relief. In such ways, suspenseful delays are integral to the structure of action sequences.

The climactic rescue sequence in *The Birth of a Nation* exhibits all three of these features. But before analyzing how they are manifested, it is necessary to briefly contextualize the sequence within the context of the film's story. The film consists of two parts, the first covering the American Civil War that is focused on the travails of two families. One family consists of the Stonemans from the North, who are abolitionists, with Austin Stoneman as the patriarch of the household, whose daughter Elsie becomes a central figure in the film's rescue sequence. Phil Stoneman is his eldest son, who also plays a role in the rescue situation. The other family is the Camerons, who represent the old South and live in Piedmont, South Carolina. Dr. Cameron is the head of this household, with the death of his daughter Flora constituting a major turning point in the story. Ben Cameron is his only surviving son after the war and plays a central role as rescuer and is Elsie's love interest. Margaret Cameron, Flora's sister, is one of the captives in the rescue sequence and is Phil Stoneman's love interest. Both families become entwined in the war when their sons enlist into the opposing armies. With General Robert E. Lee's surrender to General Ulysses S. Grant and Abraham Lincoln's assassination at the hands of John Wilkes Booth, the first part of the film concludes.

After the film's intermission, the second part depicts the oppression of white Southerners during the Reconstruction period at the hands of carpetbaggers, cynical white opportunists from the North, and by the tyrannical rule of freed black slaves. These changes are orchestrated by Austin Stoneman and his acolyte Silas Lynch, of mixed race, who is installed as lieutenant-governor of South Carolina and furthers the disenfranchisement of the white South. Alienated from Lynch's rule Ben Cameron, the only surviving brother of the Cameron family, forms the Ku Klux Klan, a development that underscores its importance given that the film's original title was *The Clansman*, with the film itself an adaptation of Thomas Dixon Jr.'s novel and play with the same title (1905).

Emboldened by his new status as Captain, Gus, a black soldier, displays his desires for Flora Cameron, who fatally jumps off a cliff at the mere thought of miscegenation. Her death becomes the catalyst for the film's story, whereby members of the newly formed Klan capture Gus and try and execute him for Flora's death. His body is disposed on the steps of Lynch's manor, motivating his black militia to patrol the streets. A confrontation begins to brew between the Klan, who aim to disarm the blacks in Piedmont, with the black militiamen who have been ordered by Lynch to fill the streets in a shock and awe tactic, as well as kill any white man in possession of a Klan costume. One of Lynch's spies discovers Ben's costume at the Cameron household with Dr. Cameron arrested, as a result, and is hauled out of his house in chains to his presumed death.

It is within this narrative context that the film's extended rescue sequence arises. But before proceeding, it is important to recognize how the film's ideological depiction of this historical period impacts upon the moral valence of the rescue scenario. The film is replete with racist imagery from white actors portraying African-Americans in blackface, to the depiction of blacks as slow-witted and sexually aggressive, to the portrayal of black rule as a travesty of justice. Silas Lynch, in particular, is a demonized figure by presenting him as a classical villain and as a drunken lecher. The glorification of the Ku Klux Klan as the deliverer of justice is especially egregious given that Gus' 'trial' resembles a murderous lynching, and the fact that the organization was known for its espousal of white supremacy through violent insurgency and lynching. The release of the film itself caused a resurgence in Klan membership. With regard to the film's account of the Reconstruction period, historian John Hope Franklin has shown that historical inaccuracies, distortions, and omissions abound within the film, including the fact that during the 1865-1866 period immediately after the end of the war, Southern state legislatures enacted a range of laws that restricted black labour and wages to maintain the plantation system (1979). The film's depiction of the Reconstruction was also informed by the Dunning School, a school of thought promulgated by professor William Archibald Dunning and his disciples that maintained the Reconstruction policies imposed by Northern Republicans were harmful to the South, portraying it as a victim of black emancipation that threatened its civil society (Stokes, 2007: 191). As shall be shown, the rescue sequence participates in and reinforces this ideological project by projecting the Ku Klux Klan as a heroic force that counters the threats on whites, particularly that on white women.

Before recounting the intertwining events that constitute the narrative action, it is worth providing an overview of the four different storylines and the evolving rescue situations. This will help clarify how the parallel editing is used to help build the moral worlds of these characters and suspense. First, there is the rescue situation concerning Elsie's captivity inside Lynch's home, which itself has the action moving across different spaces within the house [*Figure 2.7*]. Second is the rescue situation revealed in exterior shots of the streets and interior shots of the white citizens who are in danger of being lynched by the black mob [*Figure 2.8*]. The third is the rescue situation at the cabin that is about to become more desperate [*Figure 2.9*]. Finally, there is a storyline of the rescuers, shown through the summing of the Klan forces, which is also presented as occurring in different spaces in the surrounding region as members are seen to travel on route to the gathering point [*Figure 2.10*]. The parallel editing between scene segments and the ways in which this builds suspense, agency and moral valence will now be recounted; it is graphically represented in *Table 2*.

Table 2: **The Birth of a Nation (1915) Rescue Sequence Breakdown***

Sections	1. Elsie's captivity	2. Piedmont citizens	3. Besieged cabin	4. Klan forces
Section 1	(2) Lynch's lechery	(3) militiamen terror	(1) Dr. Cameron rescued by servants; escape to the cabin	(4) Klan assembles, cross-cut with (5)
Section 2	(5) Elsie captive, cross-cut with (4)	(9) Black mob	(8) Phil and Margaret storyline	(7) Klan depart
Section 3	(6) arranged marriage	(15) white townsfolk lynched	(12) militiamen besiege cabin	(10) Klan advance
Section 4	(8) Elsie faints	(16) Klan arrives at Piedmont, mob retreats. Plotlines join.	(18) militiamen besiege cabin continued, cross-cut with (19)	(13) Klan advance continued
Section 5	(11) Spies spot Elsie		(20) Klan arrive, militiamen retreat. Plotlines join.	(16) Klan arrives at Piedmont, mob retreats. Plotlines join.
Section 6	(14) Elsie gagged			

Sections	1. Elsie's captivity	2. Piedmont citizens	3. Besieged cabin	4. Klan forces
Section 7	(17) Elsie freed by Klan. Plotlines join.			(19) Klan advance on the cabin, cross-cut with (18) (20) Klan arrive, militiamen retreat. Plotlines join.

* The four plotlines in the sequence are listed in columns 2-5. Sections of the different rescue situations are numbered in chronological order of appearance in sequence.

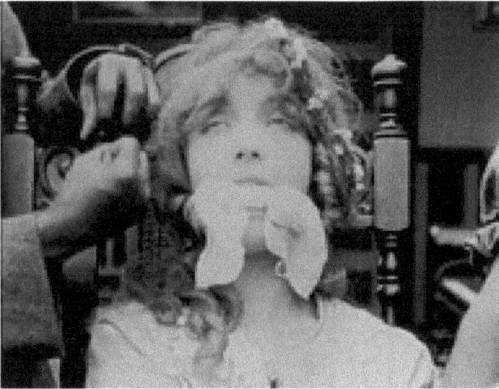

Figure 2.7 First rescue situation: Elsie.
The Birth of a Nation (1915).

Figure 2.8 Second rescue situation: helpless white citizens. *The Birth of a Nation* (1915).

53

Figure 2.9 Third rescue situation: cabin.
The Birth of a Nation (1915).

Figure 2.10 The summoning of the Clan.
The Birth of a Nation (1915).

The rescue sequence surprisingly commences through the agency of Dr. Cameron's two loyal black servants who, after pretending to mock their master, attack his captors. Phil Stoneman also aids this rescue by punching one of the captors and shooting a black militiaman. Phil then joins Dr. Cameron and his family in their wagon-driven escape to a remote cabin owned by two sympathetic Union veterans as they are pursued by black militia.

Meanwhile, back at the manor, Lynch attempts to fulfil his sexual desires by proposing to Elsie, a white woman and Austin Stoneman's daughter. She recoils in horror, retorting that Lynch should be horsewhipped, thus prompting him to lock themselves in the room. He then lecherously advances upon her, implying to the viewer that rape may be on his mind. Crucially, he also points to the town through the window, indicating his level of control and motivating the narration to cut to shots of his black militiamen terrorizing the white citizens of Piedmont.

The film, at this point, has invoked the rescue scenario prototype by having set up two enclosures of entrapment: the cabin that is about to be besieged by Lynch's black militiamen who are in pursuit, and the room in which Elsie is held captive. In addition to these, a third rescue situation is introduced in relation to the terrorized white populace of Piedmont, who, while not in a physically enclosed space, they still are bounded by their inability to repel the black militiamen. These three rescue situations consequently add complexity to the sequence and motivate the parallel editing used throughout, a technique established earlier in the film by presenting the stories of the Stoneman and Cameron families.

The film then cuts to reveal the Ku Klux Klan assembling their members, and returns to Lynch becoming more aggressive in his advances towards Elsie, then cuts to two Klan members speeding on horseback, with the film returning to Elsie's rescue situation again, a pattern that continues through the next series of shots. It is through this parallel editing that the apparent goals of the Klan temporarily shift from disarming the militiamen to rescuing Elsie, such that their efforts will appear more heroic and justified on the part of the spectator.

At this point, events begin to accelerate. Elsie's captivity storyline advances when Lynch orders for an arranged marriage, raising the spectre of miscegenation, and by implication, marital rape, introducing a deadline into the sequence that generates suspense in terms of whether the Klan will arrive in time to halt the forced wedding. Intercut with these proceedings is the gathering of Klan forces. A further plot development occurs when two Klansmen disguised as blacks arrive at Piedmont to scout the enemy, a twist on the use of blackface within the film. Soon after, Austin Stoneman returns to Piedmont and is not permitted to enter the room in which Elsie is entrapped by the guards at the door, further underscoring her captivity, and whose appearance causes Lynch to order his servants to shift her to another room. When he enters, Lynch informs Stoneman of his intentions to marry a white woman, to which Stoneman provides his approval, not yet aware that it is his daughter.

The film then cuts to the Klan now fully assembled and departing to liberate Piedmont from black rule, a rescue mission unto itself from the ideological vantage point of the film. The narrative finally shifts back to events in the cabin as Phil makes a romantic advance toward Margaret Cameron, to whom he had earlier expressed his affection. This romantic plotline continues for the remainder of the film, but this particular scene acts primarily as a delay by directing viewers' attention to a story element that is only indirectly related to the eventual rescue.

The film returns to Elsie's rescue situation. She has fainted, while Stoneman is outraged when he realizes that the white woman Lynch intends to marry is his daughter. The streets of Piedmont, crowded with an anarchic black mob, are shown next, as well as a cut to the advancing Klan forces on horseback. Elsie then rouses and smashes the window to shout for help. She is heard by the two white spies in blackface, who depart to inform the advancing Klansmen. Lynch's two servants forcibly restrain Elsie and, although her father hears her cries in the adjoining room, Lynch holds him back, demonstrating that Stoneman is too old and frail to act as a rescuer.

The narration then switches to the pursuing militiamen who discover the abandoned wagon and begin to lay siege to the captives' cabin, thereby introducing another deadline for the Klansmen to meet. Although outnumbered, the union veterans pledge to defend Dr. Cameron and his family and fire back with their weapons, revealing a degree of agency. As the Klansmen continue their advance on Piedmont, Elsie is seen to be now gagged. In the streets, the violence of the black mob reaches a crescendo as white townsfolk are lynched and tarred and feathered, with other white citizens looking on in fear, held captive, as it were, within the confines of their own homes. The mob riot introduces the last deadline of the rescue sequence, with Lynch's black forces in peak ascendency in all three rescue situations.

The Klansmen finally arrive at Piedmont and are shown to be taking losses as the black militia fire at them with their rifles, introducing an obstacle to their rescuing efforts, and thereby introducing another delay in the aim of generating suspense. Their deaths also reinforce their heroic status as fallen Klansmen who have put their lives at risk for the rescue effort. The militia is then shown to be advancing on the town in greater numbers as its occupants fire back. A group of Klansmen then arrive and are also fired upon, resulting in fatalities. But the tide soon turns in favour of the captives as the Klansmen charge the militiamen in Piedmont, who are depicted as lacking any military resolve and make a cowardly retreat along with the rioting mob. In so doing, the Klansmen achieve the first rescue by liberating the town and become the ascendant power. Elsie frees herself in jubilance. Although Lynch enters the room and attempts to run off with her, a group of Klansmen force their way in and capture him at gunpoint. Ben then lifts his hood to reveal himself to Elsie, who responds by hugging her rescuer, an act that also signifies the end of the second rescue.

The Klansmen at Piedmont are then informed of the assault on the cabin, with Ben leading the rescue charge. The militiamen have reached the cabin and make their way to the front entrance, prompting Phil and the Cameron family to barricade themselves in a backroom, with the militia now attempting to force their way into it through multiple points of entry. Fully besieged, the deadline for the final militia assault looms closer, generating mounting suspense. The editing rhythm quickens as the film cross-cuts from the Camerons inside the room, to the militia outside, continuing to break in like a crazed zombie mob, to the Klansmen speeding on horseback. This pattern continues to the point when Dr. Cameron is on the verge of bludgeoning his daughter with a pistol, implying that her possible rape by a black man is a fate worse than death. The Klansmen arrive in the nick of time, causing most of the

57

militia forces to cowardly retreat again. Ben leads the charge into the cabin, where a brief shoot-out occurs with the remaining two militiamen, posing the final obstacle to the rescue. The militiamen are then shot dead, and, with Ben's arrival, the family embraces as the Camerons reassemble. This then concludes the last rescue and the action sequence as a whole as the final moment of ascendency is achieved.

One should not underestimate the influence that this rescue sequence has had on the staging of subsequent action sequences in films to come, an influence that be can be felt to this day. Although its blatant racist ideology is highly problematic, to say the least, the rescue sequence is an exemplar that offers a model of how to construct a narratively complex action sequence. The sequence exhibits combinations of action forms, principally the rescue scenario combined with combat. In addition, the rescue sequence is a staggering twenty-eight minutes in duration, a scale of ambition that disappears until the 1960s when such instances of comparable length resurface in filmmaking. Most importantly, the sequence additionally offers a model of how to sustain spectator engagement through multiple intercut plotlines, as well as maintain suspense through the use of deadlines, and the injection of suspenseful delays, to heighten the spectator's emotional engagement.

Exemplar: Dodge City (1939) and the Western Rescue Variant

As we have seen, one of the outstanding features of the rescuer is their willingness to put themselves at risk for the sake of others who do not possess the mental or physical attributes to extricate themselves out of a situation that puts them in danger. One of the conclusions that can be drawn from this observation is that what ultimately defines the hero is precisely this willingness to act as a rescuer, in ways that overshadow other qualities he or she might possess. A character, for instance, may exhibit superior fighting skills compared to other characters in a film's story, but these are secondary enabling qualities that assist in their rescuing efforts.

Such considerations lead to an examination of a rescue variation in the western genre for two reasons. First, out of all the Hollywood film genres, it is the western in which one finds the hero in its most codified incarnation, suggesting that the rescue scenario figures prominently in the genre. Second, one form of the rescue scenario that is particularly relevant to the western consists of a community that is figuratively held captive by a villainous group that rules over them, as was the case with Lynch's hold over Piedmont through the black militia.

These rescue characteristics are what Will Wright has described as the 'classical western', exhibiting a plot that he considers prototypical to the genre (1975, 320). Amongst the plot functions that Wright claims are inherent to the classical western are those that are directly relevant to the rescue scenario variant under consideration. One significant plot function that he identifies is that "the hero is revealed to have an exceptional ability" that accords with the superior agency of the rescuer compared to the lesser abilities of the captive, as exhibited in the rescue situations covered in this chapter (1975, 42). Next are two critical plot functions that normally follow each other: "the villains are stronger than society; the society is weak" and "the villains threaten society" (1975, 45-46). These plot functions readily apply to the Piedmont rescue situation with Lynch's reign over the town as a result of the superior might of his armed militia and the direct threat that it and the crazed black mob pose to the white townsfolk. Finally, there is this trio of plot functions: "the hero fights the villains", "the hero defeats the villains", and "the society is safe" that aptly describes the resolution of the Piedmont rescue situation when the Klansmen entered the town and defeated the black militia and rendered the town safe for its white citizens (1975, 46-47).

Turning to the classical western, an analysis of *Dodge City* (Michael Curtiz, 1939) can illustrate how this rescue scenario variant operates in this genre. Set during the wild west, Dodge City is a frontier town in Kansas that is blighted by its lawlessness and a gang of outlaws led by Jeff Surrett, who engage in a range of criminal activities, including running the sheriff out of town. At the outset, the film reveals its first plot function of the classic western by presenting Surrett and his gang as superior in strength to the law-abiding townsfolk. This social situation in Dodge City also parallels that of Piedmont, where Lynch abused his power over the town, with the angry mob itself a symbol of anarchic lawlessness.

Enter Wade Hatton, played by Errol Flynn, whose star persona was associated with a heroic figure through his appearances in previous swashbucklers. Hatton and his friends have gone to Texas on a cattle drive and return to Dodge City to sell the herd. Hatton secures a purchase with a buyer named Ort, but Surrett arranges his murder to force Hatton to sell the cattle to him. This underscores the plot function that Surrett and his gang pose a threat to the town through the murder of its denizens in ways that exceed the danger that Lynch's rule posed over Piedmont. After a massive brawl in a saloon involving Rusty, one of Hatton's friends, Surrett apprehends him and takes him to be hanged. Hatton intervenes to rescue his friend while the town passively watches, thus demonstrating his superior bravery. When Surrett refuses Hatton's request to let Rusty go, Hatton adeptly pulls a gun on him, forcing Surrett's men to release Rusty. By standing up to Surrett and outmanoeuvring him, Hatton fulfils the plot function of demonstrating his special abilities in ways that contrast to the powerless townsfolk who simply look on. Such abilities also parallel those possessed by Ben Cameron and his associates in *The Birth of a Nation*, who, by donning their Klan costumes, make their special status apparent, serving a function akin to the costumes of superheroes that signal their difference from ordinary folk.[2]

After this show of bravery, leading figures of Dodge City approach Hatton and ask him to become Sherriff, a role Hatton initially turns down. However, after witnessing a child trampled

---

[2] As a sign of the influence of The Birth of a Nation, it is notable that the costumes used in the film were not based upon existing uniforms that members of the Ku Klux Klan had previously worn. These costumes were in fact designed for the film, and given the film's popularity they were subsequently massed produced by the KKK and adopted as their identifiable uniform (Kinney, 2016; Stokes, 2007, 195).

to death as a result of a noisy shoot-out, Hatton changes his mind, takes on the role of Sherriff, and commences to clean up the town by banning firearms, an act that makes the community safer but does not rid Surrett and his gang, indicating the townsfolk are still at risk. After the murder of the town's newspaper editor by Yancey, one of Surrett's men, Hatton arrests him. To avoid a lynching, Hatton takes Yancey on a train out of town, which leads to a final shoot-out with Surrett in which both Surrett and Yancey are killed. With the gang vanquished, Dodge City becomes safe, fulfilling the plot function of the classical western in ways similar to the situation of Piedmont once freed from black rule.

As Wright (1975, 34-41) observes, the classic western plot is not restricted to *Dodge City* and is exemplified in other western films such as *Shane* (George Stevens, 1953), *Canyon Passage* (Jacques Tourneur, 1946), and *The Far Country* (Anthony Mann, 1954). But the case can be made that this rescue scenario variant is found in other genres. The swashbuckler adventure film, such as *The Adventures of Robin Hood* (Michael Curtiz, 1938), is similar in plot structure to the classical western in which a community is under the autocratic control of a cruel and corrupt ruler, requiring a hero to vanquish the tyrant to rescue the populace. In addition, during the 1960s and early 1970s, conventions from the western were being incorporated into the developing police thriller. The best representative of this development was *Dirty Harry* (Don Siegel, 1971), where Clint Eastwood's star persona from the western as an anti-hero was inserted into the urban and contemporary context of San Francisco in which he rescues the city itself from crime and a terrorizing serial killer. In so doing, the film illustrates the adaptability of the rescue scenario and its pervasiveness in a range of genres.

Chapter 2: The Escape Scenario

"A word to you about escape. There is no barbed wire. No stockade. No watchtower. They are not necessary. We are an island in the jungle. Escape is impossible. You would die."

—Colonel Saito[1]

No other action form places as much emphasis on physical boundaries as the escape scenario. As the above quotes suggest with respect to the surrounding jungle, an indelible component of the concept of escape is that some form of boundary is in place that will impede the ability to leave. A closer examination of the escape scenario can illustrate how these boundaries are manifested in various escape situations in film.

The Escape Scenario Prototype

One of the defining features of the rescue scenario is the limits imposed upon the captive's ability to extricate themselves from a physically or psychologically confining situation. In the prototypical escape scenario, one finds the reversal of the rescue scenario whereby the ability of the escapee to break out from their confining situation is precisely what is showcased. Like other action forms, escape must involve effort and the undertaking of risks on the part of the escapee. If it were effortless and risk-free, much like walking out of a building unimpeded, the situation would not warrant the label of escape, let alone the categorization of an action form.

The escape sequence in *First Blood* (Ted Kotcheff, 1982) can illustrate the features representative of the prototype. John

---

[1] Quote from Colonel Saito, commander of a Japanese prison camp in *The Bridge on the River Kwai* (David Lean, 1957).

Rambo and his military comrades, all Vietnam War veterans, are initially presented as abandoned and unwanted by society; one has recently committed suicide as a result. Rambo strays into the town of Hope, in the State of Washington, in search of a meal but is spotted by Sheriff Will Teasle, who is distrustful of drifters. Teasle offers Rambo a lift in his vehicle but instead escorts him to the town's perimeter, where he leaves him. Rambo walks back towards Hope in defiance of Teasle's intentions, causing Teasle to turn back and arrest him. Rambo is then brought to the police station, where he is charged with resisting arrest, vagrancy, and possession of a concealed weapon in the form of his iconic survival knife that features prominently in the *Rambo* series.

Teasle delegates Rambo's processing to Art Galt, his sadistic and antisympathetic Deputy, who takes him into a secured space within the police station. Triggered by the barred windows, Rambo begins to have flashbacks of his incarceration in Vietnam, which makes him unresponsive to police requests, perceived by Galt as further resistance, who threatens to beat him with his club. Teasle orders Rambo to be cleaned up and, when he disrobes, Galt uses the occasion to assault him with no provocation. Rambo is then unpleasantly sprayed with a high-pressure hose, prompting Galt to cruelly laugh at his plight. Once clean, another police officer brings in a shaving kit, the sight of which makes Rambo further apprehensive, causing Galt to physically restrain him with his club. As the officer approaches Rambo with the sharpened razor, flashbacks of his internment in Vietnam are once again presented, this time with Rambo shown tied to a bamboo trellis as a Vietnamese soldier barbarically slices his chest open with a knife.

This narrative setup presents Rambo as a victim who is subjected to the unjust and abusive treatment of the police. But at a deeper structural level, the sequence draws upon the features of the prototypical escape scenario. First and foremost, Rambo is a captive bounded by walls of the secured space within the police station, features also shared with the rescue scenario. Furthermore, as a captive, Rambo is also exposed to physical harm at the hands of the brutal police, risks that are shared with the rescue scenario that also underscore its status as an action form. These dangers are further augmented in Rambo's mind through the flashbacks in which the abuse of the police is paralleled with his torture by the Vietnamese. The policemen also represent captors whose function is to maintain Rambo's confinement, another feature associated with the rescue scenario.

But unlike the rescue scenario, Rambo is in no need of a rescuer. Given his previous experience within a Special Forces Unit in Vietnam, he manages his escape through his own agency. He kicks down two officers in quick succession and escapes from Galt's grip by headbutting him. The scuffle continues with its sounds alerting a fourth officer, who enters into the cell to be promptly thrown through a window. Teasle arrives with a pistol in hand but is taken down by Rambo, causing his pistol to fire.

Alerted by the gunshot, a sixth officer unlocks the secured space only to have Rambo burst through the door and shove him through the station's window. Rambo recovers his survival knife and kicks down a seventh officer rising from his seat to assist his colleague. Rambo then rushes to the entrance of the station, taking out the eighth and final officer in the process. Bolting down the steps of the station's entrance, and no longer a captive, Rambo then commandeers a passing motorcycle and speeds off, with Teasle in pursuit in his police car.

The sequence not only exemplifies escape features but also illustrates the underlying event schema of the escape scenario. A person is held captive in some capacity, with the captivity often posing some kind of danger to the individual as well. To avoid death or physical harm, or to simply free oneself from captivity, the individual attempts to escape by their own means or is sometimes assisted by others. The escape normally entails obstacles that pose risks that the escapee either avoids by eluding captors by stealth, or are dealt with directly through combat, or a combination of both strategies. Once free, the escapee normally flees from the scene to avoid recapture.

The escape sequence in *First Blood* fits these general contours of the event schema by moving through a three-stage micro-narrative of captivity, attempted escape, and flight, with a cause-and-effect chain linking the stages. In addition, the sequence also reveals the type of characters who normally populate the scenario in its most basic form. At the minimum, the scenario must include a captive-turned-escapee and a captor. Most of the time, the captor is a human agent, but in some non-prototypical cases, the captor can be nature itself, such as in *127 Hours* (Danny Boyle, 2010), where a rock climber's right hand is pinned by a fallen boulder.

Another non-essential character type is the 'helper'. Although not manifested in the *First Blood* sequence, helpers do recur in other escape sequences, as attested in *The Adventures of Robin Hood* (1938). As Robin Hood is about to be publicly hanged, his merry men, hiding in the crowds, suddenly incapacitate the executioners and guards by firing their bows, allowing Robin Hood to abscond by leaping while handcuffed onto a guard's horse. He and his men then all speed off together. The leap itself is a stunt that demonstrates Robin Hood's athleticism and overall agency. Robin's helpers, therefore, are escaper's assistants, indicating that the difference between a helper and rescuer is relative to the status of the captive, reinforcing again the point that the distinction between a rescue and escape scenario hinges upon the agency of the captive. If agential, captives can turn into escapees, as was the case with Rambo in *First Blood*. If lacking sufficient ability to escape, captives remain captive and require rescuers to come to their aid.

The agency of the escapee parallels that of the rescuer, and in some cases, they are one and the same character. In *Dr. No* (Terence Young, 1962), James Bond is held captive by the nefarious Dr. No in a cell in his island compound. Through sheer resourcefulness, Bond escapes his imprisonment by spotting a vent in his cell and crawls through it to sabotage Dr. No's plans by causing a nuclear reactor to meltdown. As the complex commences to explode, Bond, through determination, locates Honey Ryder, his love interest and companion, and finds her handcuffed to a concrete ramp about to be drowned and frees her. Bond, therefore, fulfils the role of escapee and rescuer in the same action sequence calling upon similar abilities. In other cases, only the agency of escape is showcased. As noted, Rambo in *First Blood* takes out eight police officers in quick succession and with relative ease, employing his superior combat skills that the Hope police officers simply cannot match.

In the opening action sequence of Steven Spielberg's *Raiders of the Lost Ark* (1981), escape skills of a different order are emphasized given the obstacles encountered. In his quest for the golden idol, Indiana Jones enters a Peruvian temple. To prevent its theft, a number of traps have been built into the tunnel leading to the dais on which the idol rests, thereby invoking the heist scenario. Through his previous archaeological experience, Jones has a sense of where these traps lie, thereby differentiating his knowledge from others, such as his guide Satipo. The idol rests on a weight-sensitive pedestal, and Jones attempts to replace it with an equivalently weighted bag of sand. But, despite his efforts, the pedestal is triggered and sets in motion a set of obstacles Jones and Satipo must surmount, as well as setting in motion the escape sequence itself.

These obstacles include the collapse of the chamber in which the idol is located and darts that fire from the walls of the passage. When Satipo reaches a deep shaft that they had previous negotiated by using Jones' bullwhip as a swing, Satipo betrays Jones, posing an additional obstacle for Jones to overcome. Sapito offers the bullwhip in exchange for the idol, to which Jones agrees and tosses the idol to him. However, Sapito does not honour the agreement and drops the bullwhip into the shaft, and absconds with the idol as a set of walls descend, threatening to trap Jones within the temple and introducing a deadline into the scene. In desperation, Jones leaps over the shaft and manages to hang onto its ledge while the walls continue to descend. He scrambles up just in time to slide under the wall to discover that Sapito has been impaled by a set of spikes. As Jones retrieves the idol, a gigantic boulder rolls towards him, prompting Jones to sprint through the tunnel and leap out of the entrance.

However, rather than leaping to safety, another obstacle awaits Jones in the form of a band of Hovitos, a native tribe, who are armed and led by René Belloq, a rival French archaeologist and Jones' antagonist. Under the threat of death, Jones relinquishes the idol to Belloq in another change of hands. When Belloq triumphantly displays the idol to the Hovitos, Jones uses the opportunity to run off. Belloq then orders the Hovitos to kill Jones, and a foot chase ensues, thereby prolonging the escape sequence as it segues into pursuit mode. The film cuts to reveal a seaplane where Jones' pilot is calmly fishing and unprepared to flee at a moment's notice. This introduces another deadline, both in terms of whether Jones will make it to the craft and whether the pilot will be able to take off before the tribe kills Jones. He orders his pilot to start the plane's engine to then athletically swing from a vine into the water and swim towards the plane, as the Hovitos fire darts and arrows at him. Jones makes it to the seaplane, which then takes flight, resolving the deadline question and bringing the escape sequence to an end. In so doing, Indiana Jones exhibited escape skills that are not combative in nature but an inbuilt mental and physical ability to manoeuvre through a variety of obstacles.

Like other action forms, escape sequences possess a dramatic structure through which ascendency is orchestrated. Fundamentally, the escape scenario poses the dramatic question of whether the escapee will be successful in their escape attempt. The dramatic turning points during the attempt consist of the narrative obstacles that impede his or her progress, often in the form of boundaries, with the decisive threshold moment occurring when the escapee emerges free from their captivity and from the threat of being recaptured or killed. In continuous escape sequences, ascendency increases with every obstacle surmounted to the threshold moment, with the chance of reversal of fortune for any obstacle that poses too much of a challenge to overcome. In the *First Blood* sequence, ascendency increased with every successive police officer that Rambo was able to fight past. Rambo also navigated through boundaries as well as by sneaking through the secured door when opened, and exiting out of the precinct, with the threshold moment deferred to the end of the pursuit sequence when he eluded Teasle's capture [*Figure 3.1* and *3.2*]. In the *Raiders of the Lost Ark* sequence, ascendency increased as Jones surmounted each of the temple's traps, overcame Sapito's betrayal, and eluded capture from his arch-nemesis and the pursuing Hovitos warriors. While Jones was unsuccessful in securing the idol, he escaped with his life. Like *First Blood*, the threshold moment is deferred to the end of the chase when Jones successfully evaded capture from the Hovitos. When multiple escape attempts are featured in films like *Papillon* (Franklin J. Schaffner, 1973) and *The Dark Knight Rises* (Christopher Nolan, 2012), ascendency is manifested both at the local level of each escape, which may or may not be successful, and over the course of the narrative itself.

Figure 3.1 Obstacle and exiting first captivity boundary. *First Blood* (1982).

Figure 3.2 Exiting second captivity boundary. *First Blood* (1982).

Unlike the rescue scenario, the escape scenario possesses no inherent moral valence. The moral status of the escape depends entirely upon the morality of the characters situated within the escape context and the broader moral world internal to the film. Consequently, there are escape scenarios in which the captive-turn-escapee is presented as morally virtuous, such as Rambo, who through his previous service in the Vietnam war, is presented as honourable and sympathetic, whereas the Hope police are presented mostly as authoritarian and prone to violence, especially in the shape of the pitiless Art Galt who contrasts sharply with Rambo's initially restrained demeanour.

In other instances, the moral inverse is portrayed where the captive-turned-escapee is morally suspect if not downright evil. Parallax is a malevolent entity that feeds on fear in *Green Lantern* (Martin Campbell, 2011) and is imprisoned inside a planet by Abin Sur, a guardian of the universe. When aliens randomly crash land on the planet and fall through a sinkhole, they awaken Parallax, who sucks out their life energy, thereby granting him the power to escape from the crystal formation in which he is ensconced, and proceeds to destroy another planet and absorb its life forms.

Magneto, a mutant who has the power to manipulate metal objects, presents a more morally ambiguous character in *X2* (Bryan Singer, 2003), indicating that the escape scenario can accommodate captives of all moral shades. Within the moral world of the film, Magneto is situated in the middle of a moral spectrum; he is not as wicked as Colonel William Stryker, who wants to eradicate mutants from the Earth, but does not possess the ethical aim of Charles Xavier, another mutant, who seeks to establish peace between mutants with the rest of humanity.

In *X-Men* (Bryan Singer, 2000), the previous installment in the series, Magneto is shown to distrust humans and plots to turn world leaders at a United Nations summit into mutants. Magneto, on first appearance then, does not seem to possess aims that are substantially different from Stryker's in terms of their murderous intent. However, unlike Stryker, Magneto is presented at times sympathetically. He is a concentration camp survivor from which his suspicion of humanity derives, is shown to be sympathetic to mutants, and is ill-treated by Stryker while imprisoned.

It is within this moral context that Magneto's escape is situated. Incarcerated in a plastic cell within a larger empty chamber that neutralizes his metal morphing powers, Magneto requires the assistance of Mystique, a mutant shapeshifter, who drugs Mitchell Laurio, Magneto's guard, at a bar and injects liquified metal into his bloodstream. When Laurio arrives at the prison, the metal is undetected, and he is permitted to enter the cell to provide Magneto with his breakfast. Sensing the metal in his body, Magneto extracts it with his powers, killing Laurio in the process. Magneto then transforms the vaporized metal into globes that are fired like bullets through the plastic walls that shatter his cell, the first obstacle of his escape. Magneto then turns one of the globes into a large disc on which he levitates and moves across the empty expanse towards the chamber's entrance, while firing globes at the guards stationed there, thus surmounting the second obstacle of his escape.

As these examples have demonstrated, physical risk is intrinsic to the escape scenario. This risk parallels that manifested in rescue scenarios except in one key respect. Like the rescue scenario, captivity usually poses dangers to the captive: Rambo is physically abused while in custody in *First Blood*, Jones runs the risk of being entrapped in the collapsing temple in the escape sequence in *Raiders of the Lost Ark*, and Robin Hood is about to be executed in *The Adventures of Robin Hood*.

However, unlike the rescue scenario, it is the captive-turned-escapee instead of the rescuer who bears the burden of risks while attempting to extricating themselves from captivity. Rambo runs the risk of being throttled if not shot, and Jones could be crushed by the collapsing temple, pierced by a host of darts, fall fatally down a shaft, and be killed by the pursuing Hovitos. Captors are routinely at risk from physical danger as well, given the nature of their function, as evidenced in the X2 escape sequence. In *First Blood*, the police officers are kicked, headbutted, punched, kneed in the groin, tossed through windows, tripped, and elbowed in the face. Likewise, in The Adventures of Robin Hood escape sequence, executioners and guards are impaled with arrows. Robin Hood's helpers, too, take risks when assisting his escape, such as getting caught and tried for treason, if not running the possibility of being injured or killed.

Escape Combinations

As the examples so far discussed in this chapter reveal, the escape scenario is often found in combination with other action forms, be they vertical or horizontal combinations. The most common form of vertical combination found within escape sequences is that with the fight scenario. This is a fitting combination in that the dramatic structure of the escape scenario entails that obstacles, regularly assuming the form of captors, who are put in the path of the escapee. The function of the captors is to thwart escape attempts, with conflict naturally arising from such opposing goals. Captors in action sequences, therefore, serve the dual role of resisting inward rescue attempts and obstructing outward escape endeavours.

In addition, conflict increases the degree of risk involved in the escape attempt, thus augmenting the suspense to the sequence as well. The escape in *First Blood* would be hardly as engaging and perceived as an action sequence if the only obstacle in his path was the locked door of the secured space in the precinct, nor would it showcase Rambo's superior combat abilities. Indiana Jones' escape from the temple offers an interesting twist on the notion of a captor as well as that of the fight scenario. The set of traps laid in the tunnel that he encounters were, of course, created by the temple's designers, presumably hundreds of years prior to Jones' entry. As such, the temple designers are the guards that aggressively and actively thwart thieves through the delayed agency of the traps they have created.

The escape scenario is also regularly horizontally combined with other action forms, creating a series within a continuous action sequence. One major horizontal combination consists of the escape scenario linked with the pursuit scenario. In this combination, the escapee not only frees him or herself from captivity but tries to avoid recapture by fleeing with a captor turned capturer in pursuit. The opening action sequence in *First Blood* demonstrates this horizontal linking once Rambo escapes from the police station and flees on a motorcycle with Teasle pursuing him in his vehicle, a chase that takes them into the wilderness where eventually Teasle's vehicle tumbles down into a river allowing Rambo to elude capture.

This continuous horizontal pairing of escape with the pursuit scenario is also found in *The Rock* (Michael Bay, 1996). In the film, the FBI is trying to stop the rogue military general Frank Hummel and his military team, who are threatening to fire missiles loaded with nerve gas into San Francisco if their ransom is not met. Complicating matters, the rogue military unit has taken tourists as hostages on the island to safeguard themselves from attack. The FBI team then seeks the assistance of former SAS operative John Patrick Mason, because of his intimate knowledge of the federal penitentiary on Alcatraz Island, having been the only person who has escaped from it.

Mason is released from prison and kept in a luxurious hotel while still remaining a captive under close guard. While there, Mason freshens up, and plans his escape from FBI custody. He then meets FBI Director James Womack, the person responsible for his initial imprisonment at Alcatraz. Using a cord taken while showering, Mason tricks Womack into shaking his hand, using the opportunity to slip the cord around his wrist to hang him from the hotel balcony. The ruse distracts Dr. Stanley Goodspeed, an FBI chemical weapons specialist, and the other FBI agents that had been stationed in the hotel room to prevent Mason from escaping, effectively acting as captors.

As Goodspeed calls for help, Mason uses the opportunity to flee out of the hotel room, his provisional cell, with Goodspeed in pursuit. The escape then segues into a foot pursuit through the hotel, taking them through the kitchen, where Mason slugs

Goodspeed to slow him down. Manson then hijacks a Hummer stationed outside of the hotel while a convoy of police and FBI vehicles follow in pursuit, with Goodspeed commandeering a Ferrari to join in the chase. The pursuit involves various obstacles set in their path that are less negotiated by expert driving but rather rammed through in a path of spectacular destruction [*Figure* 3.3]. Mason then collides into a set of parked vehicles that knocks down a powerline across the street, causing the pursuing vehicles to crash into one another.

Goodspeed is the last pursuer left who takes a shortcut through a garage and drives through its window, again illustrating the destructive way in which obstacles are dealt with in the pursuit. As Mason and Goodspeed speed through the streets, an elderly woman crosses in front of the Hummer, causing Mason to collide with a streetcar and shove it off its tracks. Its passengers then fall onto the street and become themselves impediments for Mason and Godspeed. As Mason makes his getaway, Goodspeed collides into a series of parking meters and spins out. The streetcar eventually crashes into the parked vehicles, which explode and propel it into the air. Once it hits the ground, it slides its way towards Goodspeed, who makes a hasty exit from his Ferrari, which is crushed by the runaway streetcar, thus terminating his means of pursuit.

Figure 3.3 Destruction as the negation of obstacles.
The Rock (1996).

As an example of a horizontal escape-pursuit combination, the action sequence in *The Rock* leans heavily towards the pursuit component by taking up most of its duration. However, like the escape-pursuit sequence in *First Blood*, the sequence illustrates the seamlessness in which these action forms can link, suggesting deeper similarities at work. Critical to the understanding of this seamlessness is the recognition that a pursuit sequence consists of more fundamental action forms. When discussing the climactic action sequence in *Lethal Weapon* (1987) in the Introduction, I indicated that the pursuit scenario is composed of more basic action elements consisting of escape, speed, and dependent upon the goals of the pursuer, either the capture or fight scenario. With respect to the action sequence in *The Rock*, Mason's goal as the pursued is to elude capture, which is, in essence, a form of escape. The difference from the prototypical escape form is that instead of captivity manifested as a state within a confined bounded space, captivity in the pursuit scenario is expressed as a state in an unbounded space in which capture is an impending threat. To remove oneself from that threat, and given the unbounded nature of captivity in the pursuit scenario, the captive attempts to elude capture by speed, instead of primarily relying upon stealth or combat skills.

Horizontal combinations can extend in a continuous form beyond the pairing of escape with pursuit. Prior to the moment of escape in *Raiders of the Lost Ark* is the theft of the golden idol from a secure space that is not dissimilar to the secured spaces found in heist films. The action sequence in *Raiders of the Lost Ark*, therefore, consists of a heist-escape-pursuit chain that commences with the theft of the idol, then segues into the escape from the temple, and shifts to the final pursuit of Indiana Jones by the Hovitos. In theory, these horizontal combinations with other action forms can continue to unfold, limited only by the necessity for narrative closure and the bounds of audience interest and engagement.

Escape Scenario Variations

Like the rescue scenario, captivity is not always expressed in the literal sense of physical confinement in the escape scenario. Variants of the escape scenario prototype normally arise when the escapee is in a situation and is trapped by endangering conditions that the escapee seeks to extricate him or herself from. As was illustrated in the pursuit sequence in *The Rock*, the prevailing situation is the condition of impending capture by the FBI agents. One variation manifested in the typicality gradient of the escape prototype, then, is the extrication from a dangerous situation but in a way in which the escape does not end with a pursuit.

Daring Leap Escape Variant

One recurrent way in which this variation is manifested involves the escapee undertaking a dangerous and spectacular action, routinely a leap, that the pursuers or captors are unwilling to attempt, which normally brings to an end the escape sequence itself. The prison escape sequence in *Face/Off* (John Woo, 1997) ends in such a way. Sean Archer is an FBI agent who has had a facial transplant with his arch-enemy Castor Troy, a terrorist and murderer of his son, as a means to masquerade as him to extract information from Troy's brother Pollux who is interned in a high-security prison. However, Troy awakes at the clinic after the operation and orders his men to bring the surgeon of the transplant so that he can surgically place Archer's face on him, allowing Troy to now masquerade as Archer. Troy then visits the prison and makes Archer aware that he has destroyed any evidence that could prove his real identity.

It is under these circumstances Archer attempts his prison escape that follows the contours of the escape scenario prototype, with the only deviation being its resolution. About to receive shock treatment, Archer convinces Dubov, another inmate, to assist as they fight and shoot their way out of the room, killing a number of guards in the process. Archer and Dubov then make their way to the control centre of the prison, where Archer causes its power system to overload, which then instigates a riot. Dubov is shot by one of the guards and falls to his death with Archer makes his way upward to an exit. As he departs outside, Archer realizes he is on a converted oil platform surrounded by water posing another obstacle to his escape. At that moment, a helicopter arises with a guard inside who starts shooting at Archer, who tries to elude the gunfire. In an act of desperation, Archer leaps from the platform into the water far below, causing the guards in the helicopter to assume his death and fly off [*Figure* 3.4].

The daring leap that ends the opening pursuit sequence for *The Spy Who Loved Me* (Lewis Gilbert, 1977) is an even more extravagant instance of the variant. James Bond is stationed on an unspecified mission in Austria, romantically engaged with a woman in an alpine log cabin. Bond receives notification, as teletext from his watch, to leave instantly for headquarters in London. After Bond departs in ski gear, his lover notifies a foreign agent with a walkie-talkie that Bond has just left, thus revealing her duplicity. The agent is amongst a group of four armed skiers who shoot and pursue Bond down the mountain slope. As they proceed, the agents split up, with one of them following Bond through a crevice while still firing at him with his pistol. Bond then takes one of his ski poles, which doubles as a rocket gun, and ski backwards and fires the weapon at his pursuer, killing him instantly. The remaining skiers begin to converge on Bond as he approaches a huge mountain precipice. Instead of halting, Bond soars off the cliff and is airborne in a long downward descent [*Figure* 3.5]. After his skies fly off, Bond's parachute opens, patriotically revealing a Union Jack emblazoned on it but also imparting his relative safety to the viewer.

Figure 3.4 The daring leap escape variant off an oil rig platform. *Face/Off* (1997).

Figure 3.5 The daring leap escape variant off of a mountain cliff. *The Spy Who Loved Me* (1977).

Like the daring leap in *Face/Off*, the closing stunt in the opening pursuit sequence for *The Spy Who Loved Me* works in multiple capacities. First, the leap is itself a form of escape entailing considerable risk for both Archer and Bond, as a means to avoid further gunfire. Second, the action represents the dramatic threshold moment of both sequences. For Archer, the daring leap takes him off the oil rig and away from the threat of capture, for at least the time being. For Bond, the daring leap off the mountain slope constitutes a horizontal combination of the pursuit sequence with the escape scenario, an escape that is the threshold moment of the action sequence. Third, as a form of spectacular action that is akin to the explosion at the end of a car chase, these leaps, therefore, bring a sense of closure to the action sequences by marking the threshold moment more explicitly for the spectator to register.

Fleeing Escape Variant

Another important variant in the typicality gradient of the escape prototype that also does not involve pursuit are cases of fleeing. An example of this non-pursuit variant can be found in the tunnel flooding sequence in *Die Hard: With a Vengeance* (John McTiernan, 1995). Police officer John McLane investigates the theft of gold bullion from the Federal Reserve Bank of New York by Simon Gruber and his East German comrades using a convoy of large dump trucks that are escaping through one of the city's water tunnels. McLane follows them into the tunnel and discovers that the rear-guard truck had stopped midway. He shoots Gruber's men inside, commandeers the vehicle, and proceeds onward. Gruber discovers that McLane is in it by calling the vehicle and subsequently orders his men to blow up a dam retaining wall to flood the tunnel and drown McLane in the process. Meanwhile, one of the metal plates over a trench has fallen, impeding McLane's progress, who gets out of the truck and attempts to leverage the plate back up. He then hears and sees a wall of water advancing quickly and leaps back into the truck, with the looming onslaught constituting a deadline for his escape.

Unable to turn the truck around, McLane hurries in reverse to a turning point where he can spin the vehicle and accelerates forward, but the floodwater is still gaining on him. As the water reaches the speeding vehicle, McLane clambers out of the driver-side window to climb atop of the truck to grab hold of an approaching vertical air shaft. McLane manages to cling on to its grill as the water rushes past and is fired upward as the water floods the shaft. McLane's civilian partner, Zeus Carver, happens to drive past and sees its above surface spray with McLane catapulted into the air. As Carver picks up McLane, Gruber's men fire at him, with the action evolving into a vehicular freeway pursuit.

A number of points can be drawn from this example that illustrate the features of the fleeing escape variant. First, although the tunnel is a confined space, there are points of exit and is, therefore, a variation on the enclosed cell found within the escape prototype in this respect. Second, the deluge of water is presented as a perilous force of nature that points towards the necessity of fleeing. At the same time, the flood stems from the actions of Gruber's men, who are using water as a weapon in an attempt to kill McLane; this bears similarities to the traps laid in the tunnel in the *Raiders of the Lost Ark* escape sequence. Third, the scene emphasizes McLane's survival skills and his tenacious ability to endure any situation thrown at him, a hallmark of the *Die Hard* franchise as a whole, as well as the agency of the escapee more broadly.

When discussing the depiction of fleeing as an escape variant, it is necessary to also refer to their regular occurrence in disaster films. Fleeing in this capacity was briefly touched upon in the previous chapter with respect to the townsfolk who flee from the deluge of water from the burst dam in *Superman* (1978), underscoring the disaster element in the final rescue sequence. Yet such a catastrophe pales in comparison to the destruction wrought by natural disasters that are manifested in the disaster film genre and their ability to generate truly dangerous situations in films that surpass the devastation brought about by humans. Roland Emmerich's *2012* consists of a catalogue of disaster scenarios presented on a biblical scale, from earthquakes and a super-volcanic eruption to mega-tsunamis, as continents sink due to a solar flare that caused the Earth's core to overheat and destabilize its outer crust.

It is in this narrative context that the film presents an action set piece that offers an extended instance of the fleeing escape variant. Jackson Curtis, a science fiction writer and a chauffeur living in Los Angeles, begins to notice the tarmac cracking close to his parked limousine while at the Santa Monica airport. Suspicious that Mayan predictions of the 2012 cataclysms are commencing, Curtis races towards his ex-wife Kate and his children, who now reside with Kate's boyfriend Gordon. While on the route, Curtis phones Kate and warns that they are in grave danger and need to be ready to leave when he arrives. His journey, therefore, enacts the rescue scenario in which Kate and her family are captives due to their skepticism that extreme danger is imminent and are consequently unable to remove themselves from the impending perilous situation. Just as the governor of California announces on a televised broadcast that "the worst is over", a roar arises, their house shakes violently, and Kate hides underneath the dining table. Curtis arrives at their shuddering home and herds them into the limousine just prior to it collapsing. This initiates the escape component of the sequence as he heads to the airport to fly out of Los Angeles by plane.

As Curtis speeds off, the street and the surrounding neighbour-hood begin to collapse, necessitating Curtis to accelerate the vehicle or run the risk of falling into the giant chasms that are forming. Along the way, Curtis encounters a slew of obstacles that add greater desperation and suspense to their getaway. A slow-moving vehicle blocks their path, causing Curtis to drive the limousine through a number of front gardens, bashing through a series of white picket fences to get around the obstructing vehicle. Next, a portion of the road ahead lifts up, forcing Curtis to drive up it like a ramp, firing the limousine into the air. Then, a collapsing building rises in front of them, forcing Curtis to veer sharply to the right, drive through a burst sewage pipe, and swerve around a giant rolling doughnut. They then reach an elevated freeway that crumples before them and spews its vehicles onto their path. Another chasm opens up, forcing Curtis to swerve violently again and attempt to drive under an overpass before it collapses, introducing a deadline into the sequence [*Figure* 3.6]. Curtis accelerates again to race underneath, with the overpass literally scraping the top of the vehicle. Once passed, a large office building then falls down in front of them, with their only option to drive through one of its floors as its collapsing ceiling descends, creating another micro-deadline.

Figure 3.6 Overpass collapse as obstacle and deadline.
2012 (2009).

The limousine finally arrives at the airport, but they discover that the pilot of their plane lies dead, posing an obstacle of a different kind. Fortuitously, Gordon has taken some flight lessons and is cajoled into piloting. The film cuts to an overhead shot, revealing the collapsing surface crust advancing rapidly toward the airport while the plane taxies for take-off, introducing another deadline to the sequence. As the airplane reaches flying speed, it takes to the air just as the ground underneath caves in. The sequence leads the viewer to believe that Curtis and his family have finally made it to safety, but the plane has yet to reach altitude and flies through a gigantic chasm where further obstacles are tossed in their path, including subsiding buildings, destroyed freeways, and a free-falling commuter train, followed by two office towers at the point of collapse that the plane must fly between to escape. As the plane finally achieves sufficient altitude, the sequence reaches the threshold moment where its occupants are no longer in danger as they witness with horror Los Angeles submerging into the Pacific Ocean.

With its densely packed series of obstacles, and with the Curtis family continually on the brink of death, this sequence reveals that the fleeing escape variant can deliver an action form that rivals more traditional forms of action sequences through its depiction of a perilous dramatic situation. In addition, through the identification of the fleeing escape variant, one can better explain why some film critics, such as Eric Lichtenfeld (2007, 190-243), include discussions of disaster films alongside those of action films. The escape scenario is an action form that features especially prominently in its fleeing variant in disaster films making such discussions compatible and justifiable.

Given its effectiveness in conveying danger, it is not surprising to observe that the fleeing escape variant is also invoked when other overwhelming forces are in play. The most widely known of these would be the monster movie that normally features a beast of a colossal size that derives from a variety of origins from prehistoric derivation, outer space origin, or exposure to nuclear radiation. An early exemplar of the fleeing escape variant of this type appears in *The Lost World* (Harry O. Hoyt, 1925). A brontosaurus is captured in the seemingly prehistoric world of Venezuela and is brought to London. It escapes when unloaded off the steamer and runs amok through the streets, provoking mass crowd fleeing scenes. This escape variant was further conventionalized in films such as *King Kong* (Merian C. Cooper and Ernest B. Schoedsack, 1933) along with its 1976 and 2005 remakes, *The Beast from 20,000 Fathoms* (Eugène Lourié, 1953), Japanese monster movies, and the recent cycle of dinosaur films including *The Lost World: Jurassic Park* (Steven Spielberg, 1997) that revisits the scenarios of the 1925 film.

A more recent instance of the fleeing escape variant in a monster film can be found in *Godzilla* (Gareth Edwards, 2014), when the monster makes landfall in Honolulu. MUTO, an anacronym for Massive Unidentified Terrestrial Organism, is a gigantic insect-like creature that feeds off of the nuclear reactor of a Russian submarine in the forests just outside of Honolulu. As an American Special Forces team engage in attack, the MUTO deploys its scorpion-like tail that sends out an electromagnetic pulse that cuts off the electricity in the surrounding area and causes a jetfighter to crash, with its presence attracting Godzilla to the shores of Honolulu.

Meanwhile, merrymakers on a Waikiki beach become increasingly apprehensive of the growing military and police presence. A girl at the beach notices that the waters are starting to recede and calls for her father, just as a tsunami siren commences to wail, motivating the revellers to flee from the beach. Stationed offshore is the *USS Saratoga*, and on its deck is Ishirō Serizawa, a Japanese specialist on Godzilla. He is the first to spot the creature as it makes its advance by swimming under the aircraft carrier on the way to Waikiki's shores. Godzilla's arrival triggers a tsunami that rolls onto the beach and continues through the streets of Honolulu, devastating what is in its path. Crowds of people run for their lives as the massive wave moves in. The father and daughter are amongst the mass of people fleeing and hide in a nearby coffee shop just as the tsunami rushes past, with a series of overhead shots revealing the extent of the devastation. A SWAT team on a roof of a building then fires flares into the night sky, revealing the silhouette of Godzilla, who leaves a trail of destruction as it moves through the city. Soon MUTO reaches Honolulu and begins its rampage by destroying the elevated tracks of a commuter train, causing it to derail, and knocks down a helicopter that crashes into the airport, initiating a chain reaction of exploding planes as passengers in a terminal watch in horror. At this point, Godzilla arrives and battles with MUTO, who eventually flies off with Godzilla in pursuit.

In this instance, the fleeing escape variant serves as a prelude that is horizontally linked to the eventual battle between two gigantic monsters. Significantly, the sequence places emphasis on images of wreckage with people fleeing on foot to underscore the enormity of the monsters and their devastating effects, with the scale of destruction comparable to that found in a disaster film.

A similar kind of use of this variant is also found in the alien invasion film that also invokes the sensibility of a disaster film. Again, precedents for this can be found as early as *The War of the Worlds* (Byron Haskin, 1953), along with its remake *War of the Worlds* (Steven Spielberg, 2005). In these films, citizens are attacked by the Martian spaceships, which provoke them to bolt, presenting a vertical combination of the fight scenario with the fleeing escape variant. Such a combination is also manifested in *The Avengers* (2012) during the alien invasion of New York City by the Chitauri Army, in *Transformers: Dark of the Moon* (2011) when the Decepticons blitz Chicago, and in the *Green Lantern* (2011), when Parallax storms Coast City. In all these instances, the depiction of attack is coupled with shots of citizens on the run. The logic of including such scenes is identical to that of the monster movie, where the scale of destruction wrought by the invasion is intended to encourage the spectator to make associations with the devastation caused by natural disasters.

As Stephen Keane has noted (2001, 70-71), one film that became an exemplar of this combination of elements of the disaster film merged with that of alien invasion was *Independence Day* (Roland Emmerich, 1996). Drawing story elements from H. G. Wells' *The War of the Worlds* (1898) and the 1953 film adaptation, the film commences by revealing a gigantic outer space mothership entering the Earth's orbit. The mothership then deploys a series of fifteen-mile wide flying saucers that are stationed over major cities of the globe and relay transmissions with each other. Their deployment creates pandemonium, causing families to flee their homes. David Levinson, an MIT scientist, decodes the transmissions to discover they constitute a countdown for a probable coordinated attack. The spaceship hovering over Los Angeles positions itself over the U.S. Bank Tower and at the coordinated time fires a blue beam of energy, causing the structure to explode and send a fireball throughout the city, thereby instigating cataclysmic destruction and decimating the population, while those still alive attempt to flee [*Figure* 3.7]. This pattern repeats in New York City over the Empire State Building and in Washington D.C. over the White House. The fleeing escape variant is further enacted when Air Force One takes off with the President and his advisors onboard to elude the advancing fireball.

Figure 3.7 The fleeing escape variant. *Independence Day* (1996).

When reflecting on the escape scenario prototype and its variants, it is important to consider how the agency of the escapee is usually depicted, defined by the escapee's goals in relation to the relative ease or difficulty by which the obstacles in the situation are overcome. As we saw in the escape scenario prototype, their agency entailed the ability to extricate themselves from physical confinement and surmount the various obstacles put in their way. With respect to *First Blood* and *Raiders of the Lost Ark*, both John Rambo and Indiana Jones are depicted as handily overcoming the obstacles that they encounter, police officers in the first case and temple traps in the second. In these instances, the agency of the escapee is showcased but with the obstacles posing a sufficient enough challenge and level of risk such that the characters are presented as possessing special abilities that differentiate them from those around them. In the cases where the escapee requires helpers to assist, as was the case with *The Adventures of Robin Hood*, care is taken to show that the escapee possesses special abilities such that they are not wholly dependent on the helpers to escape from the situation; if not, they will remain characterized as a captive by the spectator. Robin Hood, notably, takes charge of his own escape by performing an impressive leap onto a horse, a feat of physical ability indicating his escaping prowess and the difficulty of keeping him captive.

Like the prototype, all of the escape variants discussed also underscore the agency, or lack thereof, of the escapee. In the variant in which an escape is additionally coupled with a pursuit sequence, agency is extended beyond the ability to extricate oneself from a physically confining situation but also the additional ability to elude capture. As we saw with the escape-pursuit combinations in *First Blood, The Rock,* and *Raiders of the Lost Ark*, the escapees also manifested the ability to elude, be it in the form of Rambo's aptitude in riding a motorcycle in various terrains, John Patrick Mason's knack of crashing through obstacles with the commandeered Hummer, or Indiana Jones' ability to outrun the Hovitos. In the variant in which the escapee performs a spectacular but risky act, such as Sean Archer's leap into the water, the ability to elude becomes even more pronounced since the action is one that runs an even greater risk of death.

However, an inversion of this agency exists in the fleeing escape variant. Instead of obstacles to be surmounted, the escapee recognizes that they face powers that dwarf their own abilities, such that any goals they possess are tossed aside to focus on the new goal of mere survival. At most, the fleeing escape variant can showcase an ability to remove oneself from the hostile conditions. John McLane in *Die Hard: With a Vengeance* did not attempt to confront the wall of water from the burst dam, which would have been a suicidal project, but endeavoured instead to flee. Equally, Jackson Curtis in *2012* maintained no illusions of the disparity of the power of the mega-quake and its ensuing destruction compared to his own inability to survive under those conditions. Rescue and flight remained his only life options. In some instances of the variant, such as in *Independence Day*, fleeing itself does not guarantee this ability to survive, with many citizen escapees simply perishing under the onslaught of superior forces. Agency in the escape scenario, therefore, manifests a spectrum of escaping abilities from the formidable to the weak.

Exemplar: *The Great Escape* (1963)

An examination of the extended escape sequence in *The Great Escape* (John Sturges, 1963) provides an opportunity to take a look at another instance of an escape sequence that fits within the scenario prototype. However, what is of particular interest is the fact that the sequence is produced on a much grander scale compared to the examples so far, both in relation to its duration but also because of its complexity given the number of escapees involved. Like the rescue sequences in *Superman* (1978) and *The Birth of a Nation* (1915), the escape sequence in *The Great Escape* demonstrates the ability of an action scenario to extend across the final act of a film.

Set during World War II in a German prisoner of war camp, the film commences by depicting a convoy of allied prisoners being transported to a new high-security prison specially designed to retain those Allied prisoners who had an extensive history of escaping at other prison camps. Upon arrival, prisoners are already scoping the prison in terms of its fenced perimeter and ascertaining the distance to the tree line. Group Captain Ramsey, a British officer, is brought to see Luftwaffe Colonel von Luger, who oversees the prison camp, and informs him that it is the duty of all Allied prisoners to try to escape as a means to support the war effort, particularly to re-direct German military time and resources from the front lines. As an illustration of such determination, the film next shows prisoners trying to hide amongst a crew of Russian tree cutters who are being escorted outside of the camp, but are promptly discovered and sent back. Virgil Hilts, an American Captain, then tests to see if the tower guards have blind spots by throwing his baseball at the fence perimeter and crossing the warning wire to retrieve it. But he is soon spotted and fired upon by the tower guards. Arriving by Gestapo escort shortly thereafter is Squadron Leader Roger Bartlett, who is told that if captured again while escaping, he will be executed. When Bartlett convenes a meeting with senior prisoners, he sets forth his bold plan for a mass escape involving two hundred and fifty prisoners tunnelling underneath the camp to the surrounding trees. Three tunnels are planned, codenamed 'Tom', 'Dick', and 'Harry', with the additional tunnels to allow for the contingency that if one is discovered, the other two will be available for the escape.

At its most basic level, the opening scenes function to introduce the ensemble cast of main characters who will feature prominently at the end during the final escape sequence. More significant for the analysis here, the opening sequence also stakes out the essential features of the captivity situation. These opening scenes establish the physical boundaries of captivity by revealing that the camp has two sets of fences ringing it, with guard towers stationed at the camp's perimeter. The viewer is also informed that the interior wire acts as a warning that if crossed by a prisoner, guards have orders to shoot them. In addition, work crews are rigorously checked to prevent escape via that route. The opening sequence also vividly provides access to prisoners' mental states, clearly displaying their goals, which are to divert German military resources through their attempted capture that would be otherwise directed toward Allied forces. By risking their lives through escape, they will likely save the lives of other Allied service members, and, as such, the prisoners are presented heroically.

The next part of the film consists of the allocation of prisoners into teams to undertake specific tasks in preparation for the escape. These include digging the tunnels, of course, but also obtaining additional items required for the escape such as cameras, identity cards, tools for digging, and civilian clothes. Because they must avoid detection from prison camp guards, these activities have their own obstacles. One such obstacle, and a major turning point in the film, is the guards' discovery of the tunnel labelled 'Tom', prompting the prisoners to focus on completing 'Harry' at an accelerated pace to meet the schedule. In addition, the tunnelling is not without its dangers, specifically when it collapses on Flight Lieutenant Danny Welinski. Although this middle section of the film possesses moments of suspense, the film has yet to enter into the escape scenario, strictly speaking. There is a distinction between preparing to escape and the act of escape.

The escape itself commences when the prisoners begin to sneak off through the tunnel. The sequence is split into two sections. The first takes place in the evening and centres on the prisoners making their way through the tunnel; the second occurs the next day as the escapees split in different directions and head out of German-occupied territory. In between the two is a brief scene that occurs where the Germans learn of the escape, and Colonel von Luger rounds up and counts the remaining prisoners to discover that seventy-six captives are missing. Although the scene provides important narrative information to the spectator, it also functions as a suspenseful delay by temporarily suspending the status of the escapees.

During the first section, the Allied party to enter the tunnel earliest consists of Bartlett, Flight Lieutenant Andrew MacDonald, and Lieutenant-Commander Eric Ashley-Pitt. Lying face downward, they are pulled forward on dollies towards the end of the tunnel where Hilts is stationed. Hilts digs upward to create a hole in the ground, and, when scouting the area above, he discovers the first obstacle to the escape, namely that the hole is twenty feet short from the woods, where the escapees now would run the risk of being discovered by guards and the searchlights. A master of escape through avoiding detection, Hilts solves the issue by positioning himself in the woods and setting up a rope signal that, when tugged, indicates when it is safe for the tunnel prisoners to come forward individually. Bartlett agrees, and the prisoners begin to make their way through the tunnel and to the woods, where they disperse to their allotted destinations.

The prison's air-raid siren goes off and, in the distance, bomb explosions are heard, causing the lights to be turned off in the camp as well as in the tunnel. This causes a double obstacle for the escapees to surmount. First, the journey through the tunnel has become darker and more difficult to navigate. Second, just after Welinski has summoned up his courage to overcome his claustrophobia and has entered the tunnel, the lights go out. The darkness augments his fear and prevents him from continuing the journey through the tunnel, thus blocking the passage for other prisoners. However, contingency fat lamps are ready and lit while Flight Lieutenant Willie Dickes, Welinski's best friend, comes through the tunnel to reassure and encourage him.

Once Welinski appears above ground, the blackout provides an opportunity for more prisoners to escape as a result of the darkness. Bartlett and MacDonald decide to go next, but the proceeding prisoner stumbles, thereby alerting a guard to his presence who checks the grounds as the prisoner lies motionless. Below ground, Griffith the tailor becomes impatient with the delay and eventually climbs up, without any signal to do so, with the guard catching sight of him. The guard pulls out his pistol and starts firing at Hilts. More guards arrive with the sound of gunshots heard as they enter the woods and try to capture the escaped prisoners.

It is at this point that the first section of the escape sequence ends. As indicated in the Introduction, the threat of physical risk in action scenarios can be either something that characters experience directly or is a potential inherent to the situation. The first part of the escape sequence lies primarily within the latter category. Although the journey down the tunnel is not depicted as being dangerous in and of itself, the risk of detection by armed guards is present, as demonstrated when the escape is discovered and the lethal force used by the guards. In addition, the escape situation in the first section exhibited obstacles with respect to the remaining distance to the woods, the lights going out, and Welinski's temporary loss of nerve. These obstacles possess a dramatic function by increasing suspense, but they also increase the level of risk to the escapees since with each delay, the chance of detection increases. That the escape must be undertaken under cover of the night introduces a deadline into the sequence and adds to the suspense.

Also notable in relation to the dramatic structure of the first section are the ways that boundaries and threshold moments are physically articulated. The boundaries that enclose the captives are no longer the fences that ring the perimeter of the camp but instead are expressed as the end of the tunnel and the distance to the woods. As a result, the threshold moment of escape from the camp is the moment the prisoners enter into the woods with its cover of darkness that offers relative and temporary safety from detection. Agency also takes on a distinctive inflection in this first section. Instead of the fighting abilities that Rambo uses to escape from the police precinct, the prisoners are unarmed, so they must rely upon stealth to avoid detection as well as possess a steady nerve that is not compromised by the claustrophobic conditions of the tunnel or the risk of discovery by the guards.

The second section of the escape sequence takes on a different form from the first through the extensive use of parallel editing. While the film does not follow the narrative paths of all seventy-six escapees, it does follow the events involving the main leads of the film by breaking the story down into six different lines of action, as illustrated in Table 3.

Table 3: The Great Escape (1963) Escape Sequence Breakdown*

	1st Line	2nd Line	3rd Line	4th Line	5th Line	6th Line
	Bartlett Mac-Donald Ashley-Pitt Hendley Blythe	Sedgwick	Hilts	Dickes Welinski	Cavendish	Hendley Blythe
Section 1	(1) arrival at Neustadt station	(2) steals bike	(3) laying wire across the road	(4) spot boat	(5) lift from lorry	
Section 2	(8) Gestapo on the train; Hendley and Blythe's leap	(5) travelling in desert	(7) Hilts on a motorcycle	(6) rowing down river	(17) checkpoint capture	
Section 3	(16) spotted by Kuhn; Ashley-Pitt shot	(12) spots train	(11) speeding to Swiss border	(10) continuing down river		(18) steals plane

	1st Line	2nd Line	3rd Line	4th Line	5th Line	6th Line
Section 4	(23) spotted at bus and captured; shot by German troops	(14) boards train	(13) pursued by troops	(24) board the Alta Stockholm		(20) plane crash, Blythe shot, Hendley captured
Section 5		(22) in France, meets French Resistance (25) heads toward Spain	(15) hides behind barn			
Section 6		(25) heads toward Spain	(19) Hilts encircled			
Section 7			(21) Hilts captured			

*The six narrative lines in the second part of the escape sequence are listed in columns. Sections of the narrative lines are numbered in chronological order of appearance in sequence.

Figure 3.8 Bartlett and MacDonald.
The Great Escape (1963).

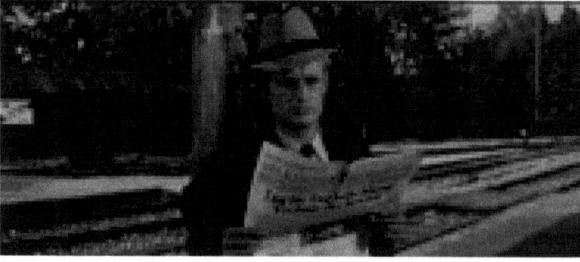

Figure 3.9 Ashley-Pitt. *The Great Escape* (1963).

Figure 3.10 Hendley and Blythe.
The Great Escape (1963).

Figure 3.11 Sedgwick. *The Great Escape* (1963).

Figure 3.12 Hilts. *The Great Escape* (1963).

Figure 3.13 Dickes and Welinski.
The Great Escape (1963).

Figure 3.14 Cavendish. *The Great Escape* (1963).

The second section commences when the first group arrives at Neustadt train station, and, to avoid detection, they split into three separate parties and enter into different carriages when the train arrives at the station [*Figures* 3.8-3.10]. At that point, the Gestapo make their appearance and also board the train, increasing the risk of capture for the escapees. The film next cuts to the 2nd line of action as Flying Officer Louis Sedgwick enters a sleepy village square, cuts the chain securing a bike, and absconds with it [*Figure* 3.11]. The 3rd line of action shows Hilts laying a wire across a road that takes out a German soldier on his motorcycle [*Figure* 3.12]. The 4th line of action sees Dickes and Welinski spot a boat along a riverbank [*Figure* 3.13]. The 5th line of action depicts Flight Lieutenant Dennis Cavendish receiving a lift from a seemingly friendly lorry driver [*Figure* 3.14]. By cross-cutting through these different lines of action, the film establishes the different modes of locomotion being used as means of escape, with each entailing different levels of the potential risk of capture.

Having established all the different trajectories of escape, the film cuts back to the 4th line of action as Dickes and Welinski leisurely row down the river, then switches to the 3rd line that presents Hilts in a German uniform and on the soldier's motorcycle while speeding off. The film returns to the 1st line of action taking place on the train where the Gestapo makes its rounds asking for passports, first stopping with Bartlett and MacDonald, who pretend to be French and then Ashley-Pitt, who is masquerading as a German. At this point, Flight Lieutenant Robert Hendley spots the Gestapo and realizes that he will not pass the inspection. He takes Flight Lieutenant Colin Blythe, who is near blind as a result of forging the documents for the escape, to the end of the train and both jump off it to avoid capture, a daring leap that bears similarities with that taken by Archer in *Face/Off* that offers a temporary respite from immediate capture. The action is also significant by creating a 6th line of action as Hendley and Blythe separate from the rest of the group.

The pace of the parallel editing hastens as the film cross-cuts from Sedgwick cycling through the countryside, to Dickes and Welinski continuing their journey down the river, to Hilts speeding along on route to Switzerland. The film then turns briefly to Sedgwick, who spots a freight train and cuts back to Hilts, who enters a border village with a Nazi military presence. Hilts is hailed by one of the military personnel, who he kicks down and then speeds off as a number of Germans fire at him and engage in pursuit on their motorcycles. Like other pursuits, obstacles are placed in their path. In this instance, Hilts adeptly steers through a narrow bridge while some of the pursuing Germans who are in a motorcycle with a sidecar crash into an adjacent fence, thereby demonstrating their lesser motorcycle-riding skills.

Hilts continues into the countryside with multiple motorcycles in pursuit. The film cuts to Sedgwick again as he abandons his bicycle to hop into one of the boxcars of the freight train just before it starts on its journey. The film returns to Hilts hiding behind a barn as a convoy of German soldiers proceeds down the road. Temporarily undetected, Hilts proceeds to take off the

German uniform, signalling his intention to make a run to the Swiss border. This passage of the pursuit sequence is therefore narratively transitional. While depicting the progress of the escapees, the sequence also functions to start to close down the 3rd storyline as the escape scenario seamlessly transitions into the pursuit mode, in addition to a vertical combination with the fight scenario marked by the firing of weapons.

At this point, the film reverts back to the 1st line of action as the train stops at the station. Herr Kuhn, the Gestapo agent who had brought Bartlett to the prison camp and warned him that he would be shot if captured again, waits at the station, underscoring the danger of capture. Bartlett and MacDonald disembark and get into the queue for an identity document check. When Herr Kuhn spots Bartlett, Ashley-Pitt rushes towards Kuhn and wrestles him to the ground, and directs Kuhn's pistol to fire at him. The sound of the gunshot and ensuing scream of a commuter alert the Gestapo present, who shoot at Ashley-Pitt as he attempts to run off, killing him in the process. In the ensuing chaos, Bartlett and MacDonald dash past the gates. The film then cuts to the 5th line of action as Cavendish, still travelling in the truck, enters into a town where the lorry driver pulls into a checkpoint lined with German soldiers, suggesting that he knew all along that Cavendish was an escapee. Cavendish is then questioned by the Gestapo and accused of being a spy on the basis of his civilian clothing, and is brought to a detention cell where he meets with other escapees who have been captured, which brings to an end the 5th line of action.

These moments in the escape sequence are consequently dramatically significant as threshold moments since the film presents events that turn against the escapees, with Ashley-Pitt shot dead and Cavendish captured. In addition, spectators are made aware of the fate of other escapees, and these adverse events set the pattern for most of the remaining plotlines.

The film returns to the 6th plotline as Hendley and Blythe reach a German airfield. Hendley sneaks upon and throttles a guard stationed at the hanger, allowing them to abscond in one of the training aircraft to make their way to Switzerland. The film next cuts back to Hilts, who has reached the German-Swiss border that is fortified with German soldiers, and as German motorcyclists bear down on him from both directions of the road. The soldiers start firing as Hilts heads off-road into the countryside, with the Germans still in pursuit. The film reverts to Hendley and Blythe in flight with the sight of the Alps, the other side of which lies Switzerland and freedom. As Hendley and Blythe prematurely celebrate, the plane's engine begins to fail and crash lands still within German territory. They escape from the burning wreckage, but a German military unit bears down upon them with a soldier firing his rifle at Blythe. Hendley surrenders to the oncoming forces as Blythe dies in his arms, thus bringing to an end the 6th line of action.

Returning to the 3rd plotline, Hilts continues to ride through the open countryside and approaches the German-Swiss border once again, which is ringed with a double barb wire fence. As a convoy of German troops advances from different directions, Hilts accelerates as he makes his run at the interior fence and jumps over it on his motorcycle in one of the film's iconic moments. Like Hendley and Blythe's daring leap, the motorcycle jump entailed physical risk to Hilts, but does not bring closure to the escape. As Hilts takes a run at the even taller second fence, the German troops fire upon him as he slides into its barbed wire and surrenders, bringing an end to the pursuit and a conclusion to the 3rd line of action.

The film then turns to the 2nd line of action where the spectator infers that the setting is within occupied France given the depiction of three German officers having a drink at a French café where Sedgwick is also seated, hiding behind a French newspaper. A waiter informs there is a phone call for Sedgwick, and as he takes the phone, the waiter and his father duck behind the counter, an action that Sedgwick wisely follows as well. An automobile then arrives and, in a drive-by shooting, guns down the German officers. Sedgwick then infers that the owners of the French café are members of the French Resistance and asks them to help him get to the Spanish border, to which they agree, serving the narrative function of helpers.

The narration then shifts to the remaining lines of action. Bartlett and MacDonald make their way to board a bus with two Gestapo officers at its door who ask them for their identity documents. Again, they pretend to be French citizens and as they board the bus, one of the officers says "good luck" in English, prompting MacDonald to spontaneously reply with a "thank you", thereby blowing their cover. The officers try to capture them, but Bartlett and MacDonald flee on foot, with additional soldiers arriving to pursue them down the streets of the town. As they flee, MacDonald is knocked down by a cyclist, causing Bartlett to separate from him. A horde of soldiers close in on MacDonald and capture him, bringing his escape attempt to an end. After fleeing along rooftops, Bartlett jumps down to speed along a street in which he encounters a police vehicle full of armed Germans. They detain Bartlett, and this time he masquerades as a German citizen. After a tense moment, they are satisfied with his responses, and they resume their search. Relieved, Bartlett picks up a newspaper to add to his disguise and pauses at a corner. From offscreen, the spectator hears "Herr Bartlett" to then reveal Untersturmführer Steinach, an SS officer who was a member who brought Bartlett to the prison camp, and who does not fall for his ruse. Pointing his pistol, Steinach orders hands up, with Bartlett resigning to his capture.

Bartlett is then taken to the same detention centre as Cavendish and is reunited with McDonald once again but as captives. From there, Bartlett, McDonald, and Cavendish are loaded onto a bus with other prisoners to be transported, presumably, back to the prison camp. When the transport vehicle stops on route, the prisoners are ordered out for a break. As they stretch their legs, the German forces set up a machine gun on a tripod and mow down all of the prisoners, with the gunfire poignantly echoing through the alpine valley, bringing the 1st line of action to a gloomy close.

The narration returns to the camp, presumably the next morning, where Colonel von Luger informs Captain Ramsey that eleven escapees will be returning to the camp while fifty of the escaping officers were shot, implying that they were executed. In a solemn moment, as the prisoners are gathered outside in silence, Ramsey reads the list of the escapees who were killed during the escape. The film finally returns back to the 4th plotline as Dickes and Welinski in their rowboat appear in a Baltic port and climb aboard the Alta Stockholm, suggesting that their remaining journey will take them to Sweden and, symbolically, to freedom. In the same spirit, the film cuts back to Sedgwick who is accompanied by two members of the Resistance who leave Sedgwick at a meadow where he meets a Spanish guide who leads him toward Spain with the Pyrenees in the distance, a final shot that brings the entire fifty-six-minute escape sequence to an end.

One of the outstanding features of the second section of the escape sequence is the way that it is narratively presented. John Sturges, the film's director, had other options in narrating the escape. For instance, instead of the parallel editing between the six plotlines, they could have been presented consecutively. One fundamental drawback to such an approach is the difficulty of indicating to the spectator how such plotlines are concurrent as op-posed to being erroneously interpreted as chronological. Through parallel editing, the spectator is more inclined to understand each of the plotlines as concurrent, in which the events in each storyline are understood to run parallel.

But there is an additional motivation to the use of parallel editing that was mentioned in the previous chapter in relation to the work of D. W. Griffith and his use of suspenseful delays. By cutting to another plotline, suspense is heightened in relation to the storyline that is left 'suspended'. For instance, when Hilts is first pursued by the German soldiers, the film then cuts to Sedgwick as he switches his mode of transport to a freight train. The spectator is not only taking in the events pertaining to Sedgwick but is also continuing to speculate on the fate of Hilts' escape. This heightening of suspense applies to all of the cross-cuts in the escape sequence in which the plotlines have yet to resolve.

Another significant aspect of this escape section is the way that it expresses boundaries. Instead of the physical boundedness of the prison camp that conforms to the escape scenario prototype, the boundaries principally assume the form of national boundaries once the escapees are outside of the prison camp. For Bartlett and MacDonald (and presumably Ashley-Pitt), their assumed destination is France, with their first relevant boundary the border between Germany and France, which they never reach. For Hendley and Blythe, their target boundary is the Swiss-German border, symbolized in the film by the Alps. As for Sedgwick, his boundary is the French-Spanish border, again symbolized as a mountain range, the Pyrenees. The Swiss-German border is also the relevant boundary for Hilts but this time expressed more viscerally as barbed wire fences in which Hilts literally gets entangled. For Dickes and Welinski, the boundary is that between Germany and Sweden, with the Alta Stockholm representative of a Swedish territorial domain. In Cavendish's case, the boundary was never established, suggesting he was the least successful of the escapees.

Obstacles and threshold moments take on their own specific inflection in the second section as well. In the first section involving escape through the tunnel, the main obstacle was detection by the guards. In the second section, however, the guards are replaced with Gestapo agents, SS officers, and German military figures positioned along routes of transportation. Document identity checkpoints loom large as well as obstacles in the 1st plotline, which are notably absent in the storylines involving Sedgwick, Dickes and Welinski.

Whereas the threshold moment in the first section was entry into the woods, the threshold moment in the second section varies in relation to the success of the escape. For Sedgwick, Dickes and Welinski, the threshold moments coincide with the crossing of the relevant boundaries that lead to freedom. For the cases of the unsuccessful escapees, the threshold moments are the point of capture or, in its most extreme instance, death. Even in these cases, unsuccessful escapees are still a win-win situation within the film's moral world. Even though they were unable to cross the boundary into freedom, they still instigated the redirection of Nazi resources from the war front, and, in that endeavour of risk and sacrifice, they attain heroic status.

The escape sequence in *The Great Escape* illustrates how an extended action sequence can manifest complexity, both with respect to its multiple-plotlines following a number of central characters, as well as through its combined action forms. Understanding the factors that contribute to action complexity will be explored in greater length in Chapter 8.

Chapter 3: The Capture Scenario

"All right, listen up, ladies and gentlemen, our fugitive has been on the run for ninety minutes... What I want from each and every one of you is a hard-target search of every gas station, residence, warehouse, farmhouse, henhouse, outhouse and doghouse in that area... Your fugitive's name is Dr. Richard Kimble. Go get him."
—Deputy Marshal Samuel Gerard[1]

One of the striking features of the capture scenario is that it is one of the most basic types of action. As we saw in the last chapter for *The Great Escape* (1963), a significant aspect of its escape sequence involved the German army and the Gestapo engaged in the capture of escaped prisoners of war. Capture is an inherent feature of the pursuit scenario as well. As was shown for the chase in *The Rock* (1996), also in the last chapter, pursuit sequences decompose to the more elemental action forms of escape, speed and capture or fight (dependent upon the aims of the pursuer). Furthermore, and as the quote from *The Fugitive* (Andrew Davis, 1993) amply illustrates, the capture scenario provides the opportunity to place narrative focus on the activities on the capturer. In order to better outline the capture scenario, it is, therefore, necessary to first differentiate it from these other related action forms.

The Capture Scenario Prototype

It is important to recognize that instances of the capture scenario can be found independent of escape situations. In such cases, individuals are captured in a manner that they have no opportunity to escape. Consider the routine occurrence of an arrest, as illustrated in *Rio Bravo* (Howard Hawks, 1959). Joe Burdette, a local town villain, shoots an innocent bystander who tried to

---

[1] Quote from Deputy Marshal Samuel Gerard, from *The Fugitive* (Andrew Davis, 1993).

intervene while Burdette was roughing up Dude, the town's former deputy sheriff. Burdette then heads to his brother's saloon for protection, after which John T. Chance, the town's sheriff, arrives with the intent to arrest him. One of Burdette's associates pulls a gun on Chance, but Dude arrives silently and shoots the gun out of his hand. Just as Burdette attempts to run off, Chance knocks him unconscious with his rifle, thereby preventing his escape, and drags him to jail with Dude's assistance.

Equally, instances of capture do not always involve pursuit, as the *Rio Bravo* arrest demonstrates. Later on in the film, Dude patrols the town but is ambushed by Burdette's men when he pauses at a water trough. He is punched unconscious and tied up. A gang member takes his hat and vest as a means to masquerade as Dude to lull Chance into a false sense of security. Once again, the film provides a case of capture with no additional escape element that would instigate a pursuit.

These instances are sufficient to outline the general features of the capture scenario prototype and its participants. The capture scenario minimally consists of two participants, namely the *capturer* and the *target*. Unlike captors whose narrative function is to prevent escape and rescue, the capturer's aim is instead to apprehend the target, who enjoys a greater level of freedom than a captive. Normally this involves capturers creating a trapping situation. Hence the often-heard term 'cornered' in crime films, which is not unlike the confinement situations found in rescue and escape scenarios. Critically, when capturers attempt to apprehend, it is not undertaken in the first instance with the intention to kill the target. If the main aim was the latter, then the aims of the capturer would be indistinguishable from the aims of participants within the fight scenario. When Chance arrives, he announces his aims to arrest Burdette in more formalized ways congruent with the law. In *Rio Bravo*'s other capture case, Burdette's men are not inhibited by any such legal obligation, so they capture Dude by stealth. But again, their aim is to apprehend, given that they tie Dude up with rope to render him immobile rather than simply kill him. Of course, in many capture situations, events escalate when the target proves resistant to arrest and starts firing at the capturers, thereby posing a lethal threat, causing the capturer's aims to consequently shift away from the intent to capture. This modification in aims mirrors a scenario shift whereby the situation horizontally evolves from a capture situation into a fight scenario.

The target in the capture scenario normally exhibits goals that oppose the aims of the capturer by attempting to escape, or by directly confronting them through force, or a combination of these strategies. Targets who successfully elude their capturers then become escapees, with the capture scenario vertically combining with the escape scenario. If the escape develops further into some form of a chase, then the situation manifests an even higher order of complexity by horizontally evolving with that of the pursuit scenario. In other instances, when the target is suddenly overpowered and consequently does not have the means to evade capture, or perhaps does not possess an awareness that they should, then the target in effect becomes a captive at the mercy of the capturers, as was the case with Dude's capture. In some cases, when the target faces the overwhelming and disproportionate power of the capturers, the target may then simply give themselves up and resign to become a captive. For instance, in *The Adventures of Robin Hood* (1938), Sir Guy of Gisbourne is made aware that Maid Marian has abetted Robin Hood's seditious activities so arrives at her residence to arrest her with his guards; Marian makes no attempt to resist and thus simply submits to her captivity.

Given the contrasting aims of the capturer and the target and the varying situations that may ensue, it is important to recognize how the event schema for the capture scenario, like other action form event schemas, is open-ended to accommodate such divergent outcomes. The proto-narrative of the capture scenario might result in success for the capturer by denying opportunities for the target to escape, be it by stealth, as was the case with Dude's capture, by superior power, as proved by the case with Burdette's arrest, or they submit without resistance to the arrest as was the case in Marian's seizure. Alternatively, the proto-narrative of the capture scenario may end with success for the target by possessing the ability to evade capture, or achieve success by overpowering the captures through force. In these instances, the proto-narrative of the capture scenario combines with either escape, pursuit, fight, or any combination of these additional action forms.

An instance of the capture scenario in *Bonnie and Clyde* (Arthur Penn, 1967) can illustrate how its proto-narrative can evolve. The Barrow gang, consisting of Clyde Barrow, Bonnie Parker, C.W. Moss, the getaway driver, Clyde's older brother Buck, and his wife Blanche, are wanted by the police after a series of robberies. They rent a motel cottage temporarily, and when ordering groceries, the delivery boy becomes suspicious, with the narrative implying that he informs the local police. In due course, a police vehicle quietly pulls into the drive of the premises, initiating the capture scenario. From a window, Clyde spots the vehicle and an armed police officer exiting the car. He then alerts the gang, who quickly gather their weapons. Clyde is the first to fire at the police, who return fire, thereby demonstrating resistance and the situation's escalating danger, as the capture predicament vertically combines with a fight scenario. A shootout ensues as police numbers increase and surround the building. Buck and Blanche exit the house from the back while being fired at; Bucks shoots a policeman in return as he makes his way to the police car blocking the exit to the drive. Buck disengages its parking brake as Clyde bursts through the garage in their vehicle with the remaining Barrow gang inside. Buck hops onto the car's running board as Clyde rams the police vehicle out of its path, thereby segueing from the fight scenario to that of escape. The gang weave their way through the police blockade as Buck grabs Blanche and pulls her into the escaping vehicle.

One important dimension of capture scenarios is the narrative perspective that the story assumes when depicting capture situations. In the *Bonnie and Clyde* example, the narrative perspective is weighted heavily toward the Barrow gang as targets not only in terms of the amount of screen-time allocated to depicting them but also by encouraging the spectator to engage with and sympathize with their situation. In contrast, the police as capturers remain unindividuated and nameless, whose identities are reduced to their narrative function as capturers. The only law enforcement officer in the film to receive individuation is Frank Hamer, a Texas Ranger, but who appears intermittently and is portrayed antisympathetically. By assuming a narrative perspective that places greater emphasis on the targets-cum-escapees, the narration puts more stress on the escape dimension of the capture scenario.

In contrast, there are instances where greater narrative focus is placed upon the capturers with the capture scenario foregrounded. A good illustration of this can be found in the police raid scene of *Point Break* (Kathryn Bigelow, 1991). Johnny Utah, a rookie FBI agent, and Angelo Pappas, his veteran partner, are on the hunt for a gang who wear masks of American ex-presidents when undertaking bank robberies. While returning back from the beach, Utah spots a group of rambunctious surfers in a jeep - Tone, Warchild, Bunker, and Archbold - the same surfers with which he had a previous altercation. Utah then runs a check on them that initially meets with the profile of the bank-robbing gang and secures a warrant for a raid.

An FBI team, consisting of Angelo, Utah, Cullen, Alvarez, and Babbit, assemble the next morning outside of Bunker's home, with Angelo providing instructions to each as to their roles in the raid. They then surround the house in ways that replicate the entrapped situation found in the escape scenario. Angelo knocks on the door that is opened by Fiberglass, one of the female gang members, pretending to have lost a dog as a means of securing entry. Meanwhile, Utah spies into the house through a window using a dental mirror and spots Tone lying on the bed, while Freight Train, another female gang member, is in the shower. Suddenly Bunker and Warchild burst into the room, alerting Tone that someone is at the door and take out an arsenal of weapons. Utah then attempts to warn Angelo of the danger, but Alvarez is unable to pass on the message given the background whir of a neighbour's lawnmower adjacent to Utah. The film then cuts to the interior for the first time, offering a narrative perspective of the targets as they arm and ready themselves for the incursion. After hearing Fiberglass' sustained refusals to open the door, Angelo finally shoves through and announces, "FBI, gorgeous". At that point, Bunker fires at Angelo with an assault rifle, but he ducks behind a wall with Fiberglass, as the capture scenario vertically combines with the fight action form.

Utah then appears from a back door and orders Bunker to drop his weapon, but he pivots instead to now fire in Utah's direction. Utah returns the fire with his pistol shooting multiple rounds into Bunker's chest. Warchild suddenly appears with a rotary shotgun and fires at Utah, who leaps out of harm's way and shoots back. Alvarez and Babbit finally burst through the back door and wrestle to the ground, and handcuff a seeming gang member, that is later on revealed to be an undercover DEA agent. Archbold then emerges and takes Fiberglass hostage at gunpoint, threatening to blow her head off and orders Angelo to back down to allow him through the front door. Demonstrating his policing experience, Angelo takes aim and fires a round into Archbold's head, killing him on the spot, providing the sequence's first embedded rescue (of Fiberglass).

The film returns to Utah and Warchild as they continue to exchange gunfire, and as Freight Train emerges from the shower to viciously attack Utah. Tone, in absolute fright, tries to escape by heading to a door through which Alvarez simultaneously charges past, causing Tone to discharge his pistol into his own foot accidentally. Babbit then takes aim at Warchild as he attempts to escape from the house, but Freight Train appears from behind and stabs him twice in the back. As she raises the scissors for the third time, Angelo grabs her hands and slams her head into a wall, knocking her unconscious, thereby enacting a second embedded rescue (of Babbit). Warchild clears the blinds from a window in preparation to exit, but Utah leaps from behind, causing them to crash through the window and take the action back outside. Warchild continues his escape efforts and enters the yard of the neighbour mowing his lawn, but Utah jumps on him again. As they wrestle, Warchild manages to pull out a large knife, increasing the risk to Utah. They continue to struggle and become more proximate to the whirling blade of the lawnmower, increasing the danger to an even higher level. Utah then forces the knife closer to the mower's spinning blades, and with contact, the knife flings out of Warchild's hand. At that moment, Warchild overpowers Utah and shoves his head to the whirling blades, using the lawnmower as an improvised weapon. With Utah's face dangerously close to the blades, Angelo at the last moment appears and fires at the lawnmower, causing it to stop, to next point his weapon at Warchild, thus ending the raid with the last embedded rescue (of Utah) and the handcuffed arrest of Warchild.

As this capture sequence demonstrates, greater narrative focus is placed upon the capturers and on the raid itself, as compared to the capture example in *Bonnie and Clyde*. Such emphasis derives partly from the fact that Utah and Angelo are central characters in the film, whereas the surfer gang is more peripheral to the film's main story. In addition, instead of depicting the FBI agents as anonymous capturers as was the case in *Bonnie and Clyde*, they are differentiated by name and are shown to have varying rapports with one another as the development of the raid is detailed, with particular focus on Utah to convey to the viewer his experience on his first raid. The moral valence of the raid leans heavily toward the capturers as well. The gang is depicted as possessing a dangerous propensity for violence given their readiness to initiate a gunfight with the FBI agents, threaten one of their own members as a hostage, and are revealed later on to be drug traffickers. In contrast, the FBI agents exhibit comparative restraint in their use of weapons by mostly returning fire when fired upon since their main priority is to arrest rather than kill. Most significantly, Angelo performs three embedded rescues during the raid, deeds of the heroic, and exhibits comparative restraint when arresting Warchild.

In other instances, the narrative focus between capturers and targets is more evenly balanced. *First Blood* (1982) achieves this equilibrium by opposing Rambo, as the protagonist, against Sheriff Teasle and his policing team, as antagonists. After Rambo's successful escape into the woods, Teasle organizes a manhunt using a pack of Dobermans and a helicopter to track him down.

The film then cuts to Rambo, who demonstrates his survival skills by making a makeshift jacket out of discarded cloth and rope to withstand the cold, to then ascend higher into the forest. The parallel editing pattern continues between the capturers and the target until Rambo reaches a cliff face of a gorge with a river down below. With the capturers in sight, Rambo starts to climb down the cliff face. At that point, Deputy Sergeant Art Galt, who had sadistically abused Rambo while interned at the precinct, arrives in a helicopter. The pilot of the helicopter catches sight of Rambo hanging precariously from a cliff ledge as Galt fires at him with his rifle. In doing so, Galt's actions reinforce the moral boundary between the intent to capture and the intent to kill.

The parallel editing pattern shifts between Galt steading himself in the helicopter, firing at his prey, to Rambo hanging on the ledge, to Teasle on a police radio demanding that Galt speaks to him. Trapped on the cliff face, Rambo enacts the daring leap escape variant by releasing his grip, springing off the cliff, and landing on a tall pine tree that breaks his downward fall. With a large gash in his right arm, Rambo hides behind the tree trunk as the helicopter descends, with Galt continuing to fire at him. Rambo then grabs a large rock that he hurls at the helicopter, causing the helicopter to swerve, and Galt to lose his balance and fall to his death, an event that temporarily pauses the capturers' manhunt. In this sequence, therefore, parallel editing is additionally used to reinforce the film's balance of narrative focus upon the capturers and the target, an equilibrium that also places equal weight upon the capture and the escape scenarios.

The dramatic structure of the capture scenario differs substantially from that of escape scenario in a number of respects. Crucially, the dramatic question that the capture scenario poses is whether the capturers will be successful in their attempt to secure their target. The difficulty of that task will depend upon the challenges the target throws toward the capturers and their comparative agency to resist seizure, and the degree of difficulty can be conceived as a spectrum. At one end of the spectrum are those instances in which the target simply yields to capture in the face of overwhelming force, as was the case with Maid Marian in *The Adventures of Robin Hood*, as well as the capture of Dude in *Rio Bravo*. Next in difficulty are those instances in which the target is able to escape but is eventually captured, as was illustrated in *The Great Escape* when Virgil Hilts temporarily eluded his pursuers but is apprehended at the Swiss border. Difficulty dramatically increases in cases where the target resists capture by engaging in combat, as had occurred in the *Point Break* raid. At the other end of the spectrum are those instances in which the challenges of capture are too difficult to overcome and result in failure, be it the Barrow gang escaping from the police raid in *Bonnie and Clyde* or Rambo's capability to elude the manhunt and evade Galt's rifle fire in *First Blood*.

Ascendency in the capture scenario is consequently contingent upon the extent of resistance that the target exhibits and the ability of the capturer to overcome such opposition. In the Maid Marian case, Sir Guy's ascendency is achieved simply by securing her compliance, with the threshold moment consisting of his guards escorting her out of the castle chamber. In the capture instance involving Burdette in *Rio Bravo*, Chance's ascendency was attained with ease through Dude's assistance in disarming one of Burdette's associates along with Chance's own powerful blow to swiftly end Burdette's bolt to the door, which constituted the threshold capture moment. Like the escape scenario, certain films present multiple attempts at capture over the course of their stories, such as *Bonnie and Clyde*, *Dillinger* (John Milius, 1973), and *The Fugitive*, where ascendency can be both exhibited at the local level of each capture situation, and over the course of the narrative itself.

In *Point Break*, the ascendency of the capturers takes on a different complexion as each of the resistant gang members presents challenges of different magnitudes that have to be overcome. The first amongst these was Fiberglass' refusal to open the door, which Angelo surmounts by eventually shoving himself through the door. Next, Utah terminates Bunker's potentially lethal assault rifle fire challenge by emptying multiple rounds into his chest and, presumably, killing him. Archbold presents a different obstacle to capture by taking a hostage, demanding passage out of the house. Angelo removes the obstruction through one shot to Archbold's head. Freight Train, initially depicted as a sexualized object in the shower, proves a more formidable challenge through her combative nature. Yet, she is dispatched by Angelo, who knocks her unconscious. Tone shoots his own foot and so proves to be no challenge whatsoever. Warchild, in contrast, provides the most resilient challenge through the use of multiple weapons. He comes closest to escape but, in the end, could not get past the neighbour's lawn. His arrest represents the threshold moment of the raid, with the progression to that point a gradual attrition waged against the targets.

Like most action scenarios, the capture scenario prototype does not possess an inherent moral valence since the capturer or the target can be either morally virtuous or villainous. As seen in *Rio Bravo*, the first capture situation presents Chance, the capturer, as morally virtuous by risking his life to arrest a murderer, whereas, in the film's other capture situation, Burdette's men as capturers are amoral outlaws with Dude as the target, depicted as morally upstanding through his efforts to stay sober and regain his dignity. The capture sequence in *First Blood* maintains the same moral valence of the initial escape sequence discussed in the last chapter, whereby the captors turned capturers continue to exhibit morally dubious aims. Teasle's efforts to capture Rambo seem more motivated out of spite than the intention to protect the town, and it is Teasle's vindictiveness toward Rambo that eventually puts the town of Hope at risk. Art Galt becomes even more venal when he breaches the moral boundary between the intent to capture and the intent to kill, even though Rambo poses no physical threat to him while hanging on a cliff ledge.

Not all films, however, necessarily present such clear-cut distinctions between the morally righteous and the villainous. As film theorist Murray Smith has maintained, there are films that exhibit a Manichaean structure in which their narrative worlds are split along the lines of good and evil; but there are other films that manifest instead a graduated moral structure in which the ethical differences between characters are morally grey (1995, 205-212). *Bonnie and Clyde* falls within the latter camp. The Barrow gang, as targets, are moral composites and, even though they do not manifest a serial killer mentality, they still use lethal force when robbing banks, as attested when Clyde shoots a bank employee in the face. But along with their violent outlaw propensity, they also exhibit positive attributes. Bonnie and Clyde demonstrate genuine affection for each other, whereas Buck and Clyde show some level of sibling attachment to one another. The police, as capturers, also do not incarnate unalloyed virtue. As indicated earlier, the police are, for the most part, unindividuated and nameless, and as their hunt for the Barrow gang progresses in the film, their use of excessive firepower is more akin to state oppression than the actions associated with an institution protecting a vulnerable community. In other words, the film does not portray the police heroically, unlike the representatives of the law in many classical westerns, such as *Dodge City* (1939). Frank Hamer, as a figure of the law, does show some personality in his determination to hunt down the Barrow gang, but this goal is tinged with vindictiveness after his humiliating capture by the Barrow gang when attempting to arrest them.

The most critical element of the moral world of the film is the historical context of the 1930s Depression and its depiction of banks that foreclosed properties and, in so doing, dispossessed communities of their homes. As Lester D. Friedman has observed, banks and their affiliated institutions are the true villains of the story:

> "Throughout the film, Clyde and his gang make clear distinctions between people and institutions. The latter represent a faceless, heartless expression of governmental ineptitude and failure, the former the human face of this political tragedy. Thus, their bank robberies represent more than simple greed or even economic desperation; they symbolize a frontal attack on the cruel policies that have humiliated the people and destroyed the backbone of rural America's social and economic organization" (2000, 47).

It is within this broader moral context that the *Bonnie and Clyde* capture scenario is additionally situated. The police are in effect a symbolic extension of the banks through their attempt to capture the Barrow gang and put an end to their robberies, actions that represent the interests of the banks rather than the community at large, members of which have been victims of their foreclosures, such as the farming family that Bonnie and Clyde meet during target practice earlier in the film. Consequently, the moral framework of *Bonnie and Clyde* is far more complex since the moral distinction between capturers and targets is less straightforward than that of *First Blood* or *Rio Bravo,* where their narrative worlds largely cleave along the lines of the good and the bad.

Given that the capture scenario prototype often involves armed law enforcement officers and targets who are resistant to arrest, it is not surprising that physical risk looms large in this action form. In capture situations, physical risk can arise with respect to both the capturer and the target. In *Rio Bravo,* when Chance enters the saloon to arrest Burdette, he runs the risk of being shot. Similarly, when Burdette's men sneak up on Dude, they are also under the threat of being shot, given Dude's previous demonstration of pistol expertise. In the *Bonnie and Clyde* capture situation, the police put themselves in clear danger when they try to trap the Barrow gang at their motel cottage, reinforced by the resulting gunfight in which two officers are shown to be shot. The police involved in the *First Blood* manhunt put themselves in danger given Rambo's superior combat skills from his previous military experience. During the *Point Break* raid, the FBI agents are shot at with an assault rifle and a rotary shotgun, punched and kicked, and stabbed with scissors; Utah almost has his face sheared off by a lawnmower blade.

Equally, targets are at physical risk in capture situations. Although Maid Marian submits to her arrest in *The Adventures of Robin Hood,* the danger was latent in this situation had she attempted to escape or tried to fight her way out of her chamber, through the opposing force of Sir Guy and his guards. Burdette in *Rio Bravo* attempts to escape but is instantly knocked unconscious by Chance, as is Dude when punched in the face by his capturers.

Miraculously, the Barrow gang in *Bonnie and Clyde* emerge unscathed from the police raid on their motel cottage, but later on in the film, they come out of the Platte City ambushes far worse, with Buck fatally wounded, Blanche blinded, Clyde shot in the arm, and Bonnie shot in her shoulder. The *Point Break* surfer gang are also resistant targets and suffer a significant toll. Bunker is shot in the chest multiple times and presumably dies from his wounds, while Archbold is shot dead when Angelo defuses the hostage-taking. Tone, through his own incompetence, shoots his own foot. Freight Train is knocked unconscious by Angelo, whereas Warchild is shoved through a window and wrestled to the ground by Utah, to be finally kicked by Angelo when arrested. Fatalities, whether they be capturers or targets, are routine in this action form.

Capture Combinations

As has been highlighted, the capture scenario prototype, given its open-ended narrative structure, readily combines with other action forms. Amongst the most recurrent combinations is the fight scenario vertically combined with the capture scenario given the recurrence of resistant targets. The combination is vertical instead of horizontal in those cases where the intention to capture persists as the situation escalates into a fight. When Chance knocks down Burdette with his rifle in *Rio Bravo*, an instance of uni-directional violence, the intention to arrest Burdette endures, as attested by Chance and Dude dragging the unconscious Burdette to jail. The intention to capture also persists in *Point Break* despite the gunfire and attacks the FBI agents face during the raid, most tellingly expressed through Warchild's arrest that brings closure to the scene. At the same time, the FBI agents fire back at the surfer gang, on occasion with lethal intent, as was the case when they shot Bunker and Archbold. In the *First Blood* capture sequence, the intention to kill splits with the intention to capture as Galt disobeys Teasle's order and fires at Rambo, provoking retaliation when Rambo lobs a stone at the helicopter. With regard to the

115

capture situation in *Bonnie and Clyde*, although there is no explicit expression of the intent to arrest by the policemen, the narrative presumption is that capture is their aim as a result of their social function as the police, and that aim continues despite the firefight with the Barrow gang. However, as the story progresses, the police dramatically increase in both number and firepower in subsequent ambushes, with the intent to kill superseding the intent to capture. The film's final ambush of the unarmed Bonnie and Clyde is an unequivocal expression of uni-directional violence and the intent to kill, poignantly expressed in its aftermath shot [*Figure* 4.1].

Figure 4.1 Aftermath shot stemming from uni-directional violence in *Bonnie and Clyde* (1967).

Another typical combination consists of capture situations vertically combining with escape scenarios. Such combinations particularly arise in instances when escapees are at large, as was the case with *The Great Escape*, or fugitives who are wanted by the police, as manifested in *Bonnie and Clyde*. In such cases, capture situations are, as it were, the obverse face of a dual-sided action combination, with escape featuring on its reverse side. The target's compulsion to escape capture is also an inherent feature of the prototype as attested by Burdette's impulse to bolt to the saloon's exit, the Barrow gang's escape strategy, and the attempted escapes by members of the surfer gang in *Point Break*. Given the propensity for escape scenarios to horizontally develop into pursuits, it is also possible to find combinations of the capture-escape-pursuit kind.

The Little Bohemia Lodge ambush in *Public Enemies* (Michael Mann, 2009) can illustrate such a combination. Melvin Purvis, an FBI agent, is on a manhunt for John Dillinger and Baby Face Nelson, who had recently robbed a bank in Sioux Falls but were wounded in the process. They retreat to the lodge to recoup, along with Red Hamilton, Homer Van Meter, and Ed Shouse, other members involved in the robbery. After gleaning information on Dillinger's whereabouts from one of his captured men, Purvis organizes an ambush. Upon arrival, and under cover of darkness and the woods, Purvis instructs his men to surround the lodge, in ways similar to the capture situations in *Bonnie and Clyde* and *Point Break*. Charles Winstead, an officer assisting Purvis, wisely advises waiting for backup since there are too many ways for Dillinger and Nelson to escape, advice that Purvis rashly ignores. As the FBI agents advance on the lodge, three men head toward a vehicle and begin to drive off. Believing them to be part of the gang, Purvis orders them to stop, and soon several agents shower the vehicle with Tommy gun bullets until it comes to a rest.

The gunfire alerts Nelson at the lodge bar, as well as Dillinger resting in his room. They both head to their respective windows and start firing at the FBI agents, with Hamilton joining in the shooting, vertically escalating the capture situation with a fight scenario. Purvis then advances towards the stationary vehicle, only to discover that two of the occupants are dead, with the third in the back seat still alive, but none are members of the gang, evidence that the capture scenario poses risks to civilians in the vicinity as well. Nelson calls out for Shouse, who comes down the stairs and commences firing at the agents outside. After a prolonged exchange of heavy gunfire, Dillinger and Hamilton breakout through an upstairs window, horizontally commencing the escape component as they flee into the nearby woods. Nelson then jumps through a window, making his escape as well, shifting the capture sequence into the woods, and splitting the action along two plotlines: one consisting of Dillinger and Hamilton's escape, the other following Nelson's getaway.

Purvis orders Agent Carter Baum to drive around the woods to head off Nelson. Meanwhile, the film cuts to Winstead and agent Clarence Hurt as they spot Dillinger and Hamilton making their escape and follow after them. Once within range, Winstead fires at the escapees with his lever-action shotgun, who are hiding behind trees. After a pause, Dillinger assumes the coast is clear, and they go forward. But Hurt has taken the high ground and fires at them with his Tommy gun, fatally wounding Hamilton. Dillinger and Hamilton make it to another building and demand from its owner the keys to his car. The film cuts back to Nelson as he makes it to the road and can hear the approach of Baum in his vehicle. Mistaking Nelson for a passer-by, Baum fatefully stops his vehicle, allowing Nelson to shoot him in point-blank range with his machine pistol through the driver-side window. Baum then slumps out of the car, with Nelson emptying further rounds into his body, to then drive off in his car. Alerted by the gunfire, Purvis makes his way to the road to find Baum dying from his gunshot wounds, and asks who shot him, and with his last dying words, Baum informs Purvis that it was Nelson.

Purvis sees another car approaching and stands on the road to block its path. As it comes to a screeching halt, Purvis finds two of his agents in the vehicle and orders the driver to turn around and pursue Nelson, as the sequence horizontally shifts gear into a pursuit sequence. As Nelson continues along the road, he picks up Van Meter and Shouse, who have also made their way to the road. With Nelson's vehicle within firing range, Purvis starts shooting, prompting Van Meter to respond in kind, thereby continuing the vertical combination of the fight scenario now situated within a pursuit. Van Meter runs out of ammo, while Purvis continues to fire at the vehicle, causing it to cannon roll into an adjacent field. Shouse dies from the accident, and Nelson and Van Meter escape from the vehicle. Purvis and the FBI agents soon arrive, and, with an intent to kill triggered by Baum's murder, Purvis guns down Van Meter as he tries to abscond again. In a desperate attempt to escape, Nelson shoots one of the FBI agents but is then shot multiple times by Purvis and other FBI men. As his body is riddled with bullets, he continues to fire his Tommy gun in one last sociopathic blaze of glory. In an epilogue to the capture sequence, the film finally cuts back to Dillinger and Hamilton, now in town and stopped in front of a pharmacy. Dillinger vainly attends to Hamilton's gunshot wounds, but he dies nonetheless.

The *Public Enemies* action sequence consequently exhibits a tripartite narrative structure of capture, escape, and pursuit that shifts the action to different settings with each development. From the vantage point of action combinations, however, the sequence is less straightforward since an ambiguity exists in the action sequence that derives from the lack of clarity of the goals of the FBI agents. The sequence commences with the capture scenario as the FBI agents surround the building. The order for the three civilians to stop their car is consistent with the intention to arrest, but once Purvis and other FBI agents fire at the vehicle, it is unclear if the intention to arrest persists since their gunfire is intended to minimally immobilize the occupants in the car who they mistake for Dillinger's gang. If the case, then the combinatory development would consist of a vertical combination of the capture situation with the fight scenario, that leads to an additional vertical combination once Dillinger's gang escapes into the woods, with the presumption of the intent to capture continuing. The sequence then horizontally transforms into an automotive chase that absorbs the capture and escape elements into the pursuit action form. The fight scenario vertically persists as Purvis and Van Meter exchange fire from their vehicles. With the crash, the sequence horizontally mutates again but into a pure fight mode with the intent to capture evidently ditched as the FBI agents fire at Van Meter and Nelson with uninhibited abandon.

Alternatively, if the FBI aborted the aim to capture at the point they fired at the civilian vehicle, which caused Dillinger and Nelson to start shooting at them from the lodge, then the action sequence takes on a slightly different combinatory form. The initial capture situation quickly horizontally shifts into a fight scenario, only to resurface later but as an incorporated element of the chase, a specific form of capture that has as its immediate goal not to arrest but the aim to halt the potential escape of the pursued. These ambiguous intentions of the FBI agents impact upon the combinatory nature of its action forms, and in a manner that increases the perceived levels of risk as the capture scenario shapeshifts with the fight action form.

Capture Scenario Variations

As can be gleaned from some of the examples discussed so far, the capture scenario prototypically, but not exclusively, manifests itself in crime films that involve law enforcement officials engaged in their institutional function of apprehending criminals, be they the law enforcement agents in *Rio Bravo*, *Bonnie and Clyde*, *First Blood*, *Point Break*, or *Public Enemies*. Even when Sir Guy arrests Maid Marian in *The Adventures of Robin Hood*, he invokes the law against treason as justification for her arrest. Variation from the prototype, therefore, comes in the form of capture situations that are not undertaken by law enforcement agents. The two most recurrent variations in the capture scenario typicality gradient are kidnapping and animal capture.

The Kidnapping Variant

The kidnapping variant is the inverse of the capturing instances that are undertaken within the confines of the law in the key respect that kidnapping is normally perceived as an activity that not only breaks the law but is also an immoral act. Consequently, unlike the prototype capture scenario where the morally virtuous and the villainous can readily swap between the capturer and the target, the moral posts of the kidnapping variant remain more fixed as the capturers are normally evil and the targets typically innocent victims. Similar to the prototype, the initial intention of kidnapping is not to kill the target; in many cases, the aim is to secure a ransom, requiring the target to be kept alive.

The kidnapping sequence in *Proof of Life* (Taylor Hackford, 2000) can illustrate. Set in Tecala, a fictional South American country, Peter Bowman is an engineer contracted to build a new dam for Quad Carbon, a multinational oil company. During Bowman's drive to his office, his usual route is diverted by a religious procession and takes an alternative path that leads to a police blockade with a queue of traffic. A motorcyclist with a passenger arrives and is instructed by a policeman to enter into the queue, but the motorcyclist makes a U-turn in the opposite direction, prompting the policeman to fire at them with his automatic weapon. The shooting incites a group of ski-masked terrorists to descend from the adjacent ravine, with one of them pointing his rifle at Bowman before he has an opportunity to call for help. As the terrorists round up individuals from the vehicles, one of the terrorists tosses a grenade under a police car, causing it to explode. Bowman, along with other hostages, are directed into covered pickups that speed off from the scene and head to the terrorists' mountain camp.

Like other action sequences, the danger in the scene is accented. The readiness for the policeman to use his weapon on a motorcyclist simply for making a U-turn is intended to bring to mind associations with failed states in South and Central America that are close to anarchy. In addition, the police presence is shown to be quickly overwhelmed by the armed terrorists, suggesting that different sources of danger lurk everywhere. The moral valence of the scene is also made clear to the viewer in relation to the status of the capturers and the targets. In the scene previous to the kidnapping, Bowman and his wife Alice have an argument concerning their stay in the country, and, while Bowman may have been guilty of being insensitive to his wife's concern's, there is nothing in his behaviour that warrants the level of punishment of a kidnapping. The terrorists, on the other hand, appear as callous opportunists with regard to who they take hostage. As the viewer learns later, a poor and defenceless mother with children is amongst the individuals kidnapped. In addition, Terry Thorne, an expert negotiator hired to resolve the crisis, informs Alice and Peter's sister that the terrorist organization who took her husband no longer has a political motive, and that kidnapping has become for the organization a major source of income, thereby characterizing the group as greedy rather than righteous. Within this narrative context, Bowman as a target is presented as an innocent victim, unlike the outlaw targets encountered in the crime films previously discussed; the terrorists as capturers are presented as amoral opportunists who kidnap not for political justice but for financial gain.

The kidnapping sequence in *Sicario: Day of the Soldado* (Stefano Sollima, 2018) provides a different take on the moral valence of the kidnapping scenario. In retaliation for a suicide bombing believed to be carried out by terrorists smuggled into the country by Mexican drug cartels, Matt Graver, a CIA officer, is provided a green light by the American government to use covert measures to combat the groups. They decide to instigate a war between the cartels by assassinating a lawyer for the Matamoros cartel, and kidnap Isabel Reyes, the teenage daughter of Carlos Reyes, the kingpin of a rival cartel, who lives in Mexico City. While returning home from her private school in a convoy of two large SUVs, Matt Graver and his operatives make their move by donning ski-masks and following her in their vehicles. When using her iPad on the journey home, Isabel notices that the cell signal has cut out. Her guard senses that something is up and orders the driver to accelerate. A blast causes the lead vehicle of the convoy to be overturned, blocking their path, and as Isabel's driver puts the SUV in reverse, a pickup rams into its rear, thereby blocking a retreat, as another of Graver's vehicles turns up with armed operatives. They then extract a terrified Isabel from the SUV and bind her wrists in zip cuffs. When brought to the operatives' car, Grazer's men place blacked-out goggles, ear muffs, and a darkened cloth bag onto her head, to ensure that she does not discover their identity. Alejandro Gillick, a covert operative involved in the mission and who murdered the lawyer, informs Isabel's guard that the kidnapping is a reprisal for the attack on the Matamoros cartel, in an attempt to sow strife between the two cartels. The film then cuts to an airport where a jet is waiting to fly Isobel out of the country to a safe house in Texas.

The initial motivation for the kidnapping by the CIA and the American government was built upon the justification of weakening the Mexican cartels. The cartels are perceived to be ruthless, profiteering from the trafficking of drugs and illegal immigrants. They are also initially believed to be responsible for the transportation of terrorists into the United States. In such a context, the CIA and the American government consider the kidnapping to be in the service of a greater good that exceeds the moral concerns of the fate of one teenage girl.

Whether these grounds are in fact justifiable is dubious, and the film is quick to undermine them and present the morally questionable operations of the CIA. Although Isabel is depicted earlier in the film as a spoiled teenager who believes she is untouchable as a result of her father's power, the viewer is nonetheless encouraged to emotionally side with her during the kidnapping, given her terrified state. Isabel is also used as a pawn in a larger game when the CIA fake a rescue of her at the safehouse. Along with her treatment, the CIA is presented as equally cold-blooded as the cartels. In a subsequent scene when Grazer is surveying satellite imagery of the kidnapping site, he appears unfazed by the deaths of the drivers and guards directly stemming from the ambush, one caused by the blast itself, the rest murdered by a policeman working for Carlos Reyes. In addition, during a debrief with Cynthia Foards, Grazer's superior, he is informed that the terrorists who carried out the suicide bombing were actually internal to the US, further undermining the morality of the kidnapping by targeting the wrong people. The sequence consequently uses the moral difficulties arising from the kidnapping to be indicative of the broader moral haze of the war on drugs itself.

The Animal Capture Variant

Capture is not restricted in film to the seizure of people but also extends to animals and creatures of fantastic or outer space origin. One type of film in which the capture of animals appears is the safari film, a sub-genre of the adventure film. Normally

123

such films involve big game hunting, such as *Safari* (Edward H. Griffith, 1940), *The Macomber Affair* (Zoltan Korda, 1947), *Safari* (Terence Young, 1956), *The Last Safari* (Henry Hathaway, 1967), and *White Hunter Black Heart* (Clint Eastwood, 1990). Human hunt films, often based upon Richard Connell's short story *The Most Dangerous Game* (1924), including Irving Pichel and Ernest B. Schoedsack's noted 1932 film adaptation, take the safari hunting premise but replace the animals targeted as prey with humans. *Predator* (John McTiernan, 1987) updates the safari hunt film by situating within a science fiction tale of an alien creature that hunts a paramilitary team for sport, and amongst its tactics is to lay lethal traps. However, another strain maintains the exotic settings of the safari film but involves the capture of animals instead, as opposed to killing them purely for sport. Such films include *Tarzan's Revenge* (D. Ross Lederman, 1938), *White Pongo* (Sam Newfield, 1945), and *Rampage* (Phil Karlson, 1963).

Amongst the best-known films in this latter category is *Hatari!* (Howard Hawks, 1962) that depicts a team of eclectic individuals who operate a business in Tanganyika by capturing wild animals that are shipped off to zoos. The film alternates between scenes of team comradery at their compound with action sequences of capturing wild animals as they complete their list of different types of animals to be caught. The film also underscores the risks involved in their business. As noted by Michael J. Anderson, one of the aims of Howard Hawks, the director, was to increase the sense of danger by emphasizing the real proximity of actors to animals during the capture scenes by recourse to non-processed images that put both actors and animals in the same shot (2009) [*Figure* 4.2].

Figure 4.2 Enhanced perception of risk as a result of proximity of actor and animals in *Hatari!* (1967).

In addition, given the abundance of wild animals in the area, a danger for the characters lurks simply by venturing off the compound. In one scene, Dallas D'Alessandro, a photographer commissioned by a zoo to take pictures of the animal captures and who accompanies the team on their excursions, takes a group of infant elephants to a nearby watering hole for a bath. Sean Mercer, the head of the team, follows her with his rifle as a precautionary measure. Sure enough, as Dallas leaves the watering hole, a protective mother elephant arrives with her calves, threatening to charge. Mercer fires a warning shot and defuses the situation. While the scene commences comedically, and serves as an opportunity to play Henry Mancini's 'Baby Elephant Walk' cue on the soundtrack, the tone shifts to emphasize the risks associated with living amongst the wildlife in the Serengeti.

In particular, the film stresses the dangers associated with the capture of wild animals. One form of danger is traversing the uneven terrain at speed. For instance, while pursuing wildebeests, a jeep blows a tire, causing it to flip over, injuring its occupants. However, the most dangerous aspect of the pursuit is the actual capture of large, powerful animals, particularly the capture of a rhinoceros, the sequences of which bookend the film. The film opens with the team surveying the plains in search of a rhinoceros. Mercer spots one with his binoculars amongst a herd of wildebeest

125

and orders the two vehicles to commence the pursuit, one a pickup truck from which the animal is lassoed with a snare on a pole, the other a jeep that herds the target animal towards the pickup. With the rhino in sight, the two vehicles pursue it until it begins to tire, causing the rhino to ram the pickup on multiple occasions. Kurt Müller, the driver of the jeep, and the 'Indian', a veteran safari hunter who rides shotgun, veer closer to the animal. The rhino then charges the jeep, hooking its horn into the Indian's leg, terminating the capture attempt as the Indian is taken to the local hospital to attend to his wound.

From the contemporary perspective of animal welfare, the use of vehicles to pursue and capture animals as staged in the film seems alarming given their evident distress. The practice dates from a bygone era before the adoption of safer and more humane means of seizure for both the capturers and the animals concerned (Player, 1967). Setting aside these issues concerning animal welfare, the film itself presents the capture sequences as a form of adventure, albeit an inherent danger of the profession, similar to other Hawks films such as the way in which aviation is portrayed in *Only Angels Have Wings* (1939) and auto-racing in *Red Line 7000* (1965) (Wollen, 80-90). Consequently, the animal capture sequences are presented in the film neutrally with respect to the moral status of the capturers and targets, given the animal's final destination to zoos serves a generally perceived greater good of zoological education. As an action form, the rhino capture sequence consists of a pursuit with the capture an embedded element within it. Most of the capture sequences in the film assume this form, with the exception of the monkey capture scene, where there is no pursuit. To capture them, rockets are hooked up to a large net that is fired over a tree in which the monkeys have been herded, thereby preventing their escape as the team collects them in their improvised body armour to minimize the danger of being bitten.

Another version of the animal capture variant entails the seizure of fantastic creatures. One such instance can be found in *The Lost World: Jurassic Park* (1997) that draws from the capture exemplars of *Hatari!*, which the film's screenwriter David Koepp has stated was an influence on the script (Smith, 1997). In this capture sequence, the targets are not wild animals but genetically engineered dinosaurs, and incorporates capture elements used in *Hatari!*, such as the pursuit of the targets in speeding vehicles and the use of nooses to rope them. However, the sequence also updates the techniques in modernized form through the use of tranquillizer guns and inflatable pads to immobilize the creatures. Crucially, the moral valence of the capture sequence contrasts sharply with the capture scenes in *Hatari!* given that the film presents dinosaur capture as corporate exploitation with little regard for the welfare of the creatures, a point reinforced as the more humane palaeontologist team watches the scene from higher ground in shocked dismay.

Another influence on *The Lost World: Jurassic Park*, and one which offers one of the earliest instances of fantastic creature capture variant, is *The Lost World* (1925), in which an expedition to South America discovers a plateau inhabited by prehistoric creatures. Amongst these is a brontosaurus that is stuck in a muddy bank of a river. Although the film does not visually depict the capture, an intertitle informs the viewer that the explorers plan to dredge the river and build a steel cage from which the brontosaurus will be placed onto a raft and transported downriver to the sea. In another example, the capture of the giant ape in *King Kong* (Merian C. Cooper and Ernest B. Schoedsack, 1933) offers a bit more visual detail as King Kong goes on a rampage through a village on Skull Island. When the ape reaches the shore, Carl Denham, a filmmaker on the expedition, lobs a gas bomb at the ape, causing him to collapse unconscious and allowing the team to enact the capture.

Peter Jackson's remake *King Kong* (2005), offers a depiction of Kong's capture with greater detail and is decidedly a more perilous affair for the capturers. The sequence commences with the rescue of Ann Darrow, who Kong has run off with and, in the process, has developed a notable attachment towards her. Darrow has feelings for Kong as well, given that he rescued her from three ravenous

Vastatosaurus rexes, the gigantic and fictional predecessors of the Tyrannosaurus rex. While Kong is asleep with Darrow in his grasp, Jack Driscoll, Ann's love interest, approaches quietly in fear of rousing Kong and beckons Ann to escape. Kong awakes at that point and begins to attack Driscoll while still holding onto Darrow. A colony of enormous bats then swarm towards Kong, prompting him to let go of Driscoll. As Kong contends with the bats, Driscoll and Darrow make their getaway by climbing down a vine overhanging the adjacent cliff. Kong spots their escape and pulls up the vine, but Driscoll grabs a nearby bat with Driscoll clasped onto him, thereby enabling them to fly off and land in the jungle below. Driscoll and Darrow then run through the jungle and head for the gates that exit onto the coast with Kong in mad pursuit.

When they reach the gates, the drawbridge over the chasm is not lowered, representing an obstacle to their escape. Like the original film, Carl Denham, the filmmaker, is intent upon capturing Kong and waits for his arrival on shore with a trap set. At the last moment, one of the crewmen for the *SS Venture*, the ship that has brought the expedition to Skull Island, slashes the rope with a machete holding the drawbridge, allowing Driscoll and Darrow to enter through the barrier as Kong leaps over the chasm. Darrow, once she has re-joined the crew, discovers, with apprehension, their capture plan using grappling hooks, rope, guns, and a large bottle of chloroform. Kong then bursts through the gates prompting the crewman to toss the hooks onto him to pull him downward. Englehorn, the Captain of the ship, tosses the chloroform bottle at Kong, further incapacitating the beast. Englehorn's crew from above shove two huge boulders, onto which a huge net is tied, that lands on Kong, crashing him to the ground. Darrow implores Englehorn to stop, a request that he ignores as he lobs another bottle of chloroform at Kong. As Driscoll drags Darrow to safety, Kong sees his love object disappearing from him, and he erupts enraged from the net, tossing the crewmen into the air and toppling over a temple from which other crewmen were firing at him.

The crew enter into escape mode with Kong now freed and head back swiftly to the two lifeboats that had originally brought them ashore, with Kong thundering after them. Two crewmen fire their rifles futilely at him to halt his approach, but Kong crushes them with one swing of his arm. The expedition group hastily jumps into the lifeboats and tries to shove off from the rocky shore before Kong arrives, setting up a deadline. Another crewman fires at Kong, who then bites off his head and tosses his body aside. Denham spots a bottle of chloroform and plans a last-ditch effort to capture Kong. Denham is then tossed into the water as Kong smashes his boat and flings it and its remaining occupants onto a rockface. Englehorn, on the remaining lifeboat, readies a harpoon gun to stop Kong's advance, and fires into the beast's leg. With Kong distracted by his wound, Denham clambers onto a rocky outcrop and throws the bottle into the beast's face. Kong gradually succumbs to the gas, and with his last conscious gesture, he reaches his hand out toward Darrow in an expression of human-like longing. Darrow breaks into tears as the soundtrack music turns mournful, leaving no doubt in the viewer's mind as to the immorality of Kong's capture.

The capture scene, therefore, is embedded within a longer action sequence combination commencing with a rescue that horizontally segues into pursuit, to then horizontally shift again into capture that is vertically integrated with the fight action mode. Notably, the capture sequence in *King Kong* (2005) mirrors the apprehension about the dinosaurs captured in *The Lost World: Jurassic Park*, suggesting that wider contemporary concerns about animal welfare are in play and have informed these capture depictions. Along with the kidnapping variant, the more recent animal capture instances tend to present a moral valence that leans towards the welfare of the target in contrast to the capture prototype in which the moral poles can readily shift, with the morality of the capture dependent upon the narrative context in which it is situated.

Exemplar: *The Fugitive* (1993)

As noted earlier in this chapter, a significant aspect of the capture scenario is the narrative perspective that the story assumes when depicting capture situations. The key factor is whether the emphasis is placed upon the capturers or the targets, or the scenario assumes a perspective that accords equal weight to both. *The Fugitive* (Andrew Davis, 1993) is a film that falls within the latter category by representing what Kristin Thompson has described as a parallel protagonist film (1999, 45-47). In such a film, instead of a protagonist-antagonist pairing in which the actions of an antagonist constitute the main obstacle to the goals of a protagonist, parallel protagonists do not necessarily have such an opposing character relationship. In *The Fugitive*, the protagonists are Dr. Richard Kimble, played by Harrison Ford, who is wrongly convicted of his wife's murder and is sentenced to death, and Deputy U.S. Marshal Samuel Gerard, portrayed by Tommy Lee Jones, who is responsible for his capture after Kimble's escape from a prison-bound bus. The fact that Harrison Ford and Tommy Lee Jones were both stars at the time of theatrical release also contributes to the sense of their equal weighting within the film. On first appearance, the aims of both are opposed since Kimble is the target and attempts to elude Gerard's capture attempts. But the true antagonists in the film are Fredrick Sykes, the one-armed man who murdered Kimble's wife, and Dr. Charles Nichols, who had hired Sykes with the original intention to kill Kimble in an effort to cover-up damaging evidence against the development of a new drug.

After Kimble's escape from the prison bus, the film presents three capture attempts. The first consists of Gerard's attempt to capture Kimble after absconding in an ambulance. The second occurs when Gerard and Kimble cross paths at a courthouse, with the third and climactic attempt that occurs in the final act is when Kimble confronts Nichols at a hotel. Throughout the film, the story cuts between the narrative perspectives of both the capturer and the target, in ways that are replicated in the capture sequences.

The first of these three sequences will be the focus here.

The first capture attempt is initiated by Gerard, who orders a fax ID of Kimble to be sent to local hospitals and state troopers. This is followed by a shot showing Kimble heading to a hospital, revealing Gerard's skill at ascertaining the motives of his target. At the hospital, Kimble tends to a wound he sustained during the bus crash, shaves his beard, and dresses as a medic to hide his true identity. Heading toward the hospital exit, he encounters a highway patrolman walking towards him with a fax of Kimble's ID in his hand. The patrolman asks him if he has seen an escaped prisoner, but does not recognize Kimble from the fax, representing a missed opportunity of capture but a successful moment of avoiding detection. Kimble exits the hospital, and an ambulance appears bearing a wounded guard from the bus crash who recognizes him. Kimble quickly places a mask over the guard's mouth to prevent him from alerting the paramedics. As the guard is wheeled into the hospital, Kimble absconds from the scene in an ambulance.

The film then cuts back to Gerard and his team, where he is informed by one of his deputies that the guard identified Kimble and that an ambulance is missing. Maintaining the parallel editing, the film shifts back to Kimble driving through a railway crossing in the ambulance with its sirens wailing. The film returns to Gerard as he and his deputies get into a helicopter, initiating the pursuit mode of the capture sequence. Kimble is then shown passing vehicles at speed, while Gerard radios to state troopers to leave the town and head toward Kimble. Eventually, the helicopter reaches Kimble, and the capturer and the target are depicted within the same shot [*Figure* 4.3]. The state trooper vehicles are shown to be catching up to Kimble as he drives the ambulance through a viaduct adjacent to a dam. Kimble spots the helicopter blocking the exit outside of the tunnel, and sees state troopers arriving at both ends of the tunnel, completing his entrapment and motivating him to swerve to a stop. As the state troopers and Gerard's team advance, Kimble leaves the ambulance and continues his escape by crouching behind stationary vehicles, while the state troopers and marshals meet in the middle of the viaduct. Momentarily, they realize that Kimble has eluded capture. Gerard passes a storm drain and then pauses, quickly grasping Kimble's avenue of escape.

Figure 4.3 Capturer and target appearing in the same shot as a result of dovetailing plotlines in *The Fugitive* (1993).

The chase shifts to the storm drain as Gerard and his deputies enter, with the narration continuing the alternate editing pattern between capturer and target. The drain splits in two, with Gerard going down one path while his other two deputies proceed down the other. Switching to Kimble, we see that he has come to a drop in the drain, which he successfully negotiates by hanging onto overhead cables. When Gerard reaches the same cables, he fails to negotiate them successfully and slips down the incline, dropping his gun in the process. Kimble seizes upon the error, picks up the weapon, and points it at Gerard in the first face-to-face encounter between the two parallel protagonists. He uses the moment to inform Gerard that he did not kill his wife. Critically, Kimble decides not to shoot Gerard when he had the opportunity, reinforcing his virtuous character, and proceeds down the drain. Gerard reaches for his second weapon hidden under his jacket, and with a gun in hand, follows Kimble. Meanwhile, Kimble reaches a dead end as the drain terminates at the dam, with a precipitous drop below. Gerard orders Kimble to put the gun down, which he does, and to put his hands over his head and get down on his knees. Figuring that risking his life is better than capture and a return to death row, Kimble jumps off the dam, thereby enacting the daring leap escape variant that also brings to an end the capture sequence. As his deputies and remaining members of the manhunt gather, Gerard organizes a further search of the river to confirm if Kimble is still on the run or has died from the fall. The film cuts to Kimble making his way to a riverbank, confirming to the viewer that he is still alive.

Given the parallel protagonist structure of the film, the capture sequence gives equal weighting to the agency of both the capturer and the target. As capturer, Gerard is presented as the consummate professional who possesses an inherent understanding of fugitives, is resolute in his objective until the fugitive is under arrest, and expertly knows how to throw down a capture net. At the site of the crash, Gerard accurately ascertained the potential radius that Kimble could have travelled and restricted the manhunt for the fugitive to a thorough local search. He correctly surmised that Kimble's first destination would be a hospital, and when in the helicopter, Gerard quickly determined the best place to ensnare Kimble in the ambulance was at the viaduct by covering both of its exits.

But yet, Kimble still escapes. The flipside of Gerard's tenacity as capturer is Kimble's aptitudes as a fugitive. Although a vascular surgeon, Kimble's character draws more upon Harrison Ford's star persona, particularly the actor's associations with Indiana Jones, to invoke the resourcefulness manifest in that adventure role. As a result, the dramatic structure of the sequence centers upon how Kimble successfully avoids capture by avoiding detection at the hospital, discovers a means to get away by appropriating an ambulance, and when cornered at the viaduct, has the presence of mind to escape via the storm drain. In addition, the dramatic structure of the sequence assumes the form associated with the escape scenario, given Kimble's successful escape. Ascendancy is therefore successively achieved at the key points in which Kimble avoids capture, with the threshold moment occurring when he executes a daring leap off the dam, temporarily eluding Gerard's capture plans. Had Gerard successfully captured Kimble, then the dramatic structure of the sequence would have taken on a different form.

The parallel protagonist form of the film is also manifested at the level of the moral valance of the final moments of the capture sequence. When Kimble had the opportunity to shoot Gerard, he chose not to and continued on with his escape. Similarly, when Gerard had Kimble cornered at the terminus of the storm drain, his primary aim was to persuade Kimble to accept arrest rather than shoot him. A moral mirroring, therefore, occurs as Kimble chooses not to cross the moral boundary to shoot as a means of ensuring his escape, whereas Gerard chooses not to cross the moral boundary to shoot as a means of enabling Kimble's capture. Unlike the moral poles of *First Blood*, where the target is virtuous, and the capturer is villainous, *The Fugitive* is unique by presenting the capturer and the target as both possessing virtue, but expressed through contrasting character traits. In doing so, the action sequence, with its parallel protagonist form, represents the yin and yang of the capture and escape scenarios and how they can be vertically combined.

Chapter 4: The Heist Scenario

"Five years have taught me one thing, if nothing else. Anytime you take a chance you better be sure the rewards are worth the risk, because they can put you away just as fast for a ten-dollar heist as they can for a million-dollar job."- Johnny Clay[1]

As noted in the Introduction, the threat of physical risk can be an element of a situation that is directly experienced by characters, or it is inherently a potential to the situation. Out of all the action forms, the heist scenario is the one that plays most with the potential of risk as a means of generating suspense. As the quote above illustrates, the risk can be the potential of capture, with a resulting prison term, and a capture that can also bear the risks of an escalation into a vertical combination with armed conflict. A closer analysis of the heist scenario prototype can reveal how such risks manifest themselves in specific heist situations in films.

The Heist Scenario Prototype

In its prototypical form, the heist scenario resembles the rescue scenario prototype in one key respect. Both involve an inward incursion into a secured space for the sake of acquiring something perceived as valuable. In the rescue scenario, that object is a person, namely a captive, whose perceived value warrants the risks taken by the rescuer to extract them from captivity. In the heist scenario, the motives are often not necessarily as honourable with the objects desired normally consisting of money or jewels; items, in other words, that are valued for their material worth.

Since the heist scenario can equally manifest itself as an endeavour that has the potential for incurring physical harm or

---

[1] Quote from Johnny Clay, career criminal from *The Killing* (Stanley Kubrick, 1956).

else an enterprise in which physical harm is actually encountered, it would be helpful first to describe specific instances of these alternatives to flesh out how the heist prototype can accommodate both. As an example of the former, consider the opening heist sequence in *Thief* (Michael Mann, 1981). The film's story focuses upon Frank, a professional jewel thief, and opens in an industrial setting in Chicago, where a vehicle is parked in an alleyway outside of a building. Inside the car is Joseph, a member of Frank's crew, who is busy monitoring chatter on the police radio, a task that implies their activity is in some way clandestine and risk-taking. The film then cuts to Barry, another crew member stationed at a telephone junction box outside of the building, who is also monitoring if any alarm signals have been triggered. The robbery then shifts inside the building where Frank is first introduced to the viewer, who places a large magnetic drill onto a safe, and commences to bore into it [*Figure* 5.1]. Once bored through the secured door, Frank hammers out its bolt with a spike and then opens the safe's set of double doors to reveal an interior set of locked doubled doors [*Figure* 5.2]. These doors are less of a challenge, as Frank handily hammers out their lock, and once opened, finds an industrial cabinet. Frank quickly rummages through its contents, throwing aside any finished jewellery, while keeping the loose diamonds contained in envelopes, demonstrating to the viewer his knowledge of what to steal. The film then cuts back outside to his two men, who are still monitoring signs of any danger, and confirm to Frank that it is safe to exit the building. Frank and Barry head to Joseph's car, deposit their respective gear in its trunk, and make their getaway.

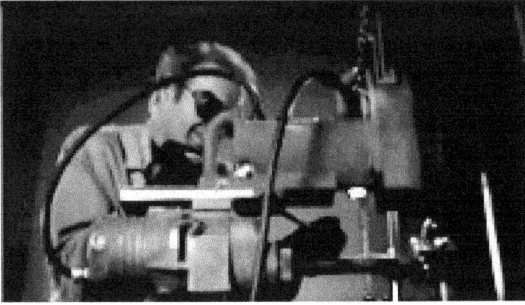

Figure 5.1 Penetrating first boundary layer in
The Thief (1991).

Figure 5.2 Second boundary layer in
The Thief (1991).

Although the opening heist in *Thief* did not involve a dangerous encounter with security guards or police, the sequence underscored the possibility of such an encounter arising by the crew monitoring of the police radio and the telephone lines and by Frank asking if the coast was clear to come out. It was through the crew's careful avoidance of detection that reduced the possibility of discovery by potentially armed guards or the police. Physical danger was, therefore, latent in the heist sequence.

Contrast this state of latency to the clear physical danger arising in the central bank robbery sequence in *Heat* (1995). Like Frank and his team in *Thief*, Neil McCauley is a professional robber with a dedicated crew. Despite attracting the attention of the police after the murder of three guards during an armoured car heist, the crew decide to progress with the robbery of the Far East National Bank, located in central Los Angeles, that distributes

137

currency, with the estimated worth around $12 million, to other branches. The night before the heist, McCauley's crew reprograms the bank's alarm system such that it turns off, along with the video surveillance systems, twenty minutes before they enter the next morning. The robbery sequence starts when McCauley enters the bank. From another entrance, Chris Shiherlis, another member of his crew, walks in and passes a guard, whose presence signals the potential for danger early at the start of the sequence [*Figure* 5.3]. The film cuts back to McCauley, now positioned against a wall to take in a clear view of the bank that is bustling with customers and bank employees, with the shot suggesting that these people too are at risk if the heist were to go amiss. Michael Cheritto, a third crew member, enters the bank and heads towards the area where a second bank guard is stationed. McCauley then spots a third guard amongst filing cabinets, suggesting to the viewer that the crew's first task will be to take out the guards.

Figure 5.3 Security guard as sign of danger in *Heat* (1995).

Cheritto lets out a cough, a signal that he is ready, motivating McCauley to slip on a ski mask, an action that Cheritto himself follows suit. Shiherlis then spins quickly around and violently bludgeons one of the security guards with a sap until he is unconscious. Cheritto clubs the guard next to him in the same manner, while McCauley orders the third guard to put his hands in the air. Shiherlis and Cheritto then proceed to constrain their guards in zip cuffs as McCauley instructs the third guard to get on his knees, while Shiherlis finally puts on his mask. After McCauley has the third guard lying prone on the floor in zip cuffs, with all of the guards now immobilized, he climbs onto a partition and addresses the customers and employees in the bank. He informs them that their intention is to harm no one and that they are only interested in taking the bank's money, and then orders them to sit on the floor and put their hands on their heads. McCauley then advances to one of the bank employees and demands the key to the vault, and after the employee feigns no knowledge of it, McCauley slugs him, drawing blood, and aggressively yanks the key from him that was hanging around his neck. McCauley hands the key to Shiherlis, who heads to the bank's vault, involving a passage through three locked doors to access an interior room in which lies plastic sealed bundles of currency, which he places into large duffle bags. Shiherlis passes two of the duffle bags to McCauley, one of which he hands to Cheritto, as the crew prepares to leave the bank after a seemingly faultless robbery.

The story then shifts to a Los Angeles Police Department precinct where Lieutenant Vincent Hanna and his team receive a tip-off that McCauley plans to rob a bank that morning, causing them to rush out to the scene of the robbery. The film returns back to Cheritto as he exits out of the bank to then return to Hanna with two of his detectives, Casals and Bosko, as they drive to the bank and order the police to cordon off the area. The film returns to Cheritto as he heads to a vehicle parked outside and gets in, with Donald Breedan, the final crew member, waiting at the wheel as the getaway driver. McCauley and Shiherlis then make their way to the getaway car and are spotted by Casals. Hanna instructs the police to wait for all of McCauley's crew to be in the car and ominously advises to "get clean shots". They then arrive at the scene and advance toward the getaway car on both sides of the street. As Shiherlis is on the verge of entering into the getaway car, he spots Casals with Sergeant Drucker hiding behind a U-Haul truck and opens fire at them with his M16 rifle.

Pandemonium then erupts. Bystanders instantly seek shelter and take to the ground with the deafening sounds of gunfire. Hanna and Bosko start firing at Shiherlis, who returns their fire and shoots Bosko in the neck, killing him. Shiherlis hastily gets into the getaway car, allowing Breedan to speed off as Shiherlis continues his gunfire through the car's rear windshield. Casals and Drucker give chase on foot, as does Hanna after checking in on Bosko. As the getaway car races away, Casals and Drucker fire at it to halt its progress. The film then cuts to the interior of the vehicle as McCauley spots ahead a police roadblock forming, which he fires at with his assault rifle, through the front windshield. An exterior shot of the getaway vehicle reveals Cheritto shooting from his backseat window as McCauley's crew fires from three directions. Casals then fires at the getaway car, shooting out its front left tire, causing Breedan to struggle to control the vehicle. Hanna, Casals, and Drucker then let loose an onslaught of gunfire, killing Breedan, with the getaway car colliding into a vehicle abandoned on the street.

With their vehicular getaway plans in tatters, McCauley and his crew attempt to escape from the closing police forces. They abandon the getaway vehicle, and while being fired upon by numerous police officers behind the roadblock, Shiherlis and Cheritto return their fire but with their superior assault rifles, allowing McCauley to press forward and shoot one of the policemen. Sensing the advance of the police from the opposite direction of the roadblock, Shiherlis pivots and starts firing at them. McCauley and Cheritto shoot at the advancing police as well, permitting Shiherlis to advance closer toward the roadblock. Shiherlis proceeds to rain further gunfire onto the roadblock, taking out an officer inside a police vehicle, to then spin around again toward the advancing police and shoot in their direction, a pattern he repeats after reloading swiftly. Meanwhile, Hanna has moved much closer to McCauley's crew, as well as Drucker, who fires at Cheritto with his shotgun.

With the police encirclement squeezing further in, McCauley's gang makes one last push to break through the cordon. Shiherlis and Cheritto press forward again, with Shiherlis firing another torrent of bullets at the roadblock. Hanna then cracks off a few shots with his assault rifle at the gang, putting further pressure on them. Close to the roadblock, McCauley fires into the police vehicles, allowing Shiherlis to break through the cordon by heading right on another street at an intersection. Cheritto tries to make a break for it as well, but is prevented by a hail of bullets, so he heads down the street in the opposite direction of Shiherlis, separating himself from the rest of the gang. Fired at multiple directions, Cheritto responds by taking out a pursuing plainclothes officer as well as a policeman shooting at him behind a police vehicle, thereby enabling him to sneak past the roadblock.

As McCauley and Shiherlis continue to fire upon the roadblock, Casals is able to get a clear shot at Shiherlis, shooting him in his shoulder that drops him to the ground. McCauley sees Shiherlis writhing in pain and heads towards him, firing one last volley at the roadblock, and takes down another officer. In an act of loyalty, if not heroism, McCauley helps Shiherlis to his feet and steers him toward an adjacent parking lot for a grocery store, as Hanna runs towards them in an effort to not let the gang slip through. Two police officers from the roadblock follow McCauley and Shiherlis into the parking lot, earning a blast of gunfire from McCauley's assault rifle, as shoppers cower behind vehicles in mortal fear. At that point, Hanna finally arrives at the parking lot with McCauley firing again, who takes out one of the pursuing police officers, and endangering bystanders in the process. McCauley and Hanna then exchange gunfire, with Hanna instructing the shoppers to get down to avoid being hit. McCauley lets loose another terrifying shower of bullets, and shoves Shiherlis into a car left open by a fleeing shopper, and gets into the driver seat. With escape within reach, McCauley reverses the vehicle, shoving away a car behind it that was blocking the exit, and speeds off before Hanna could get in one final shot.

Hanna then sprints towards the sound of gunfire, with the film cutting to Cheritto as he makes his way through an outdoor café, provoking panic, with Casals and Drucker closely on his tail. As a result of the pandemonium, a young girl is left on her own, crying for her mother. Cheritto picks her up to act as a shield, thereby exhibiting his immorality, and fires at Casals and Drucker. Hanna, coming from the opposite direction, spies Cheritto firing away, holding the girl as a shield, and steadies himself to take a clean shot, and as Cheritto turns towards him, Hanna fires, instantly killing him with a shot to the head. The sequence ends with an aftermath shot as Cheritto's body is surrounded, and Hanna takes the girl to safety, underscoring the lethal risks armed bank-robbery entails to thieves, police officers, and bystanders [*Figure* 5.4].

Figure 5.4 Aftermath shot underscoring physical risk in *Heat* (1995).

When comparing these two heist sequences, their depiction of danger contrasts sharply. In the *Thief* sequence, danger remains implicit, arising from the nature of the illegal activity, and the efforts of the gang to evade detection, given the possibility that the police could arrive, with armed escalation a likelihood. Such elements are part of the event schema of the heist scenario. But equally present in the event schema is also the realization of this likelihood, in which armed conflict comes about as a result of the heist through the presence of security guards, or the arrival of the police or equivalent security forces, as the heist sequence in *Heat* illustrates. In addition, the heist sequence in *Heat* increases the perception of physical risk through the inclusion of bystanders who are also in danger of being hit by gunfire. These two facets of the heist scenario prototype are evidenced by their reoccurrence in film. With regard to the first facet of the prototype, instances of heist sequences in which danger is manifested at the latent level can found in *Rififi* (Jules Dassin, 1955), *Point Break* (1991), *Mission: Impossible* (1996), *Charlie's Angels* (McG, 2000), and *Logan Lucky* (Steven Soderbergh, 2017). In relation to the second facet, instances of heist sequences in which physical danger is explicitly presented can be found in *High Sierra* (Raoul Walsh, 1941), *White Heat* (Raoul Walsh, 1949), *Bonnie and Clyde* (1967), *The Wild Bunch* (1969), and *The Dark Knight* (Christopher Nolan, 2008).

There are other instances of heist sequences that fall between these two poles where physical violence arises, but nothing of the order of the carnage manifested in the bank robbery in *Heat*. In the heist sequence in *The Asphalt Jungle* (John Huston, 1950), for instance, three robbers - Dix Handley, Louie Ciavelli, and Doc Riedenschneider – rob a jewellery store and use nitroglycerine to blow open its safe. But the ensuing explosion triggers alarms to ring out in the surrounding block, alerting the watchman of the building. When Louie opens the door, the watchman rushes in with a pistol in hand, but Dix slugs him, causing his gun to hit the floor and accidentally go off, shooting Louie in the stomach. Similarly, in *The Italian Job* (Peter Collinson, 1969), the violence during the heist is comparatively minor. During the robbery of the gold bullion from an armoured car, the heist crew block its path with a jeep and knock unconscious the guards in the convoy with wooden clubs. As can be ascertained by some of these film references, the heist scenario is one of the few action forms that has developed into a generic category in its own right, as a sub-genre of the crime film (Lee, 2014). However, as noted in the Introduction, even though the central and defining narrative event in these films is a heist, this does not mean the robbery plays out over a film's entire narrative. Instead, heists are primarily restricted to certain passages, with the robberies planning stages and ensuing police investigations assuming a significant amount of narrative time.

From these examples, one can adduce the main participants of the heist scenario prototype. The most important character function in the scenario is the *thief*. For a heist to occur, the agency of a thief is required who possesses a particular set of skills, most importantly the ability to steal objects of value in a secured location and avoid detection. Opposing the goals of a thief are the character types of *guards* and *capturers*, who possess slightly different aims and traits. The main function of a guard is to prevent the theft of the objects of value held in a secured location, and in so doing, constitute obstacles to the aims of the thief. In the heist sequence in *Heat*, for instance, the first thing McCauley's crew attended to at the bank was to take out the guards, representing their chief initial obstacle. Capturers, in contrast, function in the same narrative capacity as they do in capture scenarios in that their main purpose is to apprehend the thief. As in the capture scenario, capturers in the first instance do not have the intention to kill the thief in the heist scenario. Yet, if the thieves resist in lethal ways, as was the case with Shiherlis' opening gunfire in *Heat*, then vertical combination ensues as the heist escalates into the fight scenario and the capturers resultingly change their aims.

Significantly, the heist scenario prototype requires the presence of guards or capturers to offer at least some minimal resistance to the theft to avoid the perception by the viewer that the endeavour was effortless and risk-free. For instance, in the heist sequence in *Thief*, despite the fact that neither guards nor capturers materially intrude during the robbery, their potential presence is registered through the radio and alarm monitoring. In addition, as was indicated in an earlier discussion of *Raiders of the Lost Ark* (1981), the traps placed in the tunnel by the designers of the temple are in many ways similar to the designers of the secured spaces that reoccur in heist situations in films.

In this capacity, designers of secured spaced are a different form of guards by placing traps that will trigger detection and setting up boundaries to prevent the removal of the prized objects. Just as the escape scenario places emphasis upon the boundaries that function to contain the captive-cum-escapee, heist scenarios underscore the boundaries that must be penetrated to obtain access to the prized objects. As Bordwell notes, one of the main conventions of the heist film is an emphasis upon impediments (Bordwell, 2017). For the heist sequence in *Thief*, there is the implied penetration into the building itself where the jewellery is located, as well as the doubled layer set of doors to the safe [*Figure* 5.1 and 5.2]. Similarly, the presentation of the robbery in *Heat* places importance upon the entry into and exit from the bank, the outer boundary layer, as well as the three sets of secured doors that Shiherlis has to go through to access the cash [*Figure* 5.5 to 5.7].

144

Figure 5.5 First secured door in *Heat* (1995).

Figure 5.6 Second secured door in *Heat* (1995).

Figure 5.7 Third secured door in *Heat* (1995).

Given these elements of the heist scenario prototype, its event schema assumes a form that parallels that of the rescue scenario. An object of value is located within a secured location and is protected by guards, equivalent to that of captors in the rescue scenario, that is desired by a thief. To obtain the object of value, the thief must overcome the guards, and successfully navigate other obstacles such as detection traps and the penetration through

145

secured boundaries. If the prized object is successfully reached, then the thief may need to additionally get past the capturers who have arrived at the scene. In the instances where guards and capturers are potentially present, the event schema differs in the key respect that it is the design of the secured location that comes to the fore, with its attendant detection traps and secured boundaries that require successful navigation.

The heist sequence in *Mission: Impossible* can illustrate the event schema in which the emphasis is placed upon the navigation of a secured room as opposed to engagement with guards and capturers. Ethan Hunt, lead agent for the Impossible Missions Force, and his team - Luther Stickell, Franz Krieger, and Claire Phelps - aim to infiltrate CIA headquarters located in Langley to steal a list of its agents from a computer terminal located in a secured vault. Conveniently, when Ethan briefs his team as to the security in place, the film also presents to the viewer CIA Analyst William Donloe's entry into the secured room through the image-track, thereby outlining the detection traps and secured boundaries that are intended to invoke the event schema of the heist scenario.

Ethan, through voice-over, informs his team that passage to the secured vault entails a voice identity check and a six-digit access code that once passed grants access to the vault's outer-room. To access the interior vault, one needs to pass a retinal scan and to deactivate the intrusion countermeasures within, through the use of a double electronic key-card that must be inserted at its door. Next, Ethan explains that there are three systems in place protecting the vault when the analyst is not in the room including, ultra-sensitive sound detectors, thermometers that detect increases in room temperature triggered by body heat, and a pressure-sensitive floor. The only other means of access to the vault is through an air conditioning duct located thirty feet above the floor that is guarded by a laser net. This exposition on the vault's security systems is not only intended to provide the viewer greater narrative clarity as to the heist to come, but also facilitates the generation of interest by encouraging the viewer also to speculate how the IMF team will be to bypass the detection systems in place.

The film then cuts to an overhead shot of a convoy of fire trucks and emergency vehicles headed toward the CIA Langley complex, with the team disguised as firefighters. Ethan, Franz and Claire enter the building in disguise, while Luther stays in a fire truck to hack the complex's system with his computer and to give guidance to Ethan via an earphone. The team then goes past the first security boundary when entering the building as the guards at the security desk let them in when Luther triggers a bogus fire alarm in Section 21. The space provides access to the air duct, with the alarm also enabling the team to enter into an additional secured area within the building. While rushing to Section 21 escorted by an armed guard, Claire slips back to duck into a storage room to change into a dress that is more professional in appearance to blend into the other CIA analysts. Meanwhile, Donloe is presented exiting the vaulted room to head to the cafeteria, and while in the hallway, Ethan and Franz are led by the guard to a service room adjacent to the vault, who then searches for the third 'missing' fireman, as Claire enters into the cafeteria just before Donloe arrives.

The security guard heads back to the security room just as Ethan is putting away his disguise, who back kicks the guard while Franz knocks him out cold, but is prevented by Ethan from killing him, exercising a restraint that reveals his moral integrity.

Back at the cafeteria, Claire sits next to Donloe and secretly squirts nausea-inducing serum into his coffee, which will give him stomach trouble, and is shown taking a sip. The film cuts back to Ethan and Franz gaining access to the ventilation system and making their way toward the air duct above the vaulted room. The film returns to show Claire placing a miniature tracker on Donloe so that Luther can monitor his location.

Back in the air vent, Ethan places a mirrored device that redirects the lasers so that he can remove the air duct grill to gain access to the vault. Wearing a noise detection sensor on his wrist to maintain sound levels below the detection threshold, and armed with a thermometer, Ethan is lowered into the vaulted room upside down by Franz [*Figure* 5.8]. Donloe is then is shown through Luther's tracking system, as well as presented directly by the film's narration, walking back to the vaulted room, and making entry into the inner and out rooms. Franz quickly but silently pulls Ethan upwards to the top of the vault to avoid detection, as Donloe resumes his work at the computer terminal. The serum then takes effect, causing Donloe to vomit into a rubbish bin, and exits the vaulted room, allowing Ethan to continue with the theft. With Luther's guidance, Ethan is able to hack into the system and download the list of agents onto a memory disk.

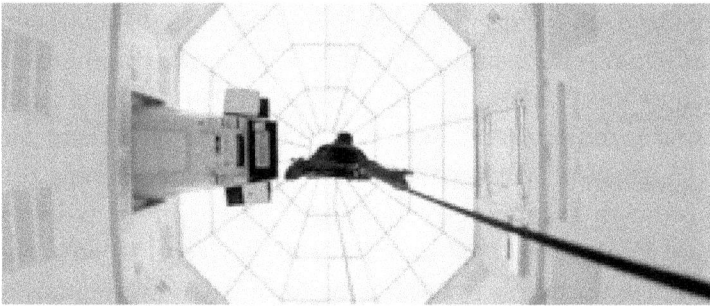

Figure 5.8 Navigating a secured space in *Mission: Impossible* (1996).

To add to the tension, a rat in the air duct heads towards Victor, the sound of its pattering reaching near-threshold detection, and in an effort to kill the rat, Victor temporarily releases his grip on the ropes suspending Ethan, who almost impacts with the pressure-sensitive floor. Further contributing to the suspense is Donloe's recovery, who then heads back to the vaulted room, as well as the thermometer that registers an increase in Ethan's body temperature, setting up two deadlines for Ethan to be removed from the room. At the same time, a bead of sweat begins to roll off of Ethan's glasses, which he catches with his hand before the drop hits the floor. Victor noisily hauls Ethan up at the last moment, almost triggering the noise detection system, and accidentally drops his knife, landing blade first into the computer terminal station just as Donloe enters and deactivates the intrusion countermeasures. Puzzled by the mysterious appearance of a knife at his terminal, Donloe gazes upward to reveal the air duct grill and laser net in place, indicating that Victor and Ethan have escaped into the air vents. However, Donloe becomes aware of the intrusion as the terminal registers a download while he was away. Before security can affect a lockdown of the building, Ethan creates a smoke distraction in the air vent that triggers an evacuation from the building allowing the IMF agents to slip away.

Like the robbery sequence in *Thief*, the heist sequence in *Mission: Impossible* lays out the event schema of the latent danger facet of the heist scenario prototype, but offers a better illustration of the micro-events involved in the passage through the secured boundaries and detection systems that are indicative of the scenario. The sequence, first of all, places emphasis upon the secured boundaries that Ethan has to pass through to access the terminal successfully. First, there is Ethan's entry into the complex. Then there is the securing of admission into Section 21, which then enables Ethan to access the air vents, with final entry into the secured vault. Second, the sequence places equal stress upon the avoidance of detection systems, namely the laser net, which requires the redirection of its rays, and the evasion of the intrusion countermeasures by monitoring and reducing noise and body heat while Ethan is within the room, and the avoidance of contact with the pressure-sensitive floor. Donloe, the CIA analyst character, also serves a detection function, given that Ethan must hide when he re-enters the vaulted room. An element of the other facet of the heist scenario prototype appears, in which physical risk is more manifest, when the guard is knocked unconscious and was nearly killed by Victor, if not for Ethan's imposition of moral limits.

Questions pertaining to moral evaluations of character behaviour invariably lead to an assessment of the moral valence of the heist scenario. As noted in the previous chapter, films can exhibit a graduated moral structure in which the ethical differences between characters are morally grey. This graduated moral structure especially arises in stories that are situated within a criminal milieu and applies equally to heist situations as to capture scenarios. In *Thief*, Frank is a criminal, and his robberies break the law but he also wants to have a family, a countervailing positive attribute. In addition, the police are portrayed in the film in a negative and corrupt light. They arrest Frank on trumped-up charges of driving with a broken taillight, only to bring him to the station to beat him up with the aim to extort a cut of the share of his earnings from his robberies.

The narrative context of the robberies in *Heat* presents a more complex moral picture. Neil McCauley and his crew are definitely portrayed as a dangerous lot — given their propensity to kill guards and police while committing robberies, and engage in a firefight with capturing forces that puts bystanders at risk. However, there are countervailing factors that make McCauley's moral complexion more complicated. Like *The Fugitive* (1993), *Heat* is a parallel protagonist film where Lieutenant Vincent Hanna's policing professionalism is paralleled with McCauley's criminal proficiency. Although McCauley is willing to kill to prevent capture and a return to jail, he does not kill for its own sake, and maintains his professional code, whereas Waingro, a former crew member, thoughtlessly kills a guard during the armoured car heist, and turns out to be a serial killer. In addition, like Frank in *Thief*, McCauley desires to settle down with Eady, his girlfriend, an aspiration that makes him a more sympathetic character, and during the bank robbery, he puts his life at risk out of loyalty to Shiherlis to take him to safety, instead of abandoning him. Such qualities exhibited by Frank and McCauley resist automatic and strict categorizations of thieves as villains and capturers as heroes.

The Italian Job (F. Gary Gray, 2003), for instance, swaps these moral poles by portraying a team of thieves as pursuing the morally just cause of seeking revenge on Steve Frazelli, who had betrayed them during an initial robbery of gold bullion and attempted to kill them. Narratively established as the villain at the outset of the film, the heist team then plans to steal the gold from Frazelli, and during the climactic heist, Frazelli's men pursue the team, turning capturers into villains in the process.

Given the similarities between the prototype rescue and heist scenarios, in terms of an inward incursion that involves an encounter with obstacles, it unsurprising that their dramatic structures resemble each other, as well as the means by which ascendency is achieved. The fundamental dramatic question that the heist scenario poses is whether the thief will be successful in their attempt to obtain the object of value located in a secured location. Dramatic turning points, therefore, hinge upon the success of overcoming these narrative obstacles, be they guards, detection systems, and secured boundaries, with the decisive threshold moment consisting of either the thief successfully obtaining the prized object from its secured location, or if the heist proves unsuccessful, then the thieves are instead captured or killed, as was the case with Cheritto in the heist sequence in *Heat*.

In continuous heist sequences, ascendency increases with every obstacle surmounted to the threshold moment, which is not the occasion in which the prized object is obtained, but the moment when the thief exits with the prized object from the secured location and also avoids capture. For the heist sequence in *Thief*, the success of the robbery is clear cut; the threshold moment occurs when Frank's crew departs from the scene undetected by the police. For the heist sequence in *Heat*, however, the success of the venture is far more qualified. Although McCauley and Shiherlis abscond with the loot, the theft comes at a significant price with Cheritto dead, Shiherlis seriously wounded, and with the future threat of capture as a result of the ensuing manhunt. Such a toll bespeaks as well to the contrast of physical risks between the latent and manifest facets of the heist scenario prototype. In the heist sequence in *Thief*, no physical danger arises with the risk kept latent. In the robbery sequence in *Heat*, there is an abundance of violence, from guards beaten senseless, to a bank employee being punched, to police officers and robbers fatally shot and critically wounded, to bystanders fleeing from the relentless gunfire.

Heist Combinations

Given that the heist scenario prototype minimally contains the possibility of thieves encountering guards and capturers who arrive at the scene of a robbery, it is unsurprising that one of its most recurrent vertical combinations is with the fight scenario, as amply illustrated by the heist sequence in *Heat* when the police arrive. Fighting is also not restricted to combat between thieves and capturers but also entails conflict between thieves and guards. A watchman is punched in *The Asphalt Jungle*; motorcade guards are beaten with wooden clubs in *The Italian Job* (1969); the armed escort guard is knocked out in *Mission: Impossible*; and the bank guards in *Heat* are bludgeoned with a sap. Not all heist sequences, though, depict guards this readily defeatable. During the armoured car heist in *Dead Presidents* (Albert Hughes and Allen Hughes, 1995), for instance, the security guards shoot back at the heist gang, with one of its members fatally shot.

Once a heist sequence combines with a capture scenario, the situation will often follow the combinatory logic exhibited in the capture scenario. It is worth pausing a moment, though, to unpick the nature of these combinations. First, when a heist sequence combines with a capture situation, as was initially the case in *Heat*, the combination is vertical in nature since the heist is not yet complete. As noted earlier, the threshold moment of ascendancy for the heist scenario is not securing the prized object, but the moment when the thief successfully escapes with the prized object by also avoiding capture. Such logic suggests then that heists vertically combine with capture since technically, the heist has yet to fully run its course. In addition, in heist situations when thieves are faced with the prospect of capture, their goals will normally turn to escape. As was the case with capture scenario, this turn to escape is also a vertical combination since the attempt to escape occurs simultaneously with the efforts of capturers to apprehend the thieves. When the intentions of the capturers turn from capture to the killing the thieves, as a result of their potentially lethal resistance, then the capture scenario horizontally segues into a fight situation as the aim to capture is replaced with the aim to kill. In the heist sequence in *Heat*, this pivotal moment occurs once Shiherlis starts shooting at Casals and Drucker, with the police's aim to 'take' McCauley's crew in the getaway changing into the aim to take them out full stop.

The heist sequence in *Heat* also involves a brief pursuit once McCauley's crew speeds off as the police chase the vehicle on foot. With the action turned into a pursuit, the chase horizontally absorbs the escape element, while vertically continuing with the heist as the crew abscond with the loot, as well as vertically continuing with the firefight. With the collision of the getaway vehicle terminating the pursuit, the action morphs back into an escape mode once again, vertically combined with the heist and the fight scenarios.

A more evident heist-pursuit combination can be found in the train robbery sequence in the western *The Wild Bunch*. A gang of ageing outlaws - consisting of Lyle, Angel, Dutch, Tector, and Sykes - led by Pike Bishop are being pursued by a posse of bounty hunters headed by Deke Thornton, Pike's ex-partner. To avoid capture, the gang cross the Rio Grande and camp at a Mexican village, ruled by the corrupt General Mapache, the local presence of the Mexican Federal Army. Pike agrees to Mapache's request to steal from an arms shipment conveyed on a U.S. Army train. Onboard the train are U.S. troops, functioning in the narrative capacity of guards, as well as Thornton's posse, present as well as potential capturers. The train stops at a water station so that the locomotive can replenish water. One of the troops checks to see if anyone is under the small bridge on which the train is parked, but not thoroughly enough as Lyle sneaks out.

Meanwhile, a locomotive engineer pulls down the trough to relay the water to the engine but discovers Angel lying within it, who orders him at gunpoint to continue with work as per normal. As the soldier continues to check the area ineffectually, Pike and Dutch then appear from under the bridge and proceed to their allotted points on the train, while Angel arrives at the locomotive cabin and watches over the other engineer. Lyle makes his way to a flatcar that is at the front of the train on which are stationed two army guards that he instructs at gunpoint to drop their weapons and sit facing towards the track ahead. Pike then joins Angel in the locomotive cabin while Dutch heads to the flatcar on which the munitions and weapons are secured. Creeping silently onto the

153

flatcar, where two other army guards are on watch, Dutch aims his rifle at them, thudding a box with its barrel, making them aware of their inability to take action. Angel heads to the end of the flatcar with the munitions and tries to uncouple it from the carriage with the troops and the posse, but the pin is stuck. Angel then signals to Pike to reverse the locomotive so that he can release the pin, and Pike instructs the engineer to roll back slightly to ensure that the flatcar does not impact upon the carriage and alert its occupants of the robbery, with the sequence thereby working in the avoidance-of-detection element inherent to the heist scenario. The film then cuts to Deke in the carriage, who checks out the window to see what the disturbance is, but only sees the engineer returning the trough to an upright position at the water station.

With the coupling opened wider, Angel releases its pin, allowing the front part of the train and the munition's flatcar to roll forward, now separated from the carriage, and in so doing, vertically combining the heist with an escape situation. Upon hearing the train begin to chug off, with most of the U.S. troops still asleep, Deke heads to the front of the carriage to see Dutch on the munition's flatcar with Angel removing the guns from the army guards, and instructs his posse to depart. The film cuts back to Dutch's narrative perspective, with parallel editing in full swing, to observe Deke's posse disembarking from one of the remaining carriages with their horses, as the escape situation swiftly horizontally shifts into pursuit mode. Sergeant McHale, the leader of the troops, finally awakes from his slumber, and looks outside the carriage to see the train speeding off with the munition's flatcar in the distance with the posse on horseback in pursuit. The posse then chases them along the track, motivating Pike to order the engineer to increase engine speed. As the train accelerates, Dutch loses his balance and falls off of the munition's flatcar and hangs precariously above the coupling, providing an opportunity for the guards to exploit. They start firing at him with their pistols, vertically combining the pursuit with the fight scenario. Aware that Dutch is in danger, Angel returns back to help him, vertically adding the embedded rescue variant to the augmented action. Pike kicks the engineers off the locomotive to assume full command of the train, while on the front flatcar, one of the guards swings round to fire at Lyle with his pistol. But Lyle is quick in reflex and shoots first with his rifle, causing the guard to fall off the train, and fires again at the remaining guard, who suffers the same fate. Closer to the munition's flatcar, Angel shoots the two remaining guards on the train and makes his way to Dutch to haul him onto the flatcar, completing the embedded rescue operation. Seeing that the posse is catching up, Pike opens the throttle to accelerate further, putting some distance between the pursuees and the pursuers.

Meanwhile, the incompetent army troops finally begin to disembark from the carriage with the intention to pursue the outlaws, but are too disorganized to pose any real threat. The train finally arrives at its rendezvous point, with Tector and Sykes waiting with horses and a wagon, as Pike slows the train to a stop. The film cuts back to the U.S. troops who have yet to disembark fully, and returns back to Pike's gang as they transfer the weapon supplies onto the wagon. Once transferred, Pike sets the train in reverse, sending it back as a weaponized driverless train with the aim to collide into the carriage, setting up a deadline for the army troops to fully disembark. As the train shuttles back, Pike and his gang head back on horseback to the Rio Grande, changing the mode of pursuit into a full horseback chase. The train meets up with the pursuing posse, forcing them off the track, temporarily impeding their progress, with the train acting as an obstacle for the group to negotiate. Deke and the posse soon realize that the train is crewless and continue with their pursuit. The film returns to the outlaws as they continue their way to the Mexican border, and cuts back to the army troops, as McHale has the train in sight as it bears down upon them. McHale urges his troops to hasten the pace, but not in time as the remaining troops and horse tumble over as the train crashes into the carriage. The posse then reaches the rendezvous point and follows the tracks of Pike's gang. The story returns to McHale, who orders a corporal to deliver a message to command that the posse had robbed the train and that the troops are in pursuit, further underscoring his ineptitude by mistaking the perpetrators of the robbery, and through his struggle to get on his horse.

The film then cuts to the pursuing posse and cuts back to the outlaws who have reached the bridge over the Rio Grande and commence to cross it. Angel lights a set of fuses at the terminus of the bridge, indicating that the gang had previous planned the demolition of the bridge through explosives as a means of escape. The story returns to the army troops reaching the rendezvous point, implying to the viewer the future gathering of three sets of opposing forces. When Deke and the posse are within sight of the bridge, Pike and Dutch fire at them, causing the fight situation to remerge vertically. While Sykes takes the wagon with the weapon supplies across the bridge, some of the planks break under the stress of its weight, causing the right rear wheel of the wagon to get stuck in the hole. The mishap then sets up a twofold deadline for the outlaws to meet with respect to the pursuing posse and the looming explosion of the charged bridge. As Pike and Tector hold off the approaching posse with gunfire, Lyle and Dutch come to Sykes' assistance and try to lift the wheel out of the hole. While lifting, the posse's gunfire becomes more insistent, with the lit fuse shown to be continuing on its fateful course. The pursuing army then arrives and starts firing at the posse, igniting an exchange of gunfire between them.

With the posse distracted, Lyle and Dutch manage to shove the wagon forward, and now freed, the outlaws hurry across the bridge with the wagon, while still maintaining gunfire with the posse. Deke takes his posse onto the bridge, unaware of the impending danger, as Pike and his outlaws take a pause from their escape to witness the explosion and the ensuing dumping of the posse into the river. A set of aftermath shots of the posse and debris in the water brings an end to the sequence and offers the threshold moment of the heist as Pike's gang absconds with a wagon full of loot.

Like the combinatory analysis of the capture sequence of *Public Enemies* (2009) in the last chapter, the foregoing analysis of the heist sequence of *The Wild Bunch* also reveals the greater complexity of combinations at work. Instead of a coarser grain analysis of the heist sequence as simply a progression from a heist, to a pursuit, to a gun battle at bridge, to end with a concluding explosion, a combinatory perspective identifies with greater detail the ebb and flow of the vertical and horizontal combinations, as fight situations emerge and fade, and as an embedded rescue variant makes an appearance. Such a perspective allows one to appreciate action sequences in terms of their combinatory complexity.

Heist Scenario Variations

Normally, the target of a heist is situated within secured locations that are stationary, such as buildings in which precious jewels are stored, banks in which money is kept, and intelligence gathering complexes like the CIA headquarters where national security data is stored. One way that the heist prototype has been innovated is to situate the target of the heist within a moving vehicle as a means to add other additional dimensions to the heist, be it increased risk, or additional action combinations, such as the combination of a heist scenario with a pursuit.

The Moving Heist Variant

One such variant can be found in *Spider-Man: Homecoming* (Jon Watts, 2017), when the Vulture, the villain of the film, steals alien technology from a convoy of moving trucks, and later on in the story, when he attempts to hijack a transport plane while in flight, containing a payload of weapons. In another example, Ethan Hunt, in *Mission: Impossible - Rogue Nation* (Christopher McQuarrie, 2015), leaps onto an Airbus 400 while taxiing for take-off, and hangs on onto it while it takes flight, in an effort to remove from the plane a pallet loaded with nerve gas canisters. Some of the most notable instances of the moving heist variant are in *The Fast and the Furious* (Rob Cohen, 2001) through a combination of speed, pursuit and highway heists. The film's opening heist sequence can serve as an example. The film starts with a container being loaded off of a boat onto a semi-trailer truck. Its contents consist of a load of Panasonic electrical home goods. A dock worker makes a call to a presumed thief, informing them that the semi-trailer truck has just departed and not to forget his share. The film then cuts to sometime later at night with the semi-trailer truck cruising down a freeway. Three Japanese sports cars then approach the truck from behind in pursuit of their prized goods. The drivers of the cars position their cars in front of and along the sides of the truck, effectively trapping the vehicle in a V formation.

In the front car, a thief stands through its sunroof with a harpoon gun, from which they fire into the windshield of the truck to yank it off as a means to gain access into the truck's cab. The vehicle on the righthand side of the truck then switches places with the front car so that it is now in front of the truck. In position, another thief arises from the sunroof to fire another harpoon, which is attached to a cable, into the passenger seat of the truck. The thief then attaches the cable to his belt and then leaps onto the truck from the front car, with the sequence thereby vertically combining the transfer action form mentioned in the Introduction with the heist scenario [*Figure* 5.9]. Pulling himself up, the thief enters the passenger side of the cab of the truck and gets whacked multiple times with a baseball bat by the truck driver. As a result, the truck weaves dangerously on the freeway, as the thief in the cab fires a tranquillizer into the truck driver, who eventually succumbs to its effects, with the thief shoving him off the driver's seat to command the vehicle. The procession of vehicles then reaches road barriers, warning of construction ahead, a set of obstacles that the gang of thieves easily negotiate by simply crashing through them. The road works ahead poses more of a challenge since the freeway has been narrowed to a single lane of traffic, requiring precision driving as the vehicles form a single line, with one of the cars tucking underneath the trailer of the truck. Having passed the roadworks, the vehicles speed off into the night, reaching the threshold moment of the heist by successfully negotiating the last obstacle in their way to offload the stolen goods.

Figure 5.9 Vertical combination of the transfer scenario and the heist in *The Fast and the Furious* (2001).

One of the notable aspects of *The Fast and the Furious* heist sequence is the heightened risk achieved by having the target of the robbery located inside of a moving vehicle. To access the truck, the thieves need to be in motion as well, making entry even more precarious, as evidenced by the leap the thief makes from car to truck. Furthermore, the vehicles are travelling at speed, so the risk of a vehicular accident adds to the physical danger manifested in the sequence. At the same time, the sequence retains elements that are recognizable in the heist scenario prototype. The truck driver, for instance, also serves the character function of a guard who attempts to prevent the theft through the use of physical force. The issue of the avoidance of detection also arises, but in the altered form of the thieves hiding their identity by wearing motorcycle helmets as a means to avoid potential identification as culprits of the crime.

However, unlike the prototype heist scenario that involves entry into and exit out of a secured space, *The Fast and the Furious* robbery primarily consists of a hijacking of a truck, through which the theft of the *secured space* itself becomes the means by which the prized goods are obtained. In addition, given the absence of capturers, and the fact that the heist takes place on an open freeway, its threshold moment takes on a different complexion as well. With no capturers, the moment of the success of the heist does not depend upon the evasion of capture, nor does its success derive from the crossing of secured boundaries to successfully obtain access to the prized objects. Without these dramatic encounters, the threshold moment of the heist sequence in *The Fast and the Furious* falls back to the last successful navigation of an obstacle, which was driving through the road works. Variations in action forms, therefore, have an impact upon its dramatic structure as well.

The Heist Typicality Gradient

The prototypical heist situations discussed so far have involved elaborate, high-stake robberies that involved a fair degree of planning and the entry into locations that possessed high security. But not all thefts in films are of this order. In *The Kleptomaniac* (Edwin S. Porter, 1905), a woman stylishly dressed enters a department store and steals items when a clerk has her back turned to her. The first robbery in *Bonnie and Clyde* involves Clyde stealing from a small-town grocery store that hardly represents a secured location. By taking a closer examination of such less prototypical instances in relation to the defining features of action forms, one can illuminate the typicality gradient of the heist scenario.

An 18-shot montage sequence in *Batman Begins* (Christopher Nolan, 2005) can illustrate some of the categorization issues that arise when considering typicality gradients. The sequence is narrated as a flashback, told from Bruce Wayne's perspective to Henri Ducard, his mentor, while training with the League of Shadows. Wayne relates his transitional period when he travelled the globe and how he immersed himself in the criminal world to understand it better. The image-track then depicts three situations to illustrate this period visually. The first two are theft situations, and the third is a shot of Wayne being taken to a prison in China, the culmination of his brief life of crime. The first theft situation shows Wayne in an open-air market, presumably somewhere in Africa, given the attire of people in the background and their ethnic appearance. He pauses at a fruit and vegetable stall, and furtively takes a plum and stuffs it into his trousers' pocket with his left hand, while distracting the market-stall owner by reaching for another piece of fruit with his right. The next shot shows him eating the plum but sharing it with an African boy, with the viewer informed through Wayne's voice-over that this was the first time he had stolen so that he would not starve, and in the process changed his conceptions about right and wrong.

The second theft situation is set in China, with Wayne inside the cab of a truck with a thief, watching workers load boxes onto another lorry. They get out of the cab, with the next shot showing sometime later the same truck being guided by another thief into the docking bay of a warehouse. As Wayne and the thief jump out, the warehouse is raided by the Chinese police, aiming their pistols at the thieves. The next shot reveals the thieves seated and handcuffed, with the police pointing out that the stolen goods belong to Wayne Enterprises, a corporation that Bruce Wayne owns.

Both theft situations are a far cry from the heist sequence in *Heat*. The theft at the market stall involves no penetration into a secured space, although there is the avoidance of a detection system of sorts, namely the eyesight of the market-stall owner that Wayne must distract to hide the theft. In addition, even though Wayne runs the risk of being caught, the film does not make apparent the element of physical danger that could arise from his action. Even Wayne's motives qualify the standard interpretation of theft as a crime for material gain, given that his motivation was hunger, with the plum shared with a boy whose longing gaze at the fruit suggested he was equally in need of food. The second theft situation is more prototypically a robbery, given the element of armed capture and a more evident possibility of physical danger, but the actual theft is elided from the montage sequence, for the viewer to infer instead its occurrence based upon the context of the action. In addition, in light of Wayne's ownership of Wayne Enterprises, it is not clear-cut that his actions count as theft.

Given the fact that these thefts appear far removed from the examples cited earlier in this chapter, it might be tempting not to consider them as instances of action in film. However, both thefts fall within the typicality gradient of the heist scenario, which is a type of action, albeit situated further away from the prototype than the other examples discussed. After all, the theft situations possess features that are shared with the heist prototype. Both thefts involve theft as a type of intentional activity, as does the prototype, and whereas the first theft manifested behaviour to avoid detection, the second theft exhibited a fuller set of heist scenario participants, in the form of thieves and capturers, as well as a more evident element of physical risk. Given these considerations, it is likely that the second theft will appear to the viewer to accord more with the heist scenario prototype than the first because of the greater degree of shared features that the former possesses compared to the latter. We can describe such processes by which a viewer perceives an accordance of a specific narrative situation with a prototype scenario as typicality perception.

Typicality perception is an important mental process because it also informs the perception of action in film more broadly. As noted in the Introduction, the feature that all action scenarios share is the manifestation of physical risk. On that score, the second theft is more likely to trigger the typicality perception of action than that of the first theft, given the greater degree of risk arising from the presence of the armed police. However, it is important to point out that the typicality perception of action is not solely triggered by the discernment of physical risk to which characters on screen are exposed. In any given narrative situation, the typicality perception of action is also triggered by the discernment of action scenarios since the presence of action scenarios has been historically associated with the presence of action in films. Fight scenes have long been associated with action, just as pursuit sequences, for instance. Consequently, the more that a narrative situation is perceived to accord with an action scenario, the greater the probability that it will trigger the typicality perception of action as well, as a broader inclusive category.

It is from such a vantage point that one can understand one of the main motivations for filmmakers to combine action scenarios. Typicality is aggregate. The more features that a given instance shares with a prototype, the more likely it will be perceived as being prototypical. Likewise, the more action scenarios that are combined in a given sequence, the greater the opportunities from which a viewer can identify accordances not just with one type of action scenario but with a multitude of action forms. It is for this reason that the heist sequence in *Heat* appears more prototypical than that of the robbery in *Thief* since more action scenarios are in play. Beyond the heist scenario that they both sequences share, the heist sequence in *Heat* additionally invokes a fight, an escape, a pursuit, a rescue, and a fleeting moment of capture. Action in film is, therefore, most prototypical not only when it involves manifest physical risk but also when it is also when it appears in aggregate scenario form.

Exemplar: *Fast Five* (2011)

As noted in the Introduction, one of the ways in which action sequences become exemplars, that is, a memorable instance of an action scenario that viewers and filmmakers refer to, is by innovating the prototype in distinctive ways. The climactic heist sequence in *Fast Five* (Justin Lin, 2011) does just that through an innovative combination of the heist scenario with a pursuit sequence that redefines how a heist is undertaken. Indeed, the film itself represented a shift in the *Fast and the Furious* franchise itself, moving away from its earlier emphasis upon street racing to a focus instead upon heists (Finke, 2011). It will be shown that such variations have implications on the sequence's dramatic structure, as was the case with the heist sequence in *The Fast and the Furious*, which itself undergoes deformation as a result of the changes to the heist scenario prototype.

To narratively contextualize the heist, Dominic Toretto, a criminal and street racer, escapes from a bus transporting him to prison with the aid of Brian O'Conner, his friend and former FBI agent, along with Mia Toretto, Dominic's sister and Brian's pregnant girlfriend. The three travel to Rio de Janeiro to avoid capture and stay with Vince, one of Dominic's former accomplices. Vince gets them involved in the theft of luxury sports cars from a train that have been impounded by the U.S. Drug Enforcement Administration, another instance of the moving heist variant. The vehicles had belonged to Hernan Reyes, a Brazilian crime lord, one of which contains a microchip detailing his finances and location of funds, causing the group to become the target of attack by Reyes' henchmen. Complicating matters, Luke Hobbs, an agent of the Diplomatic Security Service, arrives in Rio de Janeiro and works with Elena Neves, a local and law-abiding police officer, to capture the gang. Sensing the necessity to leave a country again, the gang agrees to plan a daring heist of Reyes' money, to facilitate their relocation, which is located in a vault in a Rio de Janeiro police station that is under Reyes' control. To do so, they put together a team of former criminal associates, who had also appeared in previous installments in the franchise, including Han, Roman, Tej, Gisele, Leo, and Santos. A few days before the heist, Hobbs arrests Dominic, Mia, Brian, and Vince, and while on route to the airport for extradition, the armoured convoy comes under attack from Reyes' men, killing Vince along with members of Hobbs' team, while Dominic rescues Hobbs. Seeking revenge on the attack, Hobbs agrees to participate in the heist.

On the morning of the heist, Reyes makes an inspection of the police station, which has an extra detail of police surrounding the building, forming an additional security layer. Like other heist sequences, the action commences with the penetration of a secured boundary, as Hobbs, with Elena as a passenger, slams through the station's entrance gate in an armoured vehicle, with Dominic and Brian following behind in their Dodge Chargers. The penetration spurs the police to fire at the armoured vehicle, quickly vertically escalating the heist with a fight situation. Hobbs then breaks through a set of obstructing bollards, a further boundary penetrated, as the vehicles enter into the station's underground parking lot. Bearing down onto a concrete wall, Hobbs accelerates to smash through it, representing a further boundary successfully breached, and in the process creates access to the precinct vault. Hobbs then reverses the vehicle out of the hole just created, jumps out with Elena as both start firing at the police descending upon them, and providing cover for Dominic and Brian to secure cables onto the vault that are rigged onto their cars. The film cuts to Reyes being alerted by an officer of the robbery as further police officers head toward the parking lot. Dominic and Brian get back into their Chargers and step on the accelerators to pull the vault from the wall in which it is embedded. Through the sheer horsepower of the Chargers, the vault eventually comes loose and is dragged out of the parking lot, with police vehicles in pursuit, thereby taking the action out onto the streets and into a pursuit mode.

The towed vault rolls as they take a corner as Dominic and Brian come out of the station, illustrating its destructive capacity. The police at the station fire at the vehicles as they exit the premises but to no avail. Dominic asks for directions from Mia through a two-way radio, who is at the garage and monitoring the heist's progress with a satellite-linked map. As they heed Mia's directions, a fleet of police vehicles pursue them, and at an intersection, more police lay down spikes on the road in an effort to stop them. Dominic and Brian make a sharp turn at the intersection to avoid the spikes that causes the vault to take out one of the police vehicles, as well as crash through a bank, testing their ability to maintain control of the vehicles and keep the vault in tow. They steady the vault so that it slides back on the road and continue to make their way. Two police cars then bear down in front of them, and in a coordinated response, Dominic and Brian turn sharply in opposite directions, placing the vault in the middle of the street, into which the two police cars collide.

With the Chargers facing opposite directions, Brian puts his vehicle into reverse to push the vault forward as Dominic continues to pull the vault from the opposite side. Two policemen on motorcycles then enter into the fray and commence pursuit while firing at Brian and taking advantage of his now vulnerable position. As the bullets punch holes into his windshield, Brian suddenly breaks to a stop, taking out both motorcyclists as they crash into his car. Dominic and Brian then recommence their escape and as they turn onto a wider street. Brian speeds forward in reverse and expertly executes a 180-degree hand-break turn so that he is back in front of the vault and facing the same direction as Dominic. Another fleet of police vehicles enters into the chase, prompting Brian to come up with a strategy to shake them off their tail, so he instructs Dominic to go wide, positioning their vehicles on either side of the street's median strip. In doing so, the vault takes down a street lamp, creating obstacles for the pursuing police vehicles and causing some of them to violently crash, as well as uprooting concrete bollards, sending the debris onto the road and forcing the remaining police cars to halt.

As one set of police vehicles is dispatched, another set emerges who speed closer to the two Chargers, allowing one of the officers to fire a pump-action shotgun into Brian's rear windshield. Brian, in response, weaves, causing the vault to swerve, which forces one of the police cars onto the sidewalk as pedestrians leap out of its path. Another police car accelerates towards Dominic, who also swerves to swing the vault towards the police vehicle, taking it out in the process as it crashes into a tree. A police officer within the vehicle speeding down the sidewalk emerges from the passenger window and discharges his pistol rapidly into Brian's car. Brian swerves again, with the vault demolishing a number of parked cars, with part of the wreckage strewn on the sidewalk causing the pursuing police vehicle on the sidewalk to crash into it. The remaining police vehicles drive closer to the Chargers again as the officer with the shotgun takes aim at Dominic. Before he has an opportunity to shoot, his car is rammed from the rear, revealing Han in a police car after accomplishing the embedded rescue. Han breaks suddenly, causing one of the police vehicles to collide with him and crash out in the other lane. Roman then appears, also in a police car, who swerves into the adjacent vehicles, taking out the last three pursuing police cars.

At an intersection, Han and Roman peel off as Dominic and Brian continue with another set of police emerging in pursuit. Joining into the chase is Reyes, with his second in command Zizi at the wheel, amongst a convoy of cars consisting of Reyes' henchmen. Dominic and Brian make their way to a long causeway over a body of water as the various pursuing vehicles gain upon them. Realizing their inability to elude the pursuers, Brian announces over the radio that there are too many, a point Dominic concedes. Using a remote-control device, Dominic disconnects the cable from the vault that is attached to Brian's car and spins his car around, facing the oncoming onslaught of oncoming vehicles. While revving the Charger, Dominic switches on the nitrous oxide system, delivering all the more power to his vehicle. Accelerating toward the pursuing vehicles at speed, Dominic begins to swerve, shifting the vault in the desired directions to effectively weaponize it and demolish the vehicles in his path, leaving a trail of automotive wreckage. As a result, only two pursuing vehicles remain, one conveying Reyes, the other outfitted with a large rotary gun, manned by one of Reye's men who fires at the Charger. Dominic then turns abruptly, which swings the vault around in an arc and smashes into the vehicle with the rotary gun, knocking it off the causeway into the water below. Dominic then leaps out of his vehicle as the force of the vault's collision heaves his Charger into the air to drop like a colossal hammer into Reyes' car. An aftermath shot reveals the wreckage and signals the end of the pursuit.

However, the action sequence continues as Zizi emerges with a gun from the wreckage and aims it at Dominic. Before Zizi can fire a round, he is shot multiple times by Brian, who appears suddenly in the aftermath, and adds another embedded rescue to the sequence. Hobbs and Elena then arrive in their armoured vehicle. As they march towards Dominic and Brian, Reyes collapses out of the wreckage and onto the road before Hobbs. Reyes pleads for help, but Hobbs responds by shooting him in the chest, exacting his revenge. Returning back to his capturer function, he informs Dominic and Brian that he can't let them go and that the money in the vault will stay with him, but grants them a twenty-four-hour period to escape before he hunts them down again. Dominic and Brian then depart in the remaining Charger. Hobbs then opens the vault to discover that it is completely empty. A flashback then explains to the viewer how this came about by revealing that during the chase, the vault had been transferred onto a garbage truck and switched with an empty one to act as a decoy for the pursuing police officers, and Reyes and his henchmen. The film then shifts to later on in the story when the heist team are back at their garage hideout. Tej, the team's technical expert, stands in front of the vault with computer gadgetry, attempting to hack it open, as the rest of the team watches nervously. He next places a plastic sheet over the vault's fingerprint detection device, a sheet that the film had earlier revealed possessed Reyes' fingerprints, and places his own hand upon the detection system. The vault's door then unlocks, which Tej opens to reveal bundles upon bundles of money inside, which spill onto the floor in a spectacle of abundance.

There are a number of reasons why this heist sequence is significant from an action scenario perspective. Most notably, the sequence represents a distinct vertical combination of the heist scenario with a pursuit sequence. The combination is vertical since the theft of Reyes' vault only concludes with the moment of transfer onto the garbage truck, a transfer enacted while Dominic and Brian were still pursued by the police. While the transfer marks the conclusion of the theft of the vault, it does not, however, bring closure to the theft of the money inside, the true prized object of the heist, which is deferred to the next scene. Such a deferral constitutes an important departure from the heist scenario prototype. While the heist sequence exhibits some of the hallmarks of the prototype, such as the penetration through security layers, and the avoidance of detection enacted through the decoy switch, a moment that itself temporarily avoids detection by the spectator, it also departs markedly from the prototype by deferring the moment of access to the prized object onto a later scene. In most prototypical heists, such as in *Thief* and *Heat*, the entry into a vault occurs while inside a secured space. In *Fast Five*, the heist involved the theft of a secured space instead, in the form of the vault, in ways similar to the hijacking of the truck in *The Fast and the Furious* [*Figure* 5.10].

Figure 5.10 Heist scenario innovation through theft of secured space in *Fast Five* (2011).

As noted earlier, such variations on the prototype impact on the dramatic structure of action sequences. Two aspects of the *Fast Five* heist sequence come to the fore on this issue. First, the film's narration significantly influences the viewer's interpretation of the dramatic structure of the sequence. Prior to the flashback, the threshold moment of the theft of the vault consisted of Hobbs confiscating it at the end of the pursuit sequence, representing a failure on the part of the heist team. However, when the heist is comprehended after the flashback, with the missing story elements provided, the threshold moment of the theft of the vault shifts instead to the moment of transfer onto the garbage truck, now representing a success for the heist team. Second, while the threshold moment of the theft of the vault was the transfer, the true threshold moment for the heist itself was the instant in which Tej was able to open the vault. The film, therefore, displaces the dramatic tension of the threshold moment onto another scene instead of bringing about dramatic closure within the action sequence itself. In doing so, the scene at the garage hideout, therefore, becomes another heist, albeit in abbreviated form, but one in which immediate physical threat is absent, thereby innovatively revising the notion of what a heist scene entails.

Given the sequence distinctive vertical combinations of a heist situation with the fight and pursuit scenarios, it is worth to conclude by reflecting briefly upon the deeper nature of such combinations. As noted, the event schema of the heist scenario builds in the potential for armed conflict such that when it arises

169

in a particular instance of a heist in a film, it is already narratively motivated. What constitutes a narratively motivated combination in contrast to a narratively unmotivated one is an issue that will be explored in the next three chapters.

Chapter 5: The Fight Scenario

"I want you to remember that no bastard ever won a war by dying for his country. He won it by making the other poor dumb bastard die for his country." - General George S. Patton Jr.[1]

As General Patton's words so vividly describe, no other action form incarnates the ethos of killing than the fight scenario through the expression of physical conflict. As we have seen, other action scenarios are defined by aims that do not by necessity involve killing. While not all fighting in films involves the aim to kill, it is frequently the principal aim, with the broader narrative context providing the moral grounds, or lack thereof, for the killing. But at a more fundamental level, what conceptually underpins Patton's observations on the art of war is the tacit supposition of a protagonist and an antagonist, which fleshes out the fight scenario that he paints. The bastard who wins the war is the protagonist in Patton's story, and the dumb bastard who dies for his country is the antagonist. Since these concepts are critical to the understanding of the fight scenario prototype, this chapter will provide a closer analysis of the ways in which these character functions are manifested in particular instances.

The Fight Scenario Prototype

The defining feature of the fight scenario is physical conflict. In its prototypical form, the conflict minimally consists of two combatants, which I shall label here as the *protagonist* and the *antagonist*. The physical conflict, in addition, possesses some degree of reciprocity. In other words, both parties in the physical conflict exchange attacks with each other instead of being entirely unidirectional, where one party attacks and the other party provides no semblance of physical retort. Like the heist scenario, the

---

[1] Quote from General George S. Patton, from *Patton* (Franklin J. Schaffner, 1970).

fight scenario prototype exhibits two facets. One facet consists of the one-on-one fight, normally with the fighting skills of the protagonist and the antagonist showcased, such as in the form of a duel, as illustrated in the final martial arts fight between Tang Lung and Colt in *The Way of the Dragon* (Bruce Lee, 1972). The other facet is that the protagonists and the antagonists represent large and opposing combat forces, often found in war films, but not exclusive to that genre, as demonstrated by the opening 'Battle of Hoth' sequence in *Star Wars: The Empire Strikes Back* (Irvin Kershner, 1980). Between these two facets, and like other action scenarios, the fight scenario prototype allows considerable variation with respect to how participant numbers are combined. In some fight scenes, one sole protagonist fights multiple antagonists, such as in *Ip Man* (Wilson Yip, 2008) and *Oldboy* (Park Chan-wook, 2003). While in contrast, *Pirates of the Caribbean: Dead Man's Chest* (2006) offers a 'truel' consisting of a three-way sword fight over a key, involving Jack Sparrow, who is the protagonist, with Will Turner and James Norrington as his antagonists, who also fight with each other, and with each of the participants wanting the key for different reasons. In other instances, a one-to-one fight is embedded within a larger multi-participant battle and is isolated from the rest of the conflict for dramatic purposes, such as Thorin and Azog's climactic duel in *The Hobbit: The Battle of the Five Armies* (Peter Jackson, 2014).

An instance of the one-on-one fight that can illuminate the fight scenario's underlying event schema can be found in the fight scene in *The Bourne Supremacy* (Paul Greengrass, 2004) between Jason Bourne, an assassin suffering from amnesia, and Jarda, another operative, both of which were participants in the CIA initiative Operation Treadstone that trained assassins. Seeking to recall more about an assassination he was previously involved in Berlin, Bourne stops in Munich to visit Jarda, who had also participated in the killing. The scene commences with Jarda entering into his apartment, initially seeming empty as he appears to turn off a security alarm. He then heads for the fridge, and while doing so, Bourne silently enters into the frame with his pistol pointing directly at Jarda. Sensing Bourne's presence, Jarda spins round with a gun in his hand, a weapon that he had kept in his fridge for such occasions, indicating his professional ability to discern danger and be ready to counter it. Bourne informs him that he had emptied the weapon, and Jarda, while smirking, says it felt a little light, suggesting his familiarity with weapons, and providing further clues that Jarda is Bourne's equal when it comes to combat. Bourne next instructs him to put down his weapon and handcuff himself with a zip cuff, which Jarda tightens with his teeth and then sits down.

As Bourne searches through Jarda's documents, Jarda lets on that he is aware of Bourne's amnesia, with the dialogue confirming that they had previously worked together. Jarda informs Bourne that the CIA shutdown Treadstone and that they are the last two survivors of the project, confirming his assassin status already alluded to through his behaviour, and which dramatically sets up the fight to come. Suspicious, Bourne kicks him off the chair and further interrogates him at gunpoint. As Jarda gets back onto the chair, he blurts out that he thought Bourne was there to kill him and glances at his watch. Bourne, equally adept at sensing danger, understands the significance of the glance and asks Jarda what did he do, to which Jarda ominously replies, "I'm sorry".

Ascertaining that Jarda had alerted CIA forces through the security alarm, Bourne orders Jarda to get up to leave promptly. The phone rings, temporarily distracting Bourne as he looks in its direction, with Jarda using the opportunity to strike him repeatedly, with his hands still handcuffed together, and knock the gun out of Bourne's hand. With Bourne on the defensive and Jarda initially assuming ascendency in the fight, he then grabs hold of Bourne's neck, presumably with the intent to strangle him, who tries to break Jarda's grip by slamming him into the window, swinging him around, and pounding his elbow into him. Bourne then breaks free, but Jarda is able to grab a kitchen knife from the counter, and still handcuffed, slashes dangerously with it and assumes ascendency once again as Bourne is weaponless. Bourne is able to get a couple of body blows in and then kicks Jarda into a glass shelving unit, shattering it, but before Bourne can take advantage, Jarda kicks him away as he approaches. Using one of the shelving edges, Jarda is able to sever the zip cuffs, while Bourne uses the opportunity to improvise a weapon in the shape of a tightly rolled magazine, regaining a weapon and returning equilibrium to the fight.

Duelling with their opposing weapons, Bourne gets the first hit in with the magazine and hits Jarda again in rapid succession, knocking him to the ground. Jarda quickly kicks Bourne while down, allowing him to get back up, to then engage in an exchange of blows that are more communicated through the soundtrack, as opposed to the ability of the viewer to ascertain who is hitting who through the image-track[2]. They grab hold of each other and topple to the floor, with Jarda reaching for an electrical cord, which he wraps around Bourne's neck and tries to garotte him, assuming ascendancy once again. Using his last remaining strength, Bourne lands two blows with his free hand, causing Jarda to loosen his grip of the cord. Bourne then takes the cord from his neck and wraps it around Jarda's throat, and tightly pulls at the cord until Jarda's dies through strangulation, emerging victorious from the vicious fight. With the security forces descending upon Jarda's flat, Bourne uncouples the gas main and stuffs a magazine in a toaster to act as an improvised timed fuse. Bourne then flees the premises as the security forces approach the apartment, with the ensuing explosion knocking them to the ground, allowing Bourne to escape.

Compare this one-one-one fight to the opening battle sequence involving countless participants in *Gladiator* (Ridley Scott, 2000). The battle sequence depicts Roman forces, led by Maximus Decimus Meridius, about to attack the remaining forces of the Germanic tribes in Germania. Observing the proceedings is Emperor Marcus Aurelius, who holds Maximus with deep respect. A Roman messenger had been sent out to the German forces to negotiate, but returns tied to his horse decapitated, signalling the

---

[2] Although this study does not focus upon stylistic differences by which one can evaluate the depiction of action sequences, it is notable that film scholar David Bordwell has observed that Hong Kong action sequences are far more legible in the portrayal of action than compared to the dominant Hollywood style that lacks such clarity (2001).

barbarity of the Germans and their wish to still wage war. The German leader then emerges from the forest holding the head of the messenger up high, with his forces behind him possessing visibly inferior weapons and armour. The leader then tosses the head towards the Roman army and returns to his forces, who rattle their weapons and yell with savagery. The Roman forces, in contrast, stand silent, unfazed by their taunting. As Maximus mounts his horse to lead the cavalry charge, he instructs Quintus, his second in command, to 'unleash hell' at his signal, and departs with his trained wolf. Quintus then orders his men to load the catapults, next instructs the infantry to form an advance, and tells the archers to be ready, thereby signalling the Roman army's technological and military superiority over the Germans.

The film then cuts to Maximus with his cavalry troops and orders them to hold the line when they cut off any German retreat. The film returns to the German forces, still yelling in preparation for battle, then cuts back to show the more disciplined Roman army readying their weapons. Maximus then nods for the signal to be sent as an archer fires a large flaming arrow into the air toward the battle area. At the signal, the Roman archers ignite their arrows, ready to fire with the film cutting back to Maximus and the cavalry as they begin their advance on the Germans. Returning back to the Roman army, Quintus gives the signal to fire the catapults that launch fire pots into the German forces that ignite the forest, while the flaming arrows make their descent and start decimating German swordsmen. Larger spears are then fired that impale the Germans as the Roman infantry ready themselves to advance. The film cuts back to the cavalry now progressing to the German forces at speed. A long shot is then presented, representing Marcus Aurelius' optical point-of-view, as the Roman army rain fire upon the German forces [*Figure* 6.1].

Figure 6.1 Multiple battle participants in *Gladiator* (2000).

The film then cross-cuts between the advancing cavalry and the infantry, who also move forward but in opposite directions, indicating to the viewer that the German forces are about to be squeezed. For the first time in the battle, the Germans respond to the onslaught by firing arrows at the infantrymen, but their attack is ineffectual as the arrows are blocked by Roman shields. The German forces then storm the infantrymen as they engage in direct hand-to-hand combat with each other. At that moment, with Maximus' wolf leading the way, the cavalry arrives, causing the German forces to split to defend the advancing cavalry attack. Maximus heads the assault by slaying a string of German soldiers while the German leader fends off an attack with his battle axe. Maximus charges once again, but his horse is tripped by a German with his spear, sending Maximus sprawling onto the ground. Now vulnerable, a German swings a battle axe at Maximus, which he blocks with his sword, and then sends crashing to the ground by slashing his legs. Another German attacks, but arising to his feet, Maximus fends off by stabbing him with a sword. In full warrior mode, Maximus rushes to attack more Germans and backs into Quintus, and thinking he is the enemy, raises his sword for the kill, until he recognizes his comrade in arms.

The film returns to the German leader, who is now surrounded by Roman soldiers, who they bring down by lethally piercing him with their swords. The film returns back to Maximus, who is attacked by an axe-wielding German in flames, and who floors Maximus to the ground. The German raises his axe again about to land a potentially fatal blow on Maximus, but a passing Roman horseman hacks him with his sword, executing an embedded rescue of his commander. Another German then rushes Maximus, but this time it is his wolf who comes to his aid by biting the German's sword-wielding arm and then mauls him. The film then depicts the battle in slow motion, with the combat blurred and at times illegible, but the orchestral soundtrack emerges to signal the end of the battle. Maximus and other Roman soldiers, including Quintus, begin to stand as the slain soldiers lay on the ground, offering a signal of ascendancy. Maximus then raises his sword and yells "Roma Victor", formally announcing the threshold moment of victory to his men who celebrate their conquest.

One significant issue arises when one compares these two instances of the fight scenario that extend beyond the evident contrast in participant number and which can illustrate the differences between the two facets of the prototype. Most notably, the one-on-one fight can facilitate the individuation of participants to a far greater degree than a battle situation involving a large number of combatants. In the fight sequence in *The Bourne Supremacy*, the protagonist and antagonist are individuated through their contrasting appearance, demeanour and accents. As a result, their character traits are able to inform the nature of the fight, as was the case how Jarda's and Bourne's behaviour evinced an aptitude to anticipate danger that one would expect to find with a professional assassin.

Contrast this individuation to the battle sequence in *Gladiator*. In a battle that has countless participants, only three receive individuation, namely Maximus, Quintus, and the German leader. Maximus has the greatest screen time in the battle out of all the participants, as his fights with the German forces are the most depicted. In battle, Maximus also exhibits certain qualities, such as fighting skills and valour. Quintus, in contrast, only appears in a few shots when the battle commences, as does the German leader, who is not even granted a proper name in the end credits. A one-on-one fight, therefore, permits character psychology to enter into a fight scenario to a much greater extent than in a battle sequence involving a multitude of participants.

From these two examples, one can elaborate more upon the nature of the main participants of the fight scenario prototype. As noted earlier, the minimal participants in the fight scenario are the protagonist and the antagonist. It is difficult to conceive of a physical conflict that only consists of a protagonist. Even in disaster films, antagonists are assigned to the forces of nature, with the physical conflict arising in that form.

In addition, this terminology intentionally mirrors the ways in which the main characters in narrative films have been described in screenwriting manuals (Cooper and Dancyger, 2005, 48-49; Duncan 2006, 15-23). For one thing, it is quite common for the protagonist and antagonist in a film to be also the protagonist and antagonist in a climactic fight sequence. In *From Russia with Love* (Terence Young, 1963), for instance, Donald 'Red' Grant is set up as James Bond's antagonist at the film's outset when he is assigned by SPECTRE to assassinate Bond, a pairing that is reaffirmed in the climactic fight sequence between the two on the Orient Express. Similarly, in *Face/Off* (1997), Castor Troy is presented as Sean Archer's antagonist when he shoots his son at the start of the film, with the film ending with an extended fight and pursuit sequence between the two that restates their narrative relationship as physical conflict but in a condensed action scenario form.

For another, the event structure of the fight scenario prototype is also narrative in nature, where such character relationships equally arise. Given the inherent antagonism of a physical conflict, it makes sense also to describe the main characters of the conflict using the same terms.

When it comes to the character relationships that define battles involving large numbers for both parties of the conflict, then in those cases the protagonist and the antagonist terms become plural and representative of collective agents. Consequently, in the battle sequence in *Gladiator*, the Roman army is the protagonist, and the German force is the antagonist. Instead of a fight enacted at the individual level, a battle represents a conflict that is enacted at the level of collective groups. Even in these collective situations, individuation frequently arises as a means to maintain viewer engagement with the experiences of individual characters, as was the case in the battle sequence in *Gladiator* in which the viewer was able to follow Maximus' battle experiences, and to a lesser extent, those of the German leader. In some examples from the silent Soviet cinema, the individuation of character does not go beyond the depiction of social types, such as the Odessa Steps scene in *Battleship Potemkin* (Sergei M. Eisenstein, 1925), where the citizens of Odessa are fired upon by a group of Cossack soldiers. But these experiments in characterization are exceptional and not the norm.

Despite the different character configurations within the fight scenario prototype, its underlying event schema remains the same for both facets of the prototype. At the most fundamental level, the goal of the protagonist is to defeat the antagonist through physical conflict with the defeat achieved by either killing the protagonist, or incapacitating them, or by getting them to surrender and to submit to the will of the protagonist. The goal of the antagonist mirrors that of the protagonist, with their aim to defeat the protagonist, again normally realized through the same set of narrative options.

These local goals are normally in the service of broader aims. In the fight sequence in *The Bourne Supremacy*, both Bourne and Jarda fight to the death, motivated by the broader aim to simply stay alive. In the battle sequence in *Gladiator*, the Romans battle to conquer the German people. The German forces, in contrast, fight to resist their conquest to maintain their social autonomy. Since event schemas are open-ended, the outcome of the fight can vary, where in some cases the protagonist emerges victorious, as was the case with the fight situations for *The Bourne Supremacy* and *Gladiator*. In other cases, it is the antagonist who assumes victory, such as the initial defeat of Batman at the hands of Bane in *The Dark Knight Rises* (2012), or at the larger collective level, the defeat, and the forced retreat, of the Rebel Alliance by the Imperial army during the Battle of Hoth sequence in *Star Wars: The Empire Strikes Back*. In both of these last two cases, the antagonist victory is temporary, with the fight taken up again later in the film, as occurs in *The Dark Knight Rises*, or a rematch occurring later in the film series itself, such as in *Star Wars: Return of the Jedi* (Richard Marquand, 1983).

Just as the narrative outcomes of the fight scenario's event schema can vary, so can the dramatic structure of the fight scenario. In the fight scene in *The Bourne Supremacy*, there is an oscillation as to who is ascendant in the fight at any particular moment, with both parties presented as equally skilled, despite the fact that Bourne obtains the upper hand in the end. The dramatic upshot of such dramatic design is the increased suspense the scene imparts to the viewer given the moments at which Bourne appears to be in genuine danger, be it the initial blows received at the start of the fight, the moment when Jarda possesses a knife and Bourne is weaponless, and most saliently, when Bourne is garrotted by Jarda. The dramatic structure in the battle sequence in *Gladiator* has a completely different complexion. Instead of an oscillation of ascendant moments between both parties, the Roman army assumes ascendancy from the start of the battle, through the use of their superior technology and military strategy, and maintains it until the moment that they emerge victorious through the death of the German leader, and Maximus's announcement of victory.

However, it would be incorrect to infer that such dramatic structures are restricted to these facets in such singular ways. One can find dramatic structures consisting of the gradual attrition of the protagonist's opponent equally in one-on-one fights, such as in the final battle between Lee and his antagonist Han in *Enter the Dragon* (Robert Clouse, 1973), where Lee assumes ascendancy at the start of the fight in ways that parallel the dramatic structure of the *Gladiator* battle. Conversely, there are instances of an oscillation of ascendant moments in larger battle sequences, such as in *Avengers: Endgame* (2019), where at times Thanos and his forces are ascendant, and other times it is the Avengers who possess the upper hand.

One recurrent dramatic device associated in particular within battle sequences is the 'last-minute rescue', that is used in *Star Wars*

(George Lucas, 1977), *The Lord of the Rings: The Two Towers* (2002), and *Star Wars: The Rise of Skywalker* (J.J. Abrams, 2019). In the final battle sequence in *Star Wars*, for instance, a Rebel squadron of starfighters attempts to explode the Death Star by firing torpedoes into a port to cause a destructive chain reaction. At the same time, a deadline looms as the Death Star is readied to destroy the Rebel base on a nearby planet. The Rebel squadron makes its run on the Death Star, but their forces are gradually decimated by Darth Vader and his squad of TIE fighters, with only Luke Skywalker remaining in his X-wing. As Vader lines up his shot to take out Luke, Han Solo in his Millennium Falcon suddenly appears, firing at the TIE fighters and causing them to disperse. Freed from impending death, Luke fires his torpedoes into the duct and destroys the Death Star, and saves the Rebel base as a result. The 'last minute rescue' device, therefore, displays features that are similar to an embedded rescue, but is far more dramatically significant. It not only resolves the threat of a deadline, but is also a threshold moment through an intervention that decisively turns the tide of the battle.

Talk of protagonists and antagonists as participants within the fight scenario prototype suggests a particular moral valence that sides with that of the protagonist, whether construed at the individual or at the group level. Such a moral valence especially connects with films that, at a broader narrative level, exhibit a Manichaean moral structure in which their worlds are split along the lines of good and evil. In such films, protagonists are representatives of good, whereas antagonists are representatives of evil, with the films, and many of the fight sequences, in the *Star Wars* series exhibiting such an alignment between the moral valance and character function, as the Death Star attack sequence in the first *Star Wars* film illustrates.

However, although the Manichaean split is a recurrent feature manifested in fight scenarios, not all fights in film exhibit this moral structure. Some fight situations, for instance, entail physical conflict where both participants are morally virtuous. For instance, when Robin Hood first encounters Little John in *The Adventures of*

Robin Hood (1938), he blocks Robin's path on a log over a stream. In a test of fighting ability, but also of manhood, they battle with staves atop of the log, with Little John dumping Robin Hood into the water below. While by no means a lethal contest, there is still the risk of being hit, with Robin rendered incapacitated when he falls off the log. Little John then further demonstrates his moral worth by wanting to join Robin's merry team and their righteous cause.

There are other instances in which fight situations diverge from the Manichaean norm. Amongst these are the villain versus villain fights, as illustrated in the clash between Hela, an Asgardian goddess who wants to gain control over Asgard, and Surtur, a giant fire demon who is destined to destroy Asgard in *Thor: Ragnarok* (Taika Waititi, 2017). Possessing opposing goals, Hela emerges from the water and casts gigantic spears at the demon, but to no avail as he plunges his colossal sword into her and into the crust of the planet, causing it to explode.

One can also point to those fight situations that are morally grey where it is difficult to distinguish participants on the basis of their moral nature. In *Sicario: Day of the Soldado* (2018), a convoy of armoured vehicles containing CIA agents enter into Mexico to return Isabel Reyes, the teenage daughter of a kingpin of a cartel. When they cross the Mexican border, they are escorted by Mexican police, but the operation turns out to be an ambush when cartel members in the desert fire upon them with rocket-propelled grenades, taking out two of the armoured vehicles. A policeman at the front of the convoy joins in the attack by firing at the agents using his machine gun, which is mounted on a pickup truck. Matt Graver, the leader of the covert CIA mission, responds by ordering an aerial strike on the cartel members in the desert as the agents return fire on the police. Eventually, the CIA agents kill all of the remaining police, but Isabel flees from the scene by running into the desert, motivating Alejandro Gillick, a covert operative participating in the mission, to find her. In this fight situation, there are no clear-cut morally superior participants. The CIA agents have kidnapped a teenage girl to act as a pawn in a larger war against the Mexican cartels and lie to her as to their role in the kidnapping. The Mexican police appear to be in the pay of the drug cartels and are therefore corrupt, whereas the drug cartel members are morally compromised as a result of their affiliation with the drug and human traffic trades.

In what way then does one apply the terms protagonist and antagonist to these varied fight situations in a principled manner if the moral distinction between good and evil does not readily apply? The decisive factor then does not turn on the moral valence of the fight situation but the relationship of the fight participants to the protagonist-antagonist structure of the wider story in which the fight is situated. If the fight situation replicates the protagonist-antagonist structure of the film itself, then the application of the terms is straightforward. This relationship holds true for the Death Star attack in *Star Wars*, where Luke and the Rebel Alliance are the protagonists, and Darth Vader and the Imperial forces are the antagonists. The same relationship also holds for the ambush in *Sicario: Day of the Soldado*, since the CIA agents are established as the protagonists of the film at the outset, with the Mexican cartels posited as the antagonists, as well as the corrupt Mexican police who work for them, as a result of their involvement in the drug trade and the human traffic of migrants into the USA.

In the fight situations in *The Adventures of Robin Hood* and *Thor: Ragnarok*, there is a partial replication of the protagonist-antagonist structure in that Robin Hood is the protagonist of the former, whereas Hela is the antagonist of the latter film. As a result, Robin Hood is the protagonist of the staves fight, with Little John the victorious antagonist. In contrast, Hela is the antagonist of the Asgard fight, with Surtur as the protagonist, a point further underscored by the fact that Surtur was summoned by Thor, the film's protagonist, as a means to defeat Hela, and in so doing, illustrates the relevance of the proverb 'the enemy of my enemy is my friend' to this fight scene.

In cases where neither the film's protagonist nor antagonist is involved in the fight situation, then it is necessary to establish the relationship of the fight participants to the protagonist-antagonist structure of the wider story. For instance, in *The Killer Elite* (Sam Peckinpah, 1975), Yuen Chung, a Taiwanese politician, and his daughter, along with his accompanying party, are attacked by Japanese ninjas and clash at the San Francisco airport. The CIA approaches ComTeg, a private firm that handles covert assignments, and requests that it send a crew to protect Chung and his daughter. The CIA informs ComTeg that the same organization that hired the ninjas has now contracted George Hansen for the assassination job, who is the antagonist of the film, and who had earlier in the story tried to kill Mike Locken, the film's protagonist. ComTeg then commissions Locken to lead the team to protect Chung. As a result of these relations between different parties, the protagonist-antagonist structure of the fight situation at the airport is clarified. Chung and his party are the protagonists of the airport attack, given their narrative affiliation with Locken, and the Japanese ninjas are the antagonists, given their affiliation with Hansen.

Unsurprising, the fight scenario entails physical risk to a greater extent than other action forms, given the extent to which the death of the opponent in a fight situation is often the aim of the participants. In the fight scene in *The Bourne Supremacy*, the participants are punched, kicked, and garrotted in a fight to the death. In the battle sequence in *Gladiator*, the Roman army rains down fire, spears, and arrows onto their German forces, and when the opponents engage in man-to-man combat, it is with swords and axes, which leave the ground littered with bodies after the battle. In the starfighter attack sequence in *Star Wars*, the consequence of the torpedoing the duct is the cataclysmic explosion of the Death Star, no doubt annihilating the Imperial forces inside the space station. Even Robin Hood rubs his head in pain after the staves contest in *The Adventures of Robin Hood*, in which Little John playfully knocked him on the noggin with his staff, providing, at the same time, an instance of physical conflict that is situated at the tail end of the typicality gradient of the fight scenario.

Fight Combinations

Out of all the action forms, the fight scenario is the one that vertically combines the most with other action scenarios, as has been illustrated in previous chapters. The fight scenario combines with the rescue scenario, as exemplified when Luke Skywalker and company liberate Princess Leia and engage in a firefight with her captors in *Star Wars*. The fight scenario also conjoins with the escape scenario, as amply illustrated when Rambo absconded from the police precinct in *First Blood* (1982) and had to fight his way past multiple police officers. Fight scenarios regularly co-occur with capture scenarios as well, as demonstrated in the motel capture sequence *Bonnie and Clyde* (1967) and the raid in *Point Break* (1991), where the attempted arrests triggered exchanges of gunfire between the capturers and the targets. Fight situations equally combine with the heist scenario as was shown in the bank robbery sequence in *Heat* (1995) as McCauley's crew resisted capture with lethal force. Finally, fight scenarios have also combined with pursuit situations, as illustrated by the chase element in the capture sequence in *Public Enemies* (2009) as well as the pursuit component to the heist sequence *Fast Five* (2011).

There are two reasons that best explain the propensity of fight scenarios to combine with other action forms. First, one of the chief means of creating suspense in action sequences is to put obstacles in the way of the goals of the protagonist. The larger the number of obstacles, and the greater the magnitude of the challenge they represent, then the more likely suspense will be generated with regard to the viewer's emotional stake in the outcome of the action situation. While obstacles come in different shapes and forms, one of the most dramatically effective obstacles is a character who not only represents an impediment to a protagonist's goals, but manifests that impendent as a willingness to engage in physical conflict to oppose the protagonist's aims. In other words, a character whose very essence serves the dramatic function of an antagonist. It is for this reason that the participant relations that define action scenarios are normally antagonistic. In the rescue scenario, rescuers face resistant captors. In the escape scenario, escapees meet with the resistance of captors. In the capture scenario, capturers frequently encounter defiant targets. In the heist scenario, thieves not only contend with opposing guards, but capturers as well who want to put an end to their thieving ways. In the pursuit scenario, not only do pursuees often resort to gunfire to aid their escape, but so do pursuers to facilitate capture or assist their intent to kill.

Second, and as was discussed in the last chapter, the combination of action scenarios facilitates the typicality perception of action more generally. The greater the combination of action scenarios, the greater the likelihood that the viewer will categorize the events depicted on screen as action in nature. It is for this reason that filmmakers when designing action sequences, will also include some element of physical conflict to heighten the spectator's perception of action. This inclusion of the fight scenario is not some random addition, but a combination that naturally arises from the inherent antagonisms of the participant relations that define each of the action scenarios. Action combinations in films are not only aggregate in nature; they are also emergent.

Fight Scenario Variations

One of the distinctive features of the fight scenario is the degree to which one axis of its variation can be accounted for in relation to the film genre in which it is situated. For instance, when discussing the rescue scenario, reference was made to films that fell within the superhero genre (*Superman, Thor: The Dark World*), the war film (*Rambo: First Blood Part II*), science fiction films (*Star Wars*), and historical epics (*The Birth of a Nation*). However, one would struggle to note significant variations in these rescue situations that derived specifically from the genre forms in which they are found. It would make little sense, with very little explanatory purchase to be gained, to claim that there is a superhero form of rescue, a war film type of rescue, a sci-fi kind of rescue, and a historical epic form of rescue. Consequently, it is debatable that rescue situations alter significantly in these different generic contexts. However, if one turns to fight scenarios, and claims that fight situations vary in relation to genre, then such distinctions initially appear to have more purchase on the scenario's variations. In these different cases, the mode of the physical conflict is far more generically determined.

Generic Variation

While an exhaustive summary of the full variety of fight situations in different genres is beyond the scope of this chapter, it is possible to highlight those that are particularly distinctive to the genres in which they arise. One way in which fight situations generically vary is with respect to the fighting abilities and weaponry that is utilized in the fight. Superheroes and their antagonist villains in superhero films, for instance, possess superior abilities and skills compared to most mortals, and in superhero fight sequences, it is precisely these abilities that are showcased.

For instance, in *Spider-Man* (Sam Raimi, 2002), both Spider-Man and the Green Goblin are products of bodily mutations that heighten their physical strength and consequently enhance their fighting abilities as well that differentiate them from normal human beings. In the climactic fight sequence in the film, these abilities come to the fore as Spider-Man uses his web-slinging abilities to avoid falling upon sharpened debris in an abandoned building that could impale him, whereas the Goblin uses one of his pumpkin bombs in an effort to kill him. Spider-Man withstands the explosion, further affirming his superhero resilience, while the Goblin survives a brick wall collapsing upon him, a situation that would be critically injurious if not fatal to most humans. As this example illustrates, fight situations in superhero films heighten the perception of physical danger since the punishment that the protagonist and antagonist both deliver and receive is of an order that transcends human experience.

Compare such fight sequences to those battles that are found in war films that are normally generically bound by greater commitments to realism. The opening beach landing sequence in *Saving Private Ryan* (1998) is a recreation of the World War II Normandy landings and aspires to an authentic depiction of the historical event, a point reinforced by the superimposed text that provides the date of the invasion and its geographic location. From the moment that the landing crafts open their ramps, the American troops are instantly exposed to lethal rounds of machinegun fire emanating from a German bunker perched atop a cliff. As the troops make their progress to the beach, some are shot in the water, while another drowns as a result of the weight of his combat gear. With the air abuzz with flying bullets and artillery fire, the troops find temporary respite behind the Czech hedgehogs; the iron defence crosses that the Germans stationed at the beach.

The film then assumes the narrative point-of-view of Captain John H. Miller, leader of the 2nd Ranger Battalion, whose mission is to secure the beach so that heavy armour can be moved in to progress with the Allied invasion. Miller's perspective provides the viewer with not only his shell-shocked auditory perspective but also shots of the battle from his optical point-of-view [*Figure 6.2-6.3*]. These views reconfirm the horror of the battle, but from a more personalized, individuated perspective, views that consist of soldiers cowering in fear, an explosion of a flame-thrower that ignites combatants in the area, a soldier searching for his severed arm, and military personnel in flames while exiting from a landing craft, as Captain Miller picks up his helmet from the water, awash in a sea of blood. Miller recomposes himself and orders his men to advance, and he leads the way while the American troops continue to take on causalities. Miller and his troops rest at an elevated portion of the beach that offers some level of protection from the gunfire. They lay explosive charges and blow up a section of a barbed-wire fence along the beachfront, providing a breach into which the American troops can enter.

Figure 6.2 Optical point-of-view and character individuation in *Saving Private Ryan* (1998).

Figure 6.3 Optical point-of-view and character individuation in *Saving Private Ryan* (1998).

Hiding behind a broken mass of a sea wall, Miller uses a mirror to observe a Nazi machine nest perched on top of a cliff that is preventing further advance. Miller and members of his platoon then provide covering fire on the nest, allowing some of his other troops to escape to the base of the cliff. Miller stands momentarily in clear view to distract the Nazi machine gunners to enable Private Jackson, a sniper, to scramble to a blind spot and take out the Germans in the nest, a threshold moment that allows the American troops to ascend the cliff and directly engage with the German forces hiding in the trenches. The platoon then reaches a German pillbox into which they toss in grenades, firing at the German troops as they exit from the smoke. Miller then calls in a flame-thrower, who torches the pillbox and causes the munitions stored inside to explode, turning it into a burning hell for the Germans inside who leap out in flames. Some of the German troops in the trenches surrender as their position is overrun by

American troops. The remaining Germans soldiers hide in the trenches but are shot like rats caught in a trap, as Miller calls to headquarters informing them that 'Dog One', the section of the beach that his platoon just fought for with their lives, is secured to receive heavy armour, signalling that his platoon's mission has been accomplished.

As this sequence illustrates, one of the main objectives of depictions of battles in war films is to present a fight situation in which the very environment in which combatants find themselves is fatal in the extreme. From the moment the American troops leave the landing craft, they are exposed to a barrage of machinegun fire. The water, another environment, offers no respite as bullets penetrate the soldiers swimming to the surface while another soldier drowns. The environment of the beach itself rings with the sounds of bullets and the explosions of mortar shells in which bodies are shot, fragmented, and set ablaze.

This environment created to decimate the American troops is then reciprocated by the environment that the American forces create to purge the German troops through the force of their own gunfire, grenades, and flame-thrower. This reciprocation is most noticeable through the visual rhyme of a shot of American troops aflame while decamping the landing craft, with shots of German soldiers leaping from the pillbox on fire [*Figure* 6.4]. The battle scene in *Gladiator* exhibits a similar approach to representing a fight situation in the context of war as the environment in which the German position is situated contains flaming arrows rain down upon them, along with catapulted fire pots and enormous spears. The technology used in these two battle sequences differs considerably but serves, in the end, the same function of creating a lethal environment for opposing force.

Figure 6.4 Reciprocation of lethal environments in *Saving Private Ryan* (1998).

If the fight situation in war films aspire to some level of realism, then swordfights in swashbucklers, which are routinely found within adventure films, are distinguished instead through their reliance upon conventionalized ritual, in ways similar to the sword fights in the Japanese samurai film, which are also marked by convention and ritual. In the final confrontation between Zorro and Captain Esteban Pasquale in *The Mark of Zorro* (Rouben Mamoulian, 1940), for instance, the duel is triggered by an insult, as Pasquale asks Zorro if he is willing to "translate that feeling into action," a turn of phrase that offers perfect expression to the very nature of the fight scenario. They strip off their jackets to be more suitably dressed for the duel, as Alcalde Don Luis Quintero ensures that his guards will not intervene in the fight.

As they fence, both parties demonstrate their evenly match fighting abilities through the use of swords and footwork. As Zorro moves backwards in response to Pasquale's advances, he trips over a pillow but is able to block Pasquale's opportunistic lunge. Zorro returns back to his feet, and they fence again, as well as banter, this time with Zorro advancing forward with Pasquale falling back onto a table and knocking down a pot, but is still able to block Zorro's lunge in a mirroring of action. Pasquale advances forward, this time cornering Zorro in a set of stairs, but leaps off them, extricating himself from the disadvantaged position. Pasquale advances again, pressing Zorro into a wall, in which Zorro receives a flesh wound on his shoulder, signalling Pasquale's momentary ascendency. Energized by his wound, Zorro shoves

Pasquale away and continues forward until it is Pasquale's turn to have his back to the wall. They briefly pause, and Zorro makes his lunge, fatally stabbing Pasquale, who stumbles back and knocks down a painting, revealing the mark of Zorro behind it.

As this scene attests, the swordfight is a type of fight scenario that places particular emphasis upon the combatants adhering to the codified rules of fencing, a form of fighting that is itself circumscribed by the bounds of honour, and a fight that is marked by elegance rather than an unsightly tussle, or the carnage of a military battle. Part of those constraints derives from the training received by the actors - Tyrone Power and Basil Rathbone – who themselves must avoid danger in the staging of the fight. But a significant dimension of those constraints derives from the conventions from the swashbuckler itself, what Brian Taves describes as the "code of adventure" that places emphasis upon the protagonist's preservation of honour (1993, 136-154). In swashbucklers, conflict is resolved violently, but also honourably.

The fight situations in the western, by contrast, differ from those found in the swashbuckler in two distinctive respects. First, in contrast to the civility of the sword fight, the western offers the saloon brawl, a mass participant fight, often fuelled by alcohol consumption, serving to contrast the civility of the East with the yet-to-be civilized state of the West. In *Dodge City* (1939), the brawl commences when the chorus girls at the saloon start singing 'Marching Through Georgia', a Union song, prompting Confederate loyalists to sing '(I Wish I Was in) Dixie's Land' in competition. Tex Baird, one of the associates of the protagonist Wade Hatton, tosses a bottle at a photograph of Union soldiers, claiming that the 5th Kansas infantry had chased them out of Fredericksburg, a reference to the Civil War battle that the Union lost, insulting the ex-Union soldiers present in the saloon. Yancey, a henchman for Jeff Surrett, the antagonist, tells Tex to go back to Texas, instigating a shoving match between the two that evolves into a wider brawl. In addition to the brawl being a mass slugfest, chairs and tables are used as weapons, as are bottles used to smash over the heads of others, while a few participants are tossed out of windows. An accordion player continues to play to underscore the comedic dimension of the fight, as the saloon is progressively destroyed.

The saloon brawl is consequently a symbol of the anarchic forces of the West if left untamed by the civilizing influence of Easterners, a fight situation that has wider cultural resonance. In contrast to the anarchy of the saloon brawl is the fast draw duel, fought out with pistols normally between two participants, and in which physical conflict finds its most condensed form in films. The format of the duel in film westerns likely derives from Owen Wister's influential novel *The Virginian* (1902), which not only established the conventions of the shootout, but also its use as a narrative device to resolve the conflict within the overarching story (Buscombe, 1988, 114).

Amongst the most notable instances of this fight situation, which takes the form to epic heights, is the climactic the fast draw duel in *Once Upon a Time in the West* (Sergio Leone, 1968). Stretching close to nine minutes in length, the showdown represents the culmination of the film's narrative as Harmonica, a harmonica-playing gunman and protagonist of the film, faces off with Frank, a ruthless hired gun working for a railroad tycoon, and Harmonica's antagonist. Harmonica's past identity had yet to be divulged, but a flashback inserted with the duel discloses their connection. A younger-looking Frank approaches the camera, proving to be the optical point-of-view of Harmonica as a boy, who then cruelly inserts the harmonica into the boy's mouth. As the camera tracks back, the shot reveals Harmonica supporting his older brother on his shoulders, who has a noose around his neck. Exhausted by the ordeal, Harmonica collapses onto the ground, with the film cutting back to the duel. In an instant, they draw their pistols and fire at each other, with Frank spinning round with the force of impact of the bullet to his heart. Unable to return his pistol into his holster, Frank drops his weapon and staggers forward and collapses to the ground. Uttering his last words, Frank asks, "Who are you?," and Harmonica wordlessly replies by yanking the harmonica from the cord around his neck and inserts it into Frank's mouth, mirroring Frank's gesture presented in the flashback as means to reveal his identity to him.

Out of all the fight situations, the fast draw duel is the variant that places the greatest emphasis upon the lead-up to the violence rather than the act of violence itself. Instead of showcasing a prolonged shoot out, that is also a staple of the western, the fight itself in the fast draw duel is over in an instant, with the suspenseful lead up the narrative focus, as was the case with the significant reveal of Harmonica's identity in *Once Upon a Time in the West*. In such concentrated form, the fast draw duel is also unique with respect to its dramatic structure. In the fleeting instant of gunfire exchange, there is no time to play out the oscillation of ascendancy between the participants or present the gradual attrition of an opponent until their defeat. The drama instead is a race to fire first, to which the viewer must carefully attend, thereby incorporating the speed scenario, but in a truly distinctive way.

The Sports Variant

Beyond the generic variation of fight scenarios, there is also the sports variant that cuts across the boxing film, a subgenre of the sports film - *Body and Soul* (Robert Rossen, 1947), *Rocky* (John G. Avildsen, 1976), *Raging Bull* (Martin Scorsese, 1980), *Ali* (Michael Mann, 2001), *Million Dollar Baby* (Clint Eastwood, 2004), *Creed* (Ryan Coogler, 2015); the jousting tournament - *El Cid* (Anthony Mann, 1961), *Excalibur* (John Boorman, 1981), *A Knight's Tale* (Brian Helgeland, 2001); the martial arts film as a competition - *Enter the Dragon* (1973), *Battle Creek Brawl* (Robert Clouse, 1980), *The Karate Kid* (John G. Avildsen, 1984), *Bloodfist* (Terence H. Winkless, 1989), *Kickboxer* (Mark DiSalle and David Worth, 1989), *Ong-bak* (Prachya Pinkaew, 2003); as well in sword and sandal films as gladiatorial combat - *Demetrius and the Gladiators* (Delmer Daves, 1954), *Spartacus* (Stanley Kubrick, 1960), *The Last Gladiator* (Umberto Lenzi, 1964), *The Arena* (Steve Carver, 1974), and *Gladiator* (2000). Related to the sports variant are those that take the competitive gladiatorial premise to a greater free-for-all contest, including *Death Race 2000* (Paul

Bartel, 1975), *Rollerball* (Norman Jewison, 1975), *The Running Man* (Paul Michael Glaser, 1987), *The Tournament* (Scott Mann, 2009), and *The Hunger Games* (Gary Ross, 2012).

While most sports are distinguished by their competitive physical activity, in the sports variant, that activity is specifically some form of physical combat, and as action scholar Mark Gallagher notes, often in ways that showcase their "culturally specific fighting styles" (2019, 77). In addition, what distinguishes the sports variant from merely a fight is that the former is usually governed by a set of rules that stipulate how the fight is to be conducted in terms of what type of blows and weapons are permissible, whereas a fight normally lacks such constraints. Further, the sports variant often features training sessions where combatants fight each other but in ways that still entails a risk of physical injury but in a minimized capacity, thereby placing them down on the typicality gradient, such as the training sessions in *No Retreat, No Surrender* (Corey Yuen, 1986). The sports variant also varies as to whether the aim of the fight is to incapacitate the opponent, as is normally the case in the boxing film, or to bring about their death, which occasionally arises in martial art tournaments, such as in *Enter the Dragon* and *Bloodfist*, and with fights to the death the norm in gladiatorial combat.

The final fight scene in *Bloodsport* (Newt Arnold, 1988) can illustrate the general features of the sports variant. Frank Dux, played by Jean-Claude Van Damme, is an American army captain in Hong Kong to participate in 'The Kumite', an illegal martial arts tournament. His opponent is Chong Li, the reigning champion of The Kumite, who had brutally defeated Dux's friend, motivating him further for the fight. Prior to the match, Li had defeated another opponent and killed him by breaking his neck, a breach of the rules of the contest, signalled by the presiding judges turning their back toward Li as a sign of their disapproval. As Dux and Li prepare for the match, Li's trainer secretly places a salt tablet into his waistband, indicating Li's willingness to engage in unfair play. When the referee signals the start of the match, Dux strikes quickly with a kick to Lee's head. Leaping over the referee, Dux lands another kick, knocking Li down. Li gets up, but Dux lays a series of further kicks, with Li able to land only one in response, which Dux in turn rejoinders with a boot to Li's chest.

With Dux ascendant in the fight, he tries to capitalize on his momentum by landing five successive kicks to Li's face, an action that leaves Dux temporarily vulnerable as Li grabs his Dux's leg and delivers two powerful blows, sending him to the mat. After Dux gets up, he tries to strike Li, a blow that is blocked, allowing Li to kick Dux with his shin in the abdomen, to toss him on the mat again, and to equalize the match. Dux composes himself and lets loose a dropkick to Li's head, sending him down again. Clearly rattled when shaking his head in numbness, Li then wildly lunges at Dux, who athletically summersault over him to then attack with a series of kicks and punches that leaves Li dazed. With Dux ascendant in the fight, Li pulls out the salt tablet, which he crushes with his hand, and tosses the powder into Dux's eyes, temporarily blinding him. With no sense of where his opponent is, Dux punches the air, leaving him exposed as Li takes advantage of his disoriented state through a succession of blows that puts Dux defenceless on the mat. Li prematurely celebrates, stamping and kicking Dux at will.

Sensing his impending defeat, Dux yells in a crazed state, but then meditatively quiets himself down to recall his blindfolded martial arts training, which the viewer sees in flashbacks. No longer in need of vision to sense his opponent, he blocks Li's next blow, kicks him in the stomach, and tosses to the mat. In another act of poor sportsmanship, Li shoves the referee in Dux's direction, who nonetheless is able to ascertain his identity by grabbing his robe. Regaining his ascendancy, Dux spirals his right leg in front of Li, putting on the backfoot. Li lunges again, but Dux leaps upward over Li, allowing Van Damme to perform one of his trademark splits. After one last back-kick to Li's stomach, Dux sends four consecutive spinning roundhouses to Li's head, leaving Li prostrate on the mat, from which Dux forces him to concede defeat.

As the *Bloodsport* fight scene illustrates, the main point of contrast between the sports variant and the fight scenario prototype is the additional degree of constraint imposed upon the fight. In the fight scene in *The Bourne Supremacy*, there were no constraints on the fight as the two participants made use of what was available, be it a knife, a magazine and an electrical cord. In contrast, the fight scene in *Bloodsport* had some level of constraints in that the opponents could not avail themselves of additional weapons beyond using their own bodies. In addition, a referee was present, and although he did not intervene in the match, he formally started and ended it. Unsaid rules were also in force in relation to what was considered honourable. Notably, Dux gave due respect to the officiators present and relied upon his own fighting prowess to win the match. Li, however, paid no such honour and engaged in unfair play through recourse of the salt tablet that was introduced into the match in a clandestine fashion. Boxing films, such as *Rocky* and its sequels exhibit even greater levels of constraints as the films attempt to mirror professional boxing matches and the rules that govern them.

The Unidirectional Variant

One of the defining features of the fight scenario prototype is that there is reciprocity in an exchange of attacks between the participants of the fight. But there are numerous instances in films where individuals are attacked by other characters where no such reciprocity occurs. In such instances, the violence is unidirectional instead of bidirectional. Consider an example from *The Rock* (1996) in which John Patrick Mason, a former SAS operative, and Dr. Stanley Goodspeed, an FBI chemical weapons specialist, accompany a U.S. Navy SEAL team to infiltrate Alcatraz Island. The Navy SEAL team is detected by the rogue military group controlling the island and is eliminated, leaving only Mason and Goodspeed hiding in the drainage system underneath the derelict prison. As Mason and Goodspeed converse, their voices are heard through a vent by the rogue agents above. A member of the rogue group then drops an explosive device into the drainage system, blasting Mason and Goodspeed off their feet and sending flames throughout the tunnel. They survive the blast, but another and more powerful explosive is dropped, creating an extensive firestorm in the tunnels below, which Mason and Goodspeed avoid by diving under the water [*Figure 6.5*].

In this fight situation, the attack goes unreciprocated as Mason and Goodspeed aim to survive rather than attempt to retaliate, which would probably result in their death given their limited arsenal. The unidirectional variant, therefore, retains the minimal requirement of two participants in a fight situation, but diverges from the prototype by abandoning reciprocity in favour of a unidirectional attack. In what ways then does it still make sense to describe the unidirectional variant as a fight worthy of being identified as an instance of a fight scenario? As noted in the Introduction, one of the benefits of understanding categorization as a typicality gradient is that it allows one to see the wider class of instances of an action scenario. Although the unidirectional variant does not possess reciprocity, it still retains crucial features of the fight scenario prototype, namely a situation that involves minimally two participants and an attack, features moreover that are integral to the wider class of instances of the fight scenario. The unidirectional variant manifests physical discord, but in a different form.

Figure 6.5 The unidirectional variant in *The Rock* (1996).

The Destruction Variant

Since explosions have been perceived as recurrent features of action films (Tasker, 2017, p.12), it would be helpful to use this occasion to see how they fit within an action scenario framework. Instead of viewing explosions as pure spectacle, an action scenario framework alternatively classifies explosions in relation to their narrative function within an action scenario. Viewed from this perspective, explosions are considered within the broader class of the destruction variant that takes on four principal forms.

The first is the disaster sub-variant in which the forces of nature resemble the unidirectional variant of an attack, in which their destructive powers are directed toward humankind, be they in the form of tsunamis, as depicted in *The Poseidon Adventure* (Ronald Neame, 1972); outer space objects, such as the asteroid in *Armageddon* (Michael Bay, 1998); volcanoes, as manifested in *Pompeii* (Paul W.S. Anderson, 2014); earthquakes, as showcased in *Earthquake* (Mark Robson, 1974) and *2012* (2009); and hurricanes, as presented in *The Hurricane* (John Ford, 1937) and *The Perfect Storm* (Wolfgang Petersen, 2000). Like other action scenarios, the disaster sub-variant possesses a typicality gradient, where less prototypical instances are situated further down the scale. Instead of nature wreaking full-fledged destruction, it provides a precarious environment, such as the sea storm depicted in *The Guns of Navarone* (J. Lee Thompson, 1961), and situated further down the scale, the sandstorm in the opening scene in *Close Encounters of the Third Kind* (Steven Spielberg, 1977).

The second form consists of the destruction of property variant that is situated in the fight scenario typicality gradient in which an attack on property serves as a surrogate for an attack on another character or larger social group. In *Mr. Majestyk* (Richard Fleischer, 1974), for instance, Vince Majestyk is a melon farmer who earned the ire of Frank Renda, a mobster hitman, after he had held him captive in a cabin earlier in the film. Relieved from police custody, Renda and his gang of thugs head to Majestyk's farm with the probable intent to kill him. However, Majestyk is not there, but Renda discovers a barn full of watermelons that Majestyk has harvested. Renda fires his pistol into the melon pile and then orders his thugs to do likewise. What ensues is a massacre except that it consists of automatic gunfire directed at a melon harvest, with the intention of destroying Majestyk's livelihood [*Figure* 6.6]. The destruction of property variant bears similarities with the unidirectional variant since, in both cases, attacks are unidirectional, and inanimate objects lack the agency to retaliate. But what further differentiates the destruction of property variant from the fight scenario prototype is that the unidirectional attack is instead directed at a property or an object that either stands in for or is affiliated with an opposing character or social group. As a result, instances of the variant are situated further down the typicality gradient since one of the two participants in the prototype fight scenario is rendered metonymically through an association with a property or an object.

Figure 6.6 Destruction of property variant in
Mr. Majestyk (1974).

One recurrent and spectacular way that the destruction of property variant is affected is through the use of an explosion. An example of such an instance can be found in *Bataan* (Tay Garnett, 1943), a World War II film set in the Philippines, where an American army squad blows up a bridge over a large valley as a means to prevent the advance of the invading Japanese army. In this case, the bridge is the surrogate of the Japanese army since it facilitates its advance into the Bataan Peninsula. The explosion of facilities explosions often found at the end of James Bond films, is another instance of the destruction of property variant when their destruction represents the obliteration of the antagonist's plans. In *Dr. No* (1962), for example, Bond prevents the disruption of an American rocket launch by overloading the nuclear reactor powering Dr. No's facility. In doing so, he thwarts the transmission of the disrupting radio beam, but also causes the facility to explode, thereby destroying its ability to further interfere with the American rocket programme.

The third form of destruction is also situated within the fight scenario but in the more conventional form of an attack upon another participant rather than indirectly through an attack on their inanimate surrogate. The unidirectional example from *The Rock* illustrates such a function as the explosive devices used against Mason and Goodspeed were, for all intents and purposes, weapons. The exploding artillery fire in the battle sequence in *Saving Private Ryan* that dismembered American troops is another example of explosions used in a weaponized capacity but set instead in a bidirectional conflict. The fourth form of destruction serves the narrative function to effect narrative closure on the action sequence itself. The facility explosion in the *Dr. No* sequence additionally functions in this capacity, but the convention is also used in other action scenarios, most commonly the pursuit sequence. The car chase sequence in *Dr. No* concludes with the pursuing vehicle falling down a ravine and bursting into flames, marking the end of the pursuit. Far from being pure moments of spectacle, destruction is narratively integrated into the action scenarios in which they are situated.

Exemplar: *Crouching Tiger, Hidden Dragon* (2000)

Ang Lee's *Crouching Tiger, Hidden Dragon* (2000) is a benchmark film in relation to the analysis of action in film in multiple respects. First, it is representative of the martial arts genre that had its most influential expression in Hong Kong cinema. As David Desser has noted, the genre is a distinctive narrative form in which "the protagonist or protagonists are skilled in Asian martial arts and put such skill to use in the resolution of the plot" (2000, 78). Like the heist film as a genre that centers upon the heist scenario, the martial arts film, in contrast, centers upon a particular inflection of the fight scenario, one of the genre's defining characteristics. Second, as a Chinese production, the film offers examples of action that derive from another national cinema tradition outside of that of Hollywood. Third, the film features strong female characters that are participants in the fight sequences themselves that is a welcome departure from male-dominated action in films.

Significantly, the 'Green Destiny duel', an instance of the fight scenario prototype, features women in protagonist and antagonist roles. Mu Bai, a swordsman, has entrusted the 'Green Destiny', a legendary sword to Yu Shu Lien, a female warrior, to take to their benefactor Sir Te, who resides in Beijing. One evening at Sir Te's residence, the sword is stolen by a thief, who is later revealed to be Jen Yu, the daughter of a governor who runs away from her wedding and who has been secretly learning Wudang martial art skills.

Later in the film, they meet again at a Wudang temple, and Shu Lien attempts to counsel Yu, but they enter into an argument that leads to a duel in the temple's practice chamber. As they initially standoff, Yu, the antagonist, holds the Green Destiny high, while Shu Lien, the protagonist, brandishes her own sabre. Shu Lien lunges first, causing Yu to back away, and then leaps high into the air to attack again, as Yu executes a backwards summersault to escape the path of Shu Lien's sabre. Shu Lien again goes on the offensive, swinging her sabre successively, blows that Yu successfully blocks. Yu then goes on the offensive, moving forward and thrusting her sword at her opponent. Shu Lien grabs Yu's arm and swings her sabre multiple times at Yu's head. Yu escapes Shu Lien's grasp by affecting a 360-degree spin and strikes out at her with a Green Destiny, with a backwards slice that Shu Lien slaps away with her sabre. Maintaining her momentum, Yu thrusts her sword forward twice, which prompts Shu Lien to spin and split her sabre into two, such that when she faces Yu again, she has a weapon in each hand.

With the advantage of the extra weapon, Shu Lien goes on the attack, spinning her body around and attacking with her sabres, forcing Yu to the back of the room. Yu thrusts the Green Destiny in defence, and on the second lunge, Shu Lien traps the sword between her two blades. Spinning her body horizontally, Yu breaks free from the hold but lands flat on the ground, making herself vulnerable. As Yu gets up, Shu Lien moves forward on the attack again with sabres swinging and is temporarily ascendant. Demonstrating her athleticism once more, Yu runs toward the wall and climbs up it to spin round and execute a flying attack up Shu Lien, which breaks her sabres in the process, thereby equalizing the fight [*Figure* 6.7]. Shu Lien then exhibits her own physical prowess by spinning to affect a flying kick to Yu's head.

Undeterred by her broken weapons, Shu Lien tosses the swords to the ground to avail herself of the weapons stored in the chamber. Grabbing a bendable spear, Shu Lien then lunges with it with skill, swinging it like a sword at times, and at other moments thrusting it forward as a dagger. Yu spins again to shift from defensive movements to go on the attack once more. Shu Lien holds her ground, whirling the blade end of the spear dangerously close to Yu's face. Leaping upward, she swings the spear back with a force that knocks Yu back toward a table [*Figure* 6.8]. On the offensive, Shu Lien thrusts again with her spear and spins round once more to thrust the spear toward Yu, temporarily trapping her on top of the table. Blocking the spear with her sword, Yu breaks free again, just in time to move out of the way as Shu Lien brings down the spear with strength, breaking the table. Thrusting her spear forward, Shu Lien traps Yu against a wall, who in defence grabs the spear and slices it in half with her sword. Swinging the sword again, she chops the spear down further, causing Shu Lien to retreat by spinning backward. Yu then lobs the blade end of the spear towards Shu Lien, who dodges it just in time.

Figure 6.7 Reciprocated athleticism in *Crouching Tiger, Hidden Dragon* (2000).

Figure 6.8 Reciprocated athleticism in *Crouching Tiger, Hidden Dragon* (2000).

Reaching for another weapon, Shu Lien chooses a set of sharpened hooked swords. Sensing inferior weapons, Yu then goes on the offence with a series of thrusts that Shu Lien blocks with her hooks. The two hooks lock onto each other, which Shu Lien swings round like a chain while advancing upon Yu, and then unlocks them to catch onto Yu's sword. Yu blocks an attack with her hand, kicks away Shu Lien's hook to free her sword, and lunges several times, causing Shu Lien to dodge the blade. A quick exchange of blows and blocks ensues as each of them spins in an effort to get an advantage. Shu Lien's locks Yu's sword with her hooks, but in a manner that leaves her vulnerable and Yu with the advantage. Twisting the Green Destiny, Yu shatters the hooks, causing Shu Lien to summersault over her to gain access to the arsenal of weapons stored at the chamber's wall. She quickly grabs a pair of daggers, which she fires at Yu, who leaps backs to dodge the flying weapons. Shu Lien then grabs a huge spear with a crescent as a blade and advances aggressively toward Yu, but its weighted club end proves too heavy, causing her to drop the weapon.

With a wry smile on her face, Yu senses an opportunity and swings her sword while moving forward on the offence as Shu Lien picks up a heavy metal club from the store of weapons and blocks Yu's attack. A more formidable weapon, Shu Lien swings the club around, knocking Yu to the ground, who rolls out of the way before Shu Lien sends the weapon down, breaking the stone tiles on the floor. Charging toward Yu, Shu Lien bashes the adjunct furniture as Yu dodges away. Continuing with the attack, Shu Lien charges again, swinging the rod, with one blow literally sending Yu flying backward, elevating the martial arts skills on display to a higher gravity-defying level. They pause for a moment, with Yu shaking with fear after Shu Lien's relentless onslaught. They duel again with their respective weapons until Yu spins in a series of blows with her sword, and with another flying leap, crashes the Green Destiny down onto Shu Lien's metal club, slicing it in half.

They pause again, this time exchanging barbed insults at each other. Emboldened by her ascendant moment, Yu challenges her opponent to select any weapon she wants. Shu Lien ominously selects a hefty two-hand longsword and advances again on the offence putting Yu on the backfoot. Yu backflips over Shu Lien to evade her advance as they exchange blows and blocks with quickened pace, signalling that the end of their fight is near. Yu makes a final lunge at Shu Lien, which she evades, but spins round to send her Green Destiny crashing down on the long sword, breaking the weapon, but with enough of the sword left for Shu Lien to hold against Yu's throat. Deciding not to kill her, Shu Lien slowly lowers the broken weapon and demands Yu to relinquish the Green Destiny. Yu, in violation of honour, slashes at Shu Lien's shoulder, who retreats in pain. Yu advances again, with the intent to kill, but Mu Bai arrives just in time, rescuing Shu Lien from probable death. Yu sensing a superior opponent, flies away in escape, demonstrating her superhuman martial arts abilities, with Mu Bai in pursuit, bringing to an end the duel component of a longer action sequence.

Just coming in at under five minutes, the Green Destiny duel is a densely packed instance of a one-on-one fight. Setting aside Mu Bai's rescue and Yu's escape at the end, the duel also offers an almost pure instance of a fight scenario. But what is most notable about the duel is the ways in which it reveals martial arts film conventions that distinguish it from the ways in which fight scenarios are staged in Hollywood films.

First, the Green Destiny duel exhibits a more formal structure, particularly when contrasted with the fight scene in *The Bourne Supremacy*. Instead of a brawl structured with an oscillation of ascendancy between the participants, the Green Destiny duel placed much greater emphasis upon the use of a variety of weapons that formally mark the stages of the fight's progression, and in the process, sustained viewer engagement through the changing nature of the combat. This formal structure of weapon progression is also weaved into the dramatic structure of the fight situation. Every moment that Shu Lien was on the cusp of assuming ascendancy, Yu would respond by breaking her weapon, reversing her ascendancy with the Green Destiny sword proving to be the great equalizer to Shu Lien's superior fighting prowess. In response, Shu Lien would try again with another weapon and then assume the offensive in the fight, with the same pattern of ascendancy repeated. Even the threshold moment of the duel is mirrored. Even though Shu Lien achieves the threshold moment first by holding the broken sword to Yu's throat, signalling her victory in the fight by her ability to kill her, Yu, however, gets in the last blow of the fight, which matches Shu Lien's formal victory.

Second, in addition to this more formal fight structure is the greater emphasis placed upon the athleticism of the participants, as well as the actors who play them. While fight scenes more generally place emphasis on fighting skills, the martial arts film, in particular, underscores the athleticism of the participants. In the Green Destiny duel, the participants leap, spin and perform summersaults as a means to affect stylized moments of evasion and attack. In martial arts films, athleticism becomes a crucial fighting skill. However, the supreme expression of such athleticism is the superhuman moments of gravity-defying leaps and flight. These superhuman moments in the Green Destiny duel derive from the Wuxia tradition in Chinese fiction, as manifested both in literature and in film, that includes these moments of superhuman ability (Teo, 2016). In doing so, the martial arts film gives the fight scenario its most distinctive aesthetic expression.

One of the outstanding features of the fight scenario is its ability to combine with other action forms. Despite its purity of expression of the one-on-one fight scenario prototype, the Green Destiny duel in *Crouching Tiger, Hidden Dragon* still exhibited in its concluding moment a horizontal combination with escape and a pursuit, as the sequence segued into another action scene. This ability to combine goes a long way to explain the ubiquity of this action form and the reason why the scenario is often identified with action. However, the fight scenario is not the only action form to possess such a special status. Pursuit sequences are also prototypically viewed as representative of action sequences more broadly. The next chapter will explore why.

Chapter 6: The Pursuit Scenario

"The secret is to have a story that is so based in reality that when you reach the chase, you get caught up in them emotionally and accept them as reality."[1]

Philip D'Antoni, the author of this quote, was the producer of the car chase 'trilogy' consisting of *Bullitt* (1968), *The French Connection* (1971), and *The Seven-Ups* (1973), which he also directed. One of the points that D'Antoni underscores in the quote is the importance of the film's story to secure better spectator engagement with the chase itself. As noted earlier in the Introduction, an action sequence is usually informed by the narrative in which it is situated as well as entailing consequences that have an effect upon the story that follows. In addition to its narrative dimensions, the pursuit scenario is also often viewed as prototypically representative of action sequences more broadly. Like the fight scenario, pursuit sequences demonstrate a similar propensity to combine with other action scenarios. Yet unlike the fight scenario, a pursuit sequence can be decomposed to more elemental action scenarios of escape, speed, capture or fight – dependent upon the goals of the pursuer, with these constitutive elements further heightening its prototypicality as an action form.

The Pursuit Scenario Prototype

The event schema for the pursuit scenario prototype has already been outlined in the Introduction, but it would be worthwhile to examine it in greater detail and also to analyze its decomposed elements to see how they work in tandem. As noted previously, the pursuit scenario's event schema in its most basic structure consists of character A escaping from a scene with character B in

---

[1] Philip D'Antoni cited in interview with C. Poggiali in *Shock Cinema*, 17, 200. pp. 26-27.

pursuit, often with the intent to capture or kill character A, often by means of intercept manoeuvres. As the pursuit unfolds, the characters encounter obstacles, with the scenario normally ending with the success or failure of that pursuit. We can now re-label character A as the *pursuee* and character B as the *pursuer* as the minimal character types required for a pursuit sequence to arise. Like the fight scenario prototype, the pursuit scenario prototype also accommodates the manifestation of multiple pursuers and pursuees, although the former normally occurs more frequently than the latter, such as the countless car chases involving numerous pursuing police vehicles, such as the extended pursuit in *The Blues Brothers* (John Landis, 1980).

Two additional aspects of a pursuee escaping from a particular scene warrant unpacking. First, in saying that the initiating event of a pursuit sequence is a pursuee escaping from a scene, the defining conditions of an escape situation need to be manifest. This could consist of an escape from enclosed captivity, as was the case with Rambo escaping from the police station in *First Blood* (1982), or it can assume more the nature of the fleeing variant of an impending dangerous situation where time is of the essence, and an implicit deadline is at work. Second, for an escape to evolve into a pursuit, the escapee must be fleeing from the initiating situation *at speed*. If Rambo merely strolled out of the police station instead of running down its steps to commandeer a motorcycle to flee at greater velocity, it would be unlikely the viewer would register the sequence as a pursuit. Likewise, for a pursuer to be considered in pursuit mode, they must be travelling at speed as well rather than merely following the pursuee. Therefore, speed appears to be an ineliminable element of the pursuit scenario and the primary means by which it expresses action.

A good illustration of the difference between following and pursuing, and the difference that speed makes in contrasting the latter from the former, is illustrated in the opening section of the car chase in *Bullitt*. The sequence commences with Lieutenant Frank Bullitt getting into his Ford Mustang and notices that he is being tailed by two hitmen, Phil and Mike, in a Dodge

Charger. The sequence does not suddenly enter into pursuit mode but instead depicts the hitmen following Bullitt in heavy traffic. Bullitt then turns up a street, which the hitmen do as well at the same vehicular pace. The narration shifts its perspective to the hitmen who arrive at a T-Junction with Bullitt's Mustang nowhere in sight. They turn left in search of Bullitt, who then suddenly appears behind them in their rear-view mirror as the followers now become the followed, reversing the initial cat-and-mouse structure of the sequence.

The hitmen and Bullitt continue down the streets of San Francisco, but with no notable change in pace to the vehicles, with Lalo Schifrin's jazz score contributing to the suspense. The hitmen reach another intersection and the driver of the Charger secures his seatbelt, revealed through an insert shot, thereby signalling to the viewer an imminent heightening of risk [*Figure* 7.1]. The Charger suddenly accelerates as it turns left and speeds up a street, while Bullitt cuts through the traffic in pursuit of the Charger. A sudden and dramatic shift from following to pursuing occurs in the sequence, the first functioning to build suspense, the second representing a change into action mode. This shift is not only communicated by the pace of the vehicles, which move much faster than before, but also through the soundtrack in which Schifrin's music is dropped to be replaced by the sounds of vehicular speed. The viewer hears the vehicles burn rubber as they accelerate. The sounds of their engines and gear changes become louder and more prominent. Speed is consequently apprehended both visually and aurally, but also most importantly, relative to the previous slower pace of the vehicles during the cat and mouse opening. Speed is the element that transforms a merely suspenseful sequence into an action sequence in earnest.

Figure 7.1 Insert shot signalling increased risk to come in *Bullitt* (1968).

In the pursuit scenario prototype, the main goal of the pursuee is frequently to elude capture, or if the intentions of the pursuers are more life-threatening, then the pursuee seeks to evade harm. The goals of the pursuer assume more forms in the pursuit scenario prototype given their greater variety. One recurrent goal of the pursuer is to simply kill the pursuee, as illustrated by the T-800 cyborg in *The Terminator* (James Cameron, 1984), and the shape-shifting androids in *Terminator 2: Judgment Day* (James Cameron, 1991) and *Terminator 3: Rise of the Machines* (Jonathan Mostow, 2003). When such aims are realized through physical conflict during a pursuit, the scenario vertically combines with the fight scenario.

A good illustration of such aims occurs during the first automotive pursuit sequence in *The Bourne Supremacy* (2004), in which Kirill, a Russian agent and assassin, locates Jason Bourne in Goa. Bourne spots Kirill first through his superior sense of identifying potential assassins obtained in the field, and picks up Marie, his girlfriend, in his jeep while realizing that his cover has been blown. They depart from the busy beach at speed while Kirill pursues in his sedan. Bourne heads for a bridge through an alleyway in an attempt to elude Kirill, motivated by the lethal risk he poses. Bourne and Marie then switch seats to allow Bourne to access his pistol as a passenger, preparing for the violence to come. The narration then switches back to Kirill to reveal he is still in pursuit and proximate to his prey. Bourne instructs Marie to drive through a field as a shortcut to the bridge, and as they do so, Kirill abandons his vehicle to continue the chase on foot, with his rifle case slung over his shoulder, making his intention to kill more apparent. The jeep then returns to the road leading to the bridge, with the film cutting back to Kirill, who spots them headed toward the bridge, and then returns back to Bourne and Marie, continuing a pattern of parallel editing between the pursued and the pursuer that is used routinely when depicting pursuit sequences. A very brief cutback to Kirill then shows him firing his rifle in their direction, thereby confirming his identity as an assassin, as well as combining the chase with an instance of unidirectional attack [*Figure* 7.2]. The rear window of the jeep then shatters as Marie slumps at the wheel after being shot, causing the vehicle to plummet off the bridge. As the jeep sinks deep into the river, Bourne desperately tries to save Marie, but she does not respond to his efforts, indicating her loss of life but also that Bourne survived the ordeal. A crowd begins to form on the bridge, which Kirill soon joins to confirm the kill but mistakenly assumes Bourne's death as well.

Figure 7.2 Unidirectional attack and the intention to kill in *The Bourne Supremacy* (2004).

Another recurrent goal of the pursuer manifested in the pursuit scenario prototype is to capture the pursuee. In such instances, the goals of the pursuer are identical to the goals of the capturer discussed in Chapter 3, namely the aim to apprehend the target, even in the face of resistance. Such goals are evident in the escape-chase sequence in *First Blood* (1982) when Sheriff Teasle in his police car pursues Rambo, who had absconded on a

213

motorcycle, whose intention is to capture, rather than to kill the pursuee. However, as noted earlier, situations can transform from a capture scenario into a fight scenario when the pursuee resists capture through the additional use of lethal force, motivating the pursuers to respond in kind.

Such a development in action occurs later on in the pursuit sequence in *Bullitt*. For the majority of the sequence, the action has been restricted to a pursuit mode. But when Bullitt is able to catch up with the hitmen's vehicle after nearly wiping out to avoid an oncoming motorcyclist, they vertically escalate their resolve to elude Bullitt's capture by entering into fight mode when Mike, the hitman in the passenger seat, loads his shotgun. After both vehicles negotiate traffic, Mike makes his way to the backseat while Bullitt makes the first aggressive moves by sideswiping the Charger multiple times with his Mustang in a manoeuvre to get their vehicle off the road to presumably bring the chase to an end and engage in some form of arrest. Mike then rolls down the backseat window and takes a shot at Bullitt, causing him to swerve his Mustang. Mike takes another shot, this time more proximate as the shotgun pellets strike Bullitt's windshield. Mike takes one final shot and misses, while Bullitt executes a more forceful swerve into their vehicle, forcing it to veer off the road and crash into a gas station that explodes with the impact, killing the hitmen in the ensuing fireball.

The pursuit sequence, therefore, dramatically climaxes with a vertical combination with the fight scenario, but it is worth pausing a moment to note the underlying shifts in character motivation as well. With respect to the pursued, the hitmen maintain their broader objective to elude capture, but additionally engage in lethal force as a means to get Bullitt off their tail. With respect to the pursuer, Bullitt's goals are less clear as to why he is pursuing the hitmen, but it is implicit that as a representative of the law, his goal is to capture them and his sideswiping manoeuvres are conducted to that end. They are actions that mark the occasion when the pursuit vertically shifts into vehicular capture mode. But at the same time, the sideswiping manoeuvres are aggressive, and as illustrated in the sequence, can lead to fatal consequences for the pursued. As a result, the sideswiping manoeuvres instantiate both the capture and fight action forms. Consequently, Bullitt's final swerve into the Charger was not only a more determined effort at capture, but also a move of increased physical risk for the hitmen in which the capture and the fight mode become virtually indistinguishable.

Another goal of the pursuer manifested in the pursuit scenario prototype, which slightly differs from the desire to capture the pursuee, is instead the objective to obtain a desired object that the pursuee possesses. Although a variation on the pursuer's typical goals, the variance is not sufficient to warrant the status of a variant on prototype since the actual pursuit strategies that the pursuer undertakes are near identical to those used to either capture or kill the pursuee. In addition, the goals of the pursuee remain the same, namely to elude capture, as a means to retain possession of the prized object.

Examples of such motives can be found in the climactic chase in *Mad Max 2: The Road Warrior* (George Miller, 1981) as well as the final pursuit in *Raiders of the Lost Ark* (1981). In the *Mad Max 2: The Road Warrior* chase, the Marauders, a gang of post-apocalyptic bandits, seek to possess the oil produced at an oil refinery by a community of settlers, to fuel their marauding habits. The settlers decide to break free from their besieged compound and use an armoured fuel tanker as a decoy, with Max at the wheel, as other settlers depart on a different route with the oil in other vehicles. The Marauders consequently engage in a multi-vehicle pursuit of the tanker under the belief that it contains the much sought-after oil. Similarly, Indiana Jones pursues a Nazi convoy in *Raiders of the Lost Ark* not because he seeks to capture or kill them but to repossess the Ark that was previously taken from him. In both cases, the overriding aim of the pursuers is to hijack the respective vehicles from the control of the pursuees, and are willing to additionally engage in physical conflict to achieve those ends.

Given the different pursuer goals accommodated with the pursuit scenario prototype, the dramatic structure of the pursuit scenario varies as well. Like the previous action scenarios, dramatic structure hinges upon the shifting moments of ascendancy between the conflicting goals of the participants, which come to a threshold moment.

In *The Bourne Supremacy* pursuit sequence, these conflicting goals consist of Kirill's aim to assassinate Bourne, and quite probably kill Marie in the process, whereas Bourne seeks to elude Kirill, to not only save himself but to also keep Marie out of harm's way. The first action on Bourne's part to that effect occurs prior to the chase when Bourne first spots Kirill at the city's market and identifies him as a potential assassin, depriving Kirill of the element of surprise [*Figure* 7.3]. While Bourne rushes to his vehicle, Kirill hands a photo of Bourne to a clerk in what appears to be a post office and asks if he has seen him. Although the viewer is not presented with a reply, Kirill heads to the beach, where Marie is also present, suggesting he was provided with directions.

The film then cross-cuts between Bourne speeding in his jeep, and Kirill arriving at the beach earlier than Bourne. Such parallel editing not only generates suspense with respect to the narrative question of who will be the first to get to Marie through recourse to a race-to-the-rescue editing construction. The parallel editing also institutes a pattern of representing ascendant advantage through the act of being one step ahead of the other. Although Bourne assumed his first advantage by spotting Kirill, the assassin arrives at the beach before Bourne. Furthermore, when Bourne appears, he beeps the horn of his jeep to attract Marie's attention, which unwittingly alerts Kirill as well, who now spots Bourne in the jeep, reciprocating Bourne's earlier act of identification, creating a visual reciprocity of looks that symbolically expresses the nullification of Bourne's previous advantage [*Figure* 7.4].

Figure 7.3 Reciprocal recognition in *The Bourne Supremacy* (2004).

Figure 7.4 Reciprocal recognition in *The Bourne Supremacy* (2004).

This balance is, in turn, quickly broken as Marie gets into the vehicle and Bourne speeds off, initiating the chase, as well as constituting its first ascendant moment given Kirill has to rush to his vehicle to engage in pursuit. Bourne's route is then obstructed by a bus, impeding their getaway and allowing Kirill to catch up and be within proximity, thereby diminishing again Bourne's advantage. Bourne then turns down a street, and when Kirill does the same, he finds himself behind a large lorry, with his progress now impeded, causing the advantage to return back to Bourne again. Exploiting Kirill's obstruction, Bourne quickly turns down an alley in an effort to lose Kirill, but Kirill arrives in time to catch sight of them and takes an alternate route with the aim to intercept. As Marie and Bourne switch seats, the film reveals that both vehicles are speeding along parallel paths, with the road that Bourne is on joining the route on which Kirill advances, only a few seconds behind. Bourne then instructs Marie to cut to the field and head for the bridge, which takes on greater

217

significance as a boundary beyond which lies their potential escape. When Kirill arrives at the field and decides to chase on foot, the race-against-time structure returns, this time with the window for Kirill to assassinate Bourne, quickly diminishing. When Kirill arrives at the road leading to the bridge and sees the jeep about to disappear over the bridge, he affects ascendancy not by means of continuing the pursuit but by horizontally switching to a fight mode. The shooting of Marie, and the consequent plunging of the jeep into the river below, represents the threshold moment of the sequence, but in a manner that does not wholly realize Kirill's goals given Bourne is able to survive the assassination attempt.

Like other action forms, the pursuit scenario prototype does not possess a particular moral valence in which the pursuer and the pursued assume opposite moral poles. In the examples discussed so far in this chapter, virtuous protagonists have assumed the character function of the pursuee, as illustrated in both *First Blood* and *The Bourne Supremacy*, as well as the pursuer, as evidenced in the pursuit sequences in *Bullitt* and *Raiders of the Lost Ark*. In addition, as noted in Chapter 3, just as not all capture scenarios cleave along the lines of good and evil, the same can be said for some pursuit sequences.

Consider the concluding night-time pursuit sequence in *The Driver* (1978). The film is a neo-noir set within the criminal world of Los Angeles, with its protagonist, The Driver, a professional getaway driver for hire, who has consistently eluded the police. The Detective, who is bent on capturing him, sets up a legally questionable sting operation where he pressures two arrested criminals – Glasses and Teeth – to undertake a bank heist and hire The Driver as the getaway driver. Sensing Teeth is an amateur crook, The Driver agrees to the robbery on the condition that his fee is doubled and that Teeth does not take part in the robbery. After the bank robbery, Glasses takes The Driver to an abandoned warehouse, instead of the agreed rendezvous point where The Detective awaits. Glasses pulls a gun on The Driver with the intention of keeping all of the loot. However, The Driver, apparently anticipating the double-cross, comes uncharacteristically armed and shoots Glasses dead before he can fire his weapon. The Driver then takes the loot and drives off in Glasses' pickup to hide the money inside a locker at the train station. The Driver then meets The Connection, who agrees to launder the stolen money and provide in exchange smaller bills. An exchange is arranged at the train station, and The Driver enlists The Player, his accomplice, to meet the Exchange Man. However, Teeth has become aware of the plan by extracting it from The Connection at gunpoint and shoots her after obtaining the information. Teeth then heads to the train station and steals the purse of The Player, which within it is the key to the locker containing the smaller bills.

What this narrative summary makes apparent is the murky amoral world in which the pursuit is situated where double-crossings and hidden traps prevail. The police, for instance, are normally representatives of virtue. Yet, The Detective is antisympathetic as a result of his willingness to break the law and engages in questionable behaviour to capture The Driver, a goal void of any higher ethical motive. The Driver, the target of The Detective, is a criminal who enables armed robberies for a cut of the loot and engages in dangerous high-speed pursuits. However, despite his criminality, The Driver lives by a professional code, as exhibited by driving mastery, and expressed through his isolated lifestyle, and is shown to exhibit restraint since he only kills in self-defence. In contrast, Teeth exhibits no such professionality as an amateur crook and appears out of his depth, whose actions are opportunist, and kills The Connection cold-bloodedly to ensure that she does not reveal his intentions. As a result, the moral hierarchy of the film is defined by those who exhibit superior traits and self-restraint, characteristics associated with the traditional hero, and traits that The Driver possesses through his professional code that guides his behaviour. Such a code is itself a convention within the crime film as a means to better contrast the protagonist from other shady characters in a criminal milieu (Leitch 2002, 103-104).

This moral hierarchy is expressed in the pursuit sequence as the dichotomy between the experienced and inexperienced. The chase commences with The Player getting into The Driver's pickup, who informs him that Teeth has taken her purse with the locker key, thereby laying out the goals of the pursuer as the retrieval of the prized object. The Driver then searches for Teeth in the parking lot of the train station, where The Player spots him. Suddenly, a Pontiac Firebird pulls up, and Teeth jumps in and orders its driver to go. Significantly, the character behind the wheel of the Firebird is named The Kid, which his youthful looks attest. The Kid speeds off, and The Driver takes pursuit. What follows is a series of high-speed turns, weaves through traffic, running of red lights, and an avoidance of oncoming vehicles as The Kid tries to lose The Driver. That pattern continues as The Driver demonstrates his experience by steadily gaining on the Firebird to the point where he rams their vehicle from behind in his first intercept manoeuvre. The Firebird withstands the hit, and the pursuit enters into a tunnel and vertically escalates when Teeth begins to fire at The Driver with his revolver. Stoically undeterred, The Driver continues to chase the Firebird and is able to swerve into it on a corner in an effort to stop the vehicle. The shunting continues as the chase enters into an industrial space, with The Driver weaponizing his pickup as the ramming becomes more forceful, blurring the lines between the capture and the fight scenarios.

The pursuit comes to a conclusion when they enter into a large warehouse that commences a cat-and-mouse game as they slow down their vehicles to a crawl and creep through countless aisles in search of each other. Erroneously assuming that they lost their pursuer in the warehouse maze, Teeth orders The Kid to get out of the warehouse only to discover The Driver's pickup blocking the way to the exit. As the Firebird speeds toward the exit, The Driver accelerates towards their vehicle, entering a game of chicken, and exercise of pure speed, as to which driver will first lose his nerve. The Kid swerves at the last minute, attesting to his lesser confidence, and hits a ramp, flipping the Firebird spectacularly into a concrete pit, concluding the capture component of the chase, which is underscored by a series of aftermath shots.

Teeth and The Kid are shown to survive the crash as they spill out of the wreck. Dazed, Teeth searches his surroundings for The

Driver, with the suspense augmented by the narration assuming his optical point-of-view. Teeth turns and sees The Driver standing above him with his gun pointed at him, with the camera angle and character placement within the shot emphasizing The Driver's superior position [*Figure* 7.5]. The Driver instructs Teeth to give up, once again demonstrating his restraint, but Teeth reaches for his revolver, illustrating his recklessness. The Driver handily gets in the first shot, killing Teeth on the spot. The Driver then turns to The Kid, who pleads to him that he had no part in the theft, and makes amends by tossing the Player's purse, containing the locker key, to The Driver. A shot-reverse-shot follows that metaphorically expresses The Driver's superior experience in relation to the relative inexperience of The Kid by repeating the same camera angles used in the interaction with Teeth. Perhaps sensing something of his younger self in The Kid, The Driver lets him go and instructs him to go home. The Kid then runs off in ways that convey his youth as well as his inexperience in the face of The Driver's criminal world. Morality in the film is consequently reduced to the dual characteristics of professionalism and restraint in ways that dovetail with the experience gap exhibited in the chase between the pursuer and the pursued.

Figure 7.5 Professional superiority in
The Driver (1978).

One of the defining features of the pursuit scenario is the way in which risk is uniquely manifested. While pursuit sequences often combine with gunfights, one of their distinctive forms of risk derives from the speed of the pursuit, which itself is a risky endeavour, rather than the accompanying gunplay that is more prototypical of the fight scenario. Although the nature of speed as a distinct action scenario will be covered in the next chapter, it is necessary to consider it briefly in relation to its role in enhancing risk in relation to the pursuit scenario prototype. Consider again the pivotal moment in *Bullitt* when the driver of the Charger secures his seatbelt, which offers the viewer a cue that he will soon be speeding off. But the action also communicates the driver's understanding that speeding is risky and he could get injured or killed in an accident, as confirmed by his death at the end of the chase.

In all of the pursuit sequences discussed so far in this chapter, speed is an indelible risk factor and often plays a causal role in the crashes that often conclude automotive pursuit sequences. When Bullitt swerved the Charger off the road that caused its deadly trajectory into the gas station in the pursuit sequence in *Bullitt*, it would be hard to conceive that event occurring if the two vehicles were not moving at speed. In the chase sequence in *First Blood*, Rambo takes considerable risks speeding down gravel and dirt roads without any protective wear or helmet. A leap over a fence into a field is risky for Sheriff Teasle in his police cruiser, but it is much more so for Rambo since unprotected, thus demonstrating his motorcycle riding skills.

Like the pursuit in *Bullitt*, the chase in *First Blood* ends in a crash as Teasle's police cruiser slides down a ravine and flips over, and although he emerges from the accident uninjured, the incident could have been far more hazardous. A distinctive feature of car chases, compared to other forms of pursuit, consists of the ramming of one vehicle by another, as illustrated in the pursuits in *Bullitt* and *The Driver*. As shown, such intercept manoeuvres entail particular risks to the pursuees, particularly when shunted off the road, as was the case in *Bullitt*. Another risk-associated feature often arising in car chases is the path of destruction that the pursuit leaves that is not restricted to the vehicles of the pursuer or the pursuee. As discussed in Chapter 2 in relation to the pursuit sequence *The Rock* (1996), John Patrick Mason in the

Hummer destroys not only parked vehicles, but also knocks down a powerline, endangering the police pursuing him, as well as shunts a streetcar off its tracks placing its driver and passengers at risk. The collateral damage is particularly marked in the concluding pursuit sequence in *Jason Bourne* (Paul Greengrass, 2016) in which The Asset, in a SWAT vehicle, simply plows through the traffic obstructing his path, an act of hyper-destruction, unconcerned for the injuries if not fatalities that passengers are sustaining, as a means to elude from Bourne who is pursuing him.

The examples just cited have been restricted to automotive pursuits in which speed, and its potential destructive power, is more evident than other modes of pursuit. However, risk also manifests itself in other pursuit modes that do not evidence the kind of speed manifested in car chases. Horseback pursuits, for instance, still involve speed, even though not at the same pace as automotive pursuits. This does not mean that horseback riding does not involve risk as a result, since there is the danger of being injured if a character falls off a horse, as well as the risk of being trampled. The celebrated pursuit sequence in *Stagecoach* (1939) can illustrate.

A stagecoach travelling from the Arizona Territory to Lordsburg, New Mexico, conveys a diverse assortment of representatives from society, and comes under attack from fierce Apache warriors on horseback while crossing a desert plain. A variety of strategies are used to convey the speed of the pursuit. First, we see Marshal Curley Wilcox throw stones at the horses pulling the stagecoach in an attempt to get them run faster, providing an inferential cue that their pace will increase as a result. The action is additionally captured with a camera set-up atop of the moving stagecoach that offers a point-of-view shot from the standpoint of being onboard the carriage, heightens the sense of its speed [*Figure* 7.6]. The film then cuts to reveal the Apache on horseback in a shot taken from a camera car that offers a dual sense of motion: the first deriving from the Apache on horseback galloping in haste, the second from the perception that the camera itself is moving quickly [*Figure* 7.7].

Figure 7.6 Heightened sense of speed of the pursuee in *Stagecoach* (1939).

Figure 7.7 Heightened sense of speed of the pursuers in *Stagecoach* (1939).

This telegraphing of the speed of both the pursuer and the pursuee to the viewer also augments the perceived risk of actions that characters undertake under such circumstances. Risky actions that may endanger both the character and the actor performing the action are normally understood as stunts, and if too dangerous, are often performed by stunt doubles. Stuntwork is by no means restricted to the pursuit scenario. As we have observed in relation to the daring leap escape variant discussed in Chapter 2, jumps from a great height are stunts since they pose significant risks to both the character and the actor performing the leap. With respect to the stunts in the pursuit sequence in *Stagecoach*, these were performed by the legendary stuntman Yakima Cannutt (Buscombe 1992, 67-68). Amongst the stunts was a 'transfer' by one of the Apache who leaps from his horse onto one of the horses pulling the stagecoach, which Cannutt reported he performed as stunt double for the character at a speed of forty-five miles per hour, suggesting not only the risk posed to the character and stunt double, but also a sense of the pace of the chase itself (Cannutt 1979, 110).[2]

Foot chases, which are manifestly slower than automotive and horseback pursuits, would not initially seem to possess sufficient pace to exhibit the levels of risk that are normally associated with pursuits undertaken at greater velocity. Yet running with pace is not risk-free and certainly is more hazardous than merely walking given the greater likelihood of injury through falling or twisting one's ankle.

In addition, filmmakers often include additional elements, such as obstacles, to heighten the sense of perceived risk in foot pursuits. The foot chase component in the pursuit sequence in *Point Break* (1991) can illustrate. The chase commences when FBI agents Johnny Utah and Angelo Pappas stake-out a bank that Utah believes the Ex-Presidents will rob. Sure enough, Utah's hunch proves correct when the Ex-Presidents arrive and park their Lincoln in front of the bank and quickly make their robbery while wearing their characteristic American ex-Presidents masks. Utah draws his weapon and orders them to freeze, but the Ex-Presidents speed off, so he discharges his weapon at their vehicle. Pappas then pulls up for Utah to hop in and they pursue after them in their vehicle. The chase continues through heavy traffic as Pappas rams their Lincoln successively in an effort to intercept them, but the Ex-Presidents are still able to elude capture. Pappas rams them again, and as the vehicles shove against each other, they head into a parking lot, causing Pappas' sedan to collide into a booth. Utah leaps out of the car and takes the chase on foot, transforming his mode of locomotion in the process.

The foot chase at this moment is in a transitional mode since Utah is pursuing a moving vehicle instead of both the pursuer and the pursuee running on foot. The Ex-Presidents pull their trashed

---

[2] One should also note the risks posed to horses in stuntwork, which often resulted in injury or death. Amongst the most notorious means was the 'running W' set up in which wires were tied to a horse's legs causing it to fall spectacularly, a practice that was eventually banned. See 'Stunt' entry in Edward Buscombe (ed). 1988. *The BFI Companion to the Western*. London: British Film Institute. pp. 225-226.

Lincoln into a gas station and commandeer another vehicle from a customer. While Bodhi, the leader of the Ex-Presidents, pauses to torch the Lincoln to destroy incriminating evidence, Utah is able to catch up and leaps onto Bodhi, and they grapple in the fire. Punching Utah and shoving his head under the hood of the car, Bodhi eludes Utah's attempted capture and takes flight on foot. Utah pursues again, with the chase turning to full foot pursuit mode. The chase takes them into the adjacent neighbourhood, and when Bodhi spots a police car, he bashes through the gate of a yard with its outdoor toys and swings posing the first set of obstacles to negotiate. Bodhi then collides into a woman watering her lawn, who falls onto the ground, causing Utah to leap over her. The next set of obstacles consist of cyclists and a garbage truck, which Bodhi successively dodges, while Utah runs into the garbage man and shoves him onto the road. As they speed down the street, the audio track provides the sounds of Bodhi's gasps for air and their rapid footsteps, audio cues commonly associated with a foot chase, which serve the same soundtrack function of the roar of engines and squealing of tires used to signal speed in an automotive pursuit.

Recognizing that Utah is still on his tail, Bodhi ups the obstacle ante by turning into someone's front yard and with a leap over the porch, he enters into their home. While running through the house, he encounters a woman with laundry who tosses it at him, a projectile, while not injurious, still momentarily obstructs his view. He pushes her aside. Utah follows the same path into the house and leaps over the woman now lying on the floor as Bodhi makes it through to the back garden onto an alley. This time the obstacle Bodhi encounters assumes the form of a tall fence that he scales as Utah follows suit undeterred by the impediments placed in his way.

The pursuit continues down a passageway between two homes as Bodhi enters into another home through its backyard. Entering into the house, Bodhi locks the patio door behind him, placing another obstacle in Utah's path, who picks up a pot in response and tosses it through the glass, the shards of which he passes through to crashes onto a table and land onto the floor. The ruckus alerts the homeowner, who promptly beats Utah with her vacuum cleaner, posing a different sort of obstacle through a brief vertical combination of the chase with a unidirectional fight variant. Utah gets up and heads to the front door to discover Bodhi waiting for him with a pitbull in his grasp, which he tosses at Bodhi as an animate projectile. Utah punts the dog away as if a football, in a move that suggests his college football past. The chase continues down another passageway where Bodhi leaps over another fence, but one that leads out of the neighbourhood and onto an aqueduct. Bodhi carefully scrabbles down the ravine and jumps down to the aqueduct below, whereas Utah tumbles down, and when he leaps into the aqueduct, he twists his knee, causing an old injury to flare up, thereby bringing a conclusion to the chase. Utah pulls his gun as he sees Bodhi running off and eluding capture, but cannot bring himself to fire at him, so he fires his weapon into the air in an act of frustration.

Despite the comparatively slower pace of the foot chase in *Point Break* with respect to horseback or automotive pursuits, it is fast enough to be potentially injurious in the face of the obstacles placed in Bodhi and Utah's path, exhibiting the event structure of the pursuit scenario prototype. The neighbourhood yards and homes resemble a parkour obstacle course where domestic objects, such as a vacuum cleaner and a pet dog, become weaponized. In addition, Utah bears a pistol, and although he draws it only at the last moment, the danger of gunfire is latent. The chase also ends with Utah's injury, underscoring the physical risks of the pursuit. Although foot chases tend to fall on the opposite end of the typicality tail of the pursuit scenario with respect to its speed compared to an automotive chase, they can compensate that risk through other means.

Pursuit Combinations

As has been noted at the outset, one of the distinctive features of the pursuit scenario compared to other action scenarios is that it is inherently a combinatory form in the sense that it minimally includes the escape and speed scenarios. If the intention of the pursuer is to apprehend the pursuee, then the pursuit will also include a capture scenario, as is illustrated in the opening pursuit sequence in *Star Trek* (J.J. Abrams, 2009) when, James T. Kirk as a boy takes his father's vintage Corvette out for a joy ride but is pursued by a police officer on a hover-cycle, who corners the boy at a canyon cliff edge. But if the intention is to kill, and which is realized as physical conflict, as was the case with Kirill in *The Bourne Supremacy*, then the pursuit incorporates the fight scenario. Given these goal-orientated outcomes, one can therefore describe the capture and fight elements of the pursuit scenario as being emergent combinations since either outcome arises naturally out of the prototype.

In contrast, heist and rescue combinations can be described as contingent combinations, since they are not inherent constituent elements of the pursuit scenario, but arise instead from some variation on the prototype that externally introduces a heist or rescue element. For these reasons, the heist sequence in *Fast Five* (2011) represents a contingent combination of the pursuit scenario with the heist action form, since heists are not inherent elements of a pursuit, nor does the heist scenario lead to expectations that a chase will necessarily arise from a specific heist sequence. The combination therefore results from a deviation from prototype. Similarly, the need to be rescued is neither a defining feature of the pursuer or the pursuee. A pursuer is not in a situation that requires escape since that would entail captivity of some kind, the antithesis of the ability to pursue. Likewise, if the pursuee has the ability to escape, then they are not necessarily in need of rescue, given the agency that they possess. However, there are sufficient instances of pursuits that involve rescues in films to be identified as a variant that involves contingent combinations, a case that will be shortly explored.

Pursuit Scenario Variants

When discussing fight scenario variations in the previous Chapter, it was noted that one type of variation exhibited derived from the film genre in which it is situated. With respect to the pursuit scenario, although there are some broad correlations between genre and pursuit variance, the scenario, however, is less determined by genre than the fight scenario. While one can speak of horseback pursuits emerging in historical adventure films, samurai movies, and westerns; car chases appearing in crime films and police thrillers; and spacecraft pursuits occurring in sci-fi films, given their different historical contexts, it is more difficult, however, to make finer-grained correlations between genres and variants. For instance, the espionage film contains automotive pursuit sequences, as the *Bourne* franchise attests, but it would be erroneous to conclude on that basis that car chases in spy films express themselves differently from how they would appear in urban crime thrillers. The same applies to horseback pursuits in westerns and historical adventure films. Instead of the generic context being the primary driver of variation in the pursuit scenario, what is more significant is how the *modes of locomotion* and the *modes of pursuit* can combine in different ways and can result in innovation through novel combinations.

Combinatory Variation

So far, we have been treating pursuit sequences in almost pure form in which the mode of pursuit is consistent throughout the action sequence, and the modes of locomotion for the pursuee and the pursuer are the same. But a cursory glance at pursuit sequences in film can quickly offer counter-examples in which the modes of pursuit can vary within a pursuit sequence as well as their modes of locomotion.

Consider the pursuit sequence in *Point Break* again in its entirety. The pursuit commences with a car chase, and after the collision with the parking booth, Utah briefly pursues the ex-

Presidents on foot as they continue their escape in their Lincoln. When the ex-Presidents switch vehicles at the gas station, and Utah fails to capture Bodhi, the pursuit then transforms into a foot chase between Bodhi and Utah. This pursuit sequence, therefore, manifests a tripartite structure in which its first part is in automotive pursuit mode, with the modes of locomotion for the pursuee and pursuer, on the whole, identical since the performance specifications of the cars, and driving ability, are not presented as distinguishably different.

Following after the first part of the pursuit sequence is a transitionary phase in which the pursuit mode becomes composite — a foot-car chase — as the modes of locomotion between the pursuee and pursuer temporarily diverge since the ex-Presidents flee in their car while Utah pursues on foot, offering a prelude to the final component of the sequence. After this transitional phase, the pursuit switches from its temporary composite mode to return to a unitary state, but this time expressed differently as a foot chase by exhibiting the same means of locomotion for both the pursuee and the pursuer.

What such anatomy reveals is that a pursuit sequence can be combinatory just like an action sequence with respect to its combinations of action scenarios and that such combinations exhibit parallel horizontal and vertical dimensions. The pursuit sequence in *Point Break*, for instance, reveals horizontal combinations at the level of the mode of pursuit as it moves from an automotive mode, to a composite automotive-foot mode, to finally assume a foot mode. As a result, such changes in its pursuit mode transform the complexion of the chase over the course of its duration. In contrast, vertical combinations entail transformations from unitary to composite pursuit states when the modes of locomotion of the pursuee and the pursuer diverge. When Utah decides to continue the pursuit on foot, he not only changes his mode of locomotion while the ex-Presidents continue their attempted escape unchanged in their automobile, he also momentarily *increases* the number of modes of locomotion in the chase.

Consequently, one can describe this transformation in pursuit states as vertical in nature since it consists of a change in magnitude of the number of modes of locomotion that can co-occur during the chase. The Seven Mile Bridge chase in *True Lies* (1994), for instance, features terrorists as the pursuees, escaping in two vans and a limousine, while the pursuers fly after them in two helicopters and a pair of Harrier jump jets. The pursuit, therefore, features four modes of locomotion simultaneously. Differentiating the vans from the limousine presents two co-occurring modes of automotive locomotion for the pursuees, while the pursuers use helicopters and Harriers, adding two additional co-occurrent modes of locomotion to the pursuit.

As the *True Lies* chase illustrates, filmmakers can innovate pursuit sequences with an array of options as a result of these combinatory dimensions. They can innovate through horizontal combinations to design a pursuit sequence that morphs through different pursuit modes, such as a chase that starts on horseback, shifts to foot mode, and ends with a motorcycle chase. Alternatively, filmmakers can innovate through vertical combinations by adding or subtracting the number of modes of locomotion during any given moment of the chase, be they foot, boat, helicopter, or automotive modes of locomotion.

The Pursuit-Rescue Variant

As noted earlier, the combination of the pursuit scenario with the rescue scenario is a contingent amalgamation since the rescue scenario does not naturally arise from the pursuit scenario prototype. The reason why this is the case is that the pursuee normally exhibits the intention to escape from the pursuer, as well as possesses the agency to attempt to do so. Yet, there are instances in which the character being pursued resembles less the traditional pursuee but more the captive found in the rescue scenario. In these instances, the captive is in a predicament in which they are moving at speed and are unable to control their mode of locomotion, which poses a danger to them. In addition, the character undertaking the pursuit is more akin to a rescuer since their goal is to rescue the captive instead of the usual aims to either capture or kill them. The pursuit-rescue variant, therefore, represents a true amalgam of action scenario prototypes in which the dramatic personage of the rescue scenario is combined with a pursuit situation involving speed.

An instance of the pursuit-rescue variant can be found in the final stage of the chase sequence in *True Lies* discussed previously. The terrorists in the two vans are taken out by the Harriers, which fire missiles at them and blow up a section of the bridge. Meanwhile, Harry Tasker, an American secret agent in one of the helicopters, continues the pursuit of the limousine, in which his wife Helen is held captive at gunpoint by Juno Skinner, an antique dealer, working with the terrorists to smuggle in nuclear warheads. While Juno barks orders at the chauffeur, Helen uses that moment of distraction to try and snatch the gun out of her hands. In the ensuing struggle, the chauffeur is accidentally shot in the head, and as he collapses, he places his foot on the limousine's accelerator, sending the vehicle careening down the freeway, and headed towards the gap in the bridge, thereby setting up a rescue deadline.

To narratively underscore Helen's captive situation, Harry informs his fellow agent that the vehicle is "out of control", implying that Helen does not have the agency to extract herself from the endangering situation. Helen and Juno continue their brawl in the vehicle, with Helen reaching the threshold moment when walloping Juno's head with a champagne bottle, knocking her unconscious. Speeding through the burning wreckage of one of the exploded vans, the limousine catches fire, adding an additional layer of risk. Observing his wife's predicament, Harry orders the helicopter pilot to fly down to the limousine in an attempt to rescue her before the limousine reaches the break in the bridge. Standing through the sunroof of the vehicle, Helen sees the danger lying ahead and tries to grab hold of Harry's outreached hand, who hangs precariously from the helicopter. At the final moment, their hands clasp, allowing Harry to lift Helen out of the vehicle just before it flies off the bridge, thereby capping off the pursuit-rescue variant, and the pursuit sequence as a whole, with a clear instance of the transfer scenario.

The pursuit-rescue variant has its own variations that once again alter the terms of the pursuit-rescue format but still in a recognizable form. In one sub-variant, the pursuee and the pursuer roles are retained, but the goals of the pursuee are loftier than merely the effort to elude capture since the broader aim is to rescue someone who is inside the escaping vehicle. Such a scenario arises in the night-time pursuit sequence in *Batman Begins* (2005).

Rachel Dawes, Gotham City's assistant district attorney and love interest of Batman's alter-ego Bruce Wayne, when visiting Arkham Asylum, is sprayed by Dr. Jonathan Crane with a psychotropic hallucinogen that induces fear after she discovers his plans to poison Gotham City's water supply with it. Given that the spay delivering the toxin was in concentrated form, Rachel runs the risk of the effects of the toxin becoming permanent after a short period of time, setting up a deadline for rescue. Batman arrives and takes out Crane's armed guards and sprays Crane with a similar toxin, and is able to extract the information that he is working with Ra's al Ghul, Batman's antagonist. The police arrive and lay siege to the asylum in an effort to capture Batman, setting up the conditions for escape, the initiating event of a pursuit. Sergeant James Gordon, a trustworthy policeman, also arrives and enters the building and agrees to help by carrying Rachel, who is semi-conscious, to the Batmobile while Batman sends out a signal that causes a swarm of bats to swoop into the asylum, providing cover for their escape from the building.

Batman takes Rachel from Gordon and places her in the Batmobile, a special vehicle designed by the military to leap over rivers. Batman promptly speeds off, running over a police car in his haste, and heads to his cavernous base lying beneath Wayne Manor, with the aim to administer an antidote before the effects of the hallucinogen become permanent. The police pursue after the escaping vehicle in their police cars, while an overhead helicopter joins the chase, adding another mode of locomotion to the multi-vehicle pursuit. In an attempt to lose the pursuing vehicles, Batman enters into a parkade and heads up its ramps to its roof level, with the police following, assuming they have Batman cornered. In a demonstration of the Batmobile's leaping abilities, Batman makes his escape by firing rockets into an impeding wall and then accelerates at speed to leap onto an adjacent building, where he speeds off from rooftop to rooftop, to finally returns to the road by soaring onto on overpass.

The police regain their pursuit as the chase enters into a tunnel under repair that presents a number of obstacles for the vehicles that the Batmobile simply bashes through, whereas a police car collides into a median. The police then try to set up a blockade, but Batman handily navigates through and then drops a number of miniature tire bombs, causing further spectacular crashes with the vehicles behind him. The chase then exits the tunnel onto a freeway as the helicopter rejoins the pursuit, highlighting its presence on the freeway with its spotlight. Batman responds by turning off the lights of the Batmobile, temporally making it invisible as the vehicle seemingly disappears into the darkness.

Sensing that time is running out before Rachel permanently lapses into drug-induced psychosis, he instructs her to stay alert. He then turns on the lights of the vehicle back on again to speed off and ram through a highway barrier through which the remaining pursuing vehicles are unable to pass through, thereby ending the chase component of the sequence to become a pure race against time. As Batman speeds down the last leg toward his base, the viewer is provided with Rachel's hallucinatory optical point-of-view shot and then begins to slip into unconsciousness, once again underscoring the urgency of the situation and adding to the suspense. The Batmobile then soars through a waterfall into Batman's base, who hurries to administer the antidote, thereby ending the sequence with Rachel's rescue. This instance of the pursuit-rescue subvariant is distinctive not only through the way it expresses a rescue through a pursuit mode, but also by emphasizing the substantial difference in modes of locomotion between the pursued and the pursuers.

In another sub-variant, what is pursued is neither a pursuee nor a captive but a speeding object that endangers the lives of captives. In Chapter 1, when discussing the multiple rescues that constitute the extended rescue sequence in *Superman* (1978), it was noted that one rescue situation entailed Superman pursuing a nuclear missile directed toward the town Hackensack who is able to capture it and redirect its trajectory to explode in the Earth's upper atmosphere. In this instance, the pursuee returns but as an inanimate object moving at speed. The captives do not play a direct role in the pursuit per se, but act as a destination of the pursuee that are held captive and without the agency to alter the pursuee's course. In this instance, the pursuer acts heroically and displays at the same time the ethos of the superhero.

Exemplar: *Mad Max: Fury Road* (2015)

There are a number of reasons why the first pursuit sequence in George Miller's *Mad Max: Fury Road* (2015) warrants a closer examination as an exemplar. First, the film departs from the previous installments in the *Mad Max* series by featuring Imperator Furiosa, a woman, as the main protagonist in the pursuit sequence, and is one of the main protagonists in the narrative as a whole, a point that has been highlighted in feminist analyses of the film (Barrett, 2017; Du Plooy, 2019). Second, the sequence is illustrative of how its multi-vehicle pursuit innovates the pursuit scenario prototype. Third, this multi-vehicle element is additionally significant since a variety of automotive modes of locomotion are also manifested. Fourth, the exotic vehicle customization featured in the chase bears thematic significance as well since the mutated nature of the vehicles mirrors the abnormality of the characters involved in the pursuit, whose deformities derive from the film's post-nuclear setting. Fifth, the mutated nature of the vehicles, and their distinctive modes of combat, function to increase the level of risk in an already hazardous pursuit. Lastly, the pursuit sequence features a number of notable stunts that further underscore the risks to character and stunt performer.

To better understand the initiating event of the pursuit, it is necessary to provide the narrative context from which it springs. In the wastelands of the post-apocalyptic Australian desert lies the Citadel, a mutant enclave possessing a bountiful water supply, many of whom suffer from radiation sickness. The enclave is ruled by Immortan Joe, a grotesque figure who himself appears to suffer from radiation sickness revealed through his blistered skin, and the breathing apparatus that he wears. Immortan Joe presides over a community of impoverished peasants and supplies then water at his pleasure. His power is enforced by the War Boys, an army that defends the Citadel from the surrounding fiefdoms, and who treat Immortan Joe with reverence and are willing to sacrifice their lives on his behalf in the belief that Valhalla awaits them in their afterlife.

Imperator Furiosa then enters into this story, notably with a shot of her back that reveals that she has been branded, signifying that she is owned like livestock by Immortan Joe, but who also serves as a warrior, bestowed with the honour of driving the War Rig, an armoured, articulated petrol truck. Furiosa is sent on a mission, accompanied by a group of War Boys in hot rods and on motorcycles, as well as perched atop the War Rig, to obtain petrol from Gas Town and ammunition from the Bullet Farm, two adjacent enclaves in which they have trading relations. In addition to this storyline is the plotline concerning Max Rockatansky, the lead character that reappears in previous installments in the franchise, who is captured at the start of the film by the War Boys and is used as a fresh blood supply to Nux, a War Boy, whose radiation sickness manifests itself as tumours on his shoulder. This initial narrative focus suggests to the viewer that Max will be the main protagonist of the film, but as the story develops, it becomes apparent that Furiosa is the other main protagonist in a dual protagonist story as they overcome their initial antagonism and work together as a team.

It is in this narrative context that the initiating event occurs. While on route to Gas Town, Furiosa suddenly steers the War Rig off the road, informing Ace, one of the accompanying War

Boys, that she is headed East but withholds her true mission. At the Citadel, Furiosa's actions are spotted by Corpus Colossus, a lookout, through an optical magnifying instrument, and alerts Immortan Joe, who rushes in response to a large safe within the Citadel, to find the chamber empty, a space in which his wives were kept in captivity to function as 'breeders' to provide his offspring. Miss Giddy, a nanny of sorts, is left to confront Immortan Joe, who informs him that his wives pleaded with Furiosa to take them away. It is at this point that the viewer is able to piece together Furiosa's true motives in which her veering off the road was not merely an attempt to escape but also a rescue mission to free Immortan Joe's wives from captivity, thereby reaffirming her hero status.

A rallying call is made to the remaining War Boys in the Citadel to mount their pursuit of Furiosa in the War Rig and to capture Immortan Joe's wives. Despite his ill health, Nux fights with Slit, another War Boy, for the right to possess the steering wheel of Nux's hot rod, and eventually persuades The Organic Mechanic, the Citadel's medic, that he is ready for war by bringing Max, his 'blood bag', who ends up affixed at the front of Nux's vehicle, an action that will eventually bring the two plotlines together. The film then cuts to the exterior desert to reveal Immortan Joe's automotive armada, a mix of modes of locomotion consisting of souped-up militarized hot rods, trucks, motorcycles, and most bizarrely, a large vehicle used to convey an ensemble of drummers and a musician whose instrument is a cross between a guitar and flame thrower, a rig that is akin to a mobile concert that provides accompanying mad rock music for an equally crazed pursuit. The pursuers fire coloured-flares into the air, a signal for the armed forces of Gas Town and the Bullet Farm to join in the pursuit. Ace relays the information to Furiosa, who again hides her true motives.

However, joining the pursuit are not Immortan Joe's allies but the Buzzards, a rival horde in spiked vehicles who view the presence of the War Rig and War Boys as a hostile intrusion into their territory, and in doing so, constitute an additional set of pursuers in the chase sequence. Furiosa confirms to Ace that they will forge ahead with one of the War Boy's hot rods taking the lead at the front of the convoy. However, the Buzzards have laid a trap in the road, causing the lead hot rod to flip into a spiked pit that resembles the spiked vehicles in which they ride. The Buzzards continue the attack and ram a motorcycle, knocking it and its riders to the ground. The War Boys retaliate by tossing explosive spears onto the spiked vehicle, but not enough to deter its path as it smashes through another War Boy motorcyclist. Armed with a large horizontal circular saw, the spiked vehicle begins to cut into the War Rig's armoured tires as the War Boys on top of the rig continue to rain down explosive spears onto it. A hot rod suddenly appears from the front of the War Rig and fires an explosive harpoon into the spiked vehicle, dispatching it and its Buzzards occupants. This temporary ascendant moment in the pursuit/battle is nullified by two other spiked vehicles flanking the War Rig on its left side. The Buzzards again deploy a circular saw into the rig's rear tires, motivating both Ace and Furiosa to fire their weapons at the vehicle, which flips with the ensuing explosion and collides with the other spiked vehicle.

Furiosa and the War Boys assume ascendancy once again, but through the smoking wreckage a larger, and more monstrously spiked truck, emerges armed with a dual circular saw and large digging scoop, followed in tow with another spiked vehicle. The film then cuts to an aerial shot revealing Immortan Joe's armada gaining on the War Rig, with Nux driving his hot rod assuming the lead, with Max held captive in a rig at the front of the vehicle, and linked to Nux through a long chain, with Split at the back ready for attack. Nux decides first to take on the Buzzards and accelerates forward, permitting Split to lob an explosive spear at the large spiked truck. The Buzzards in the smaller vehicle swerves into Nux's hot rod in retaliation. Morsov, a War Boy stationed atop of the War Rig at its rear, then fires a tethered harpoon into the smaller spiked vehicle as Split lobs another explosive spear into it as well. The spiked vehicle begins to swerve wildly and dangerously close to Max, with the tether ripping out its top. While Morsov prepares to throw an explosive spear into the spiked vehicle, one of the Buzzards inside fires a crossbow at Morsov, impaling him with its arrows. Knocked down by their impact, Morsov slowly arises, spraying his mouth with chrome paint, a ritual to prepare for a sacrificial attack and entry into Valhalla. He grabs two explosive spears and leaps into the spiked vehicle below, while Split, at the same time, tosses an additional armed spear at it for good measure as it explodes in a ball of flames.

The remaining spiked truck advances upon the War Rig, causing Furiosa to sound the War Rig's horn to alert the War Boys of its impending attack, and it is at this point that one of the wives emerges from one of the War Rig's tankers, confirming its precious cargo. The War Boys in the hot rod with harpoon weaponry station themselves in front of the spike truck and fire explosive harpoons and spears into it, but the truck zooms forward unabated, bashing the hot rod out of its way. Nux then backs his hot rod in the path of the spiked truck to provide Split's a turn to attack, as the War Boys on top of the War Rig lob explosives at it. Furiosa and Max then glance at each other, an initial sign that their paths will cross later in the story. Split then tosses an explosive spear at the spiked truck, causing it to accelerate like an enraged beast, but Nux is able to speed away in time to avoid the fate of the War Boys in the harpoon vehicle. Another wife emerges from hiding, just as the spiked truck's dual circular saw is deployed into War Rig's cabin, while the truck digger scoop proceeds to attack the War Boys atop the rig. Nux spins his hot rod around to allow Slit to attack the spiked truck again, as the War Boys in a concerted effort fire explosives at the truck's hydraulics. Suddenly, the dual circular saw whips off, slicing the explosives riding atop of Nux's hot rod, which fall beneath the spiked truck causing it to flip over, the threshold moment when the War Boys successfully resisted the Buzzards' attack.

With the Buzzards dispatched, Nux and Slit return to their original goal of retrieving Immortan Joe's wives from the War Rig. However, complicating their retrieval is the emergence of a colossal sand storm into which Furiosa directs the War Rig. Ace finally twigs that something is amiss and chokes her, demanding what she has done. Furiosa violently jabs her fingers into his eyes, sending Ace to the desert floor. As Nux and Slit are about to mount an attack, Furiosa swerves the War Rig into their hot rod, destroying its front right tire. From the opposite side, another War Boys vehicle attacks with a flamethrower, motivating Furiosa to swerve into it in response. Seeing the War Rig speeding off into the storm, Nux instructs Slit to remove Max from the rig in the front to place him in the back of the hot rod as a means to counterbalance the vehicle's lost wheel. The film cuts back to the pursuing armada and to Immortan Joe inside his custom vehicle, who gazes at its compass that spins uncontrollably as a result of the approaching sand storm, an initial signal that Furiosa may be able to lose the pursuers inside the desert vortex temporarily. As Furiosa presses forward into the storm, the War Rig's entry into it constitutes a boundary moment for the pursuit, as the War Boys on a pursuing motorcycle are simply blown away through the force of the wind.

Meanwhile, atop of Nux's hot rod, Slit is on the verge of breaking Max's neck with the chain, but Max is able to grab him and toss him to the open back of the hot rod. Kicking Slit violently, Max is able to boot him off the vehicle just before Nux makes his entry into the storm. The force of the wind nearly blows Max off the vehicle but is kept on by the chain linking him with Nux. In the distance, Nux spots the War Rig and swerves to mount his final attack. Within the sand storm, a huge tornado arises, constituting an obstacle of a different order, as the War Boys in the flame-throwing hot rod also make their last gamble at capture. Yet Furiosa swerves the War Ring into their vehicle, nudging it into the tornado, sending the hot rod and its occupants sucked into the vortex.

Emboldened by the sight of the hot rod exploding into flames in the air, Nux seizes the opportunity to die in glory and enter into Valhalla. Opening the valves to the tanks containing petrol, Nux lets it spill into the vehicle, transforming it into a speeding bomb while spraying chrome paint into his mouth in preparation for his suicidal act to explode into the War Rig. Sensing Nux's intentions,

Max smashes his fist through the rear window in an effort to halt Nux's plan as the hot rod careens in front of the War Rig. Nux then breaks open a flare to ignite the petrol, but Max seizes it out of his hand. Nux then slams on the breaks as the War Rig collides into the hot rod, smashing it to smithereens as its occupants are tossed into the desert, with the last shot of the pursuit consisting of the War Rig disappearing into the protective cloak of the storm.

As this summary description of the first pursuit sequence in *Mad Max: Fury Road* shows, the sequence is complex, consisting of multiple elements that innovate the pursuit scenario prototype. At the most fundamental level, the sequence innovates by having Imperator Furiosa, a woman, assume the role as protagonist, setting her against Immortan Joe, the film's antagonist. This change is not only significant in relation to the *Mad Max* franchise, in which Max Rockatansky played the lead role in previous installments, but also speaks to the generally gendered nature of action films, whose protagonist tend, on the whole, to be male. Furiosa's agency is particularly underscored in the pursuit sequence by portraying her as a rescuer, whereas Max spends most of his time as a captive, deprived of agency, until the moment he is able to wrest free from Slit.

In addition, Furiosa's agency fits in the broader feminists' themes of the film itself in which women function under Immortan Joe's rule as reproductive agents, whose captivity is marked by being kept in a large safe. There is also the thematic opposition between the War Boys, who incarnate a masculine death culture through their subservience to a vision of martial glory in the belief that their life sacrifice will secure entry in their afterlife into Valhalla. Compare this to the Vuvalini, a matriarchal clan from which Furiosa is a descendant, which is introduced later on in the film, and is affiliated with the nurturing and life-affirming aspects of agriculture, as metaphorically expressed through the Keeper of the Seeds character, whose bag of seeds hold the promise of social renewal. The film also reworks the pursuit scenario prototype through its multi-faceted nature.

On the one hand, the pursuit falls within the remit of the pursuit-rescue variant, in which Furiosa simultaneously incarnates the rescuer function, with the wives narratively functioning as the captives to be rescued, as well as serving the narrative function of the pursuee through her intention to escape from the oppressive control of Immortan Joe. Similarly, the film modulates the motives of the pursuers in which Immortan Joe's wives constitute the prized objects that are to be captured, as expressed when Slit announces the change in pursuit goals to bringing home "the booty", whereas the aims of the Buzzards as pursuers are more deadly with the evident intent to kill as a reprisal for entering into their territory. Indeed, one of the distinctive features of the first pursuit sequence is how it introduces complexity through the depiction of two separate sets of pursuers. At one point in the chase, the War Boys constitute one set of pursuers who pursue two different sets of pursuees - the Buzzards and the War Rig Convoy - with the Buzzards acting in the dual capacity as pursuees and pursuers when they chase down the War Rig convoy [*Figure* 7.8 and 7.9]. The first pursuit sequence in *Mad Max: Fury Road* consequently is not merely multi-vehicle in nature but is also permutative with respect to the relations between vehicular sets.

Figure 7.8 The Buzzards as pursuees and pursuers in *Mad Max: Fury Road* (2015).

Figure 7.9 Vehicular sets in *Mad Max: Fury Road* (2015).

While the first pursuit sequence represents the pursuit-rescue variant, it also manifests the vertically emergent nature of the fight scenario within the pursuit prototype. As Nux eloquently puts it: "If I'm gonna die, I'm gonna die historic on the Fury Road!". The road, therefore, is not only an arena of pursuit and speed but also one of combat. In addition, the pursuit sequence not only diversifies its modes of locomotion with respect to their customized hot road appearance but also through their distinctive modes of combat. The War Rig resembles a whaling ship in the desert able to harpoon its prey. The vehicles of the Buzzards, in contrast, appear as militarized porcupines with spikes that can impale while additionally wielding spinning circular saws. One War Boys' hot rod employed an array of harpoon guns, while another was fitted with a flamethrower. As noted earlier, the appearance of these customized vehicles bears thematic significance as well. Appearing as if cobbled together from the refuse of a post-nuclear scrap heap, their transfigured nature metaphorically expresses the deformed nature of the mutants at the wheel. Immortan Joe's Gigahorse, for instance, was constructed from two Cadillac bodies, obscenely stacked upon one another, mirroring Immortan Joe's own grotesque bricolage of bodily and junk-yard elements (Abrams, 2015).

The levels of risk presented in the first pursuit sequence in *Mad Max: Fury Road* is of an entirely different order that sets it apart from other standard chases, but remains consistent with the risks manifest in the chases in the *Mad Max* series, particularly in *Mad Max 2: The Road Warrior* and *Mad Max Beyond Thunderdome*

(George Miller, 1985). While a standard chase normally offers the risks associated with speed, collisions with obstacles, vehicular ramming, and often gunplay, the weaponized dimensions of the vehicles in the first pursuit sequence escalate risk to an even higher level through its unique combination of the hazards of the combat mission with the perils of pursuit. Augmenting the perception of risk stemming from this distinct combination of action forms is the risk associated with the stuntwork performed in the sequence itself, whether relating to the hazards faced by a character or that by the stunt performer.

In terms of risk to character, Morsov's suicidal leap, for instance, onto the spiked vehicle below presents a risk in its most lethal form through which Morsov ends his life. In terms of risk to Chris Patton, the stunt actor who portrayed Morsov and who performed the dangerous stunt with the assistance of a special harness rig, any extra-diegetic knowledge of the dangers of the stuntwork will also be mapped onto that of the fictional character. If the stunt is risky for the stunt performer, then it must be even more so for the character in question who does not benefit from the safety precautions taken in its production. Through such action combinations and through such stuntwork, the first pursuit sequence in *Mad Max: Fury Road* heightens the perception of risk in ways that make it distinctive not only as a chase sequence but also a significant exemplar of a combinatory action form.

Chapter 7: The Speed Scenario

"It is really flying, and it is impossible to divest yourself of the notion of instant death to all upon the least accident happening." - Thomas Creevy

"When a body is moving at very high velocity, it then, to all intents and purposes, becomes a projectile, and is subject to the laws attending projectiles." - C.H. Greenhow[1]

When the steam locomotive appeared during the 1800s, it was observed at the time as amongst the technological marvels of modernity through its "annihilation of space and time" (Schivelbusch 1986, 33). Travel times to destinations drastically diminished as the perception of the space traversed during travel dramatically shrunk. However, and as the above quotes from the period attest, the steam locomotive's annihilation of space and time was also perceived to come with the price of substantial risk. As social historian Schivelbusch notes, a dominant metaphor by which the steam locomotive was understood during that era was to understand it as a projectile due to its velocity, which had a greater impact than a speeding cannonball, and though such force, could result in 'instant death' through an accident, mainly through a collision (1986, 53-54). As this chapter shall show, these notions in which speeding objects are conceived as projectiles that entail risk through their velocity are inherent with the speed scenario.

The Speed Scenario Prototype

Before delineating the fundamental features of the speed scenario prototype, it is first necessary to contrast it with the

---

[1] Quotes cited in Wolfgang Schivelbusch. *The Railway Journey: The Industrialization of Time and Space in the Nineteenth Century*. Oakland: University of California Press, 1986. p. 15; p. 54.

more basic concept of movement that some action scholars view as being essential to action in films (Anderson, 1998; Tasker, 2015). Yvonne Tasker, for instance, claims that "both the action body and action spectacle is characterized by movement" (2015, 5). In this chapter, I want to finesse this notion of movement, to outline instead why the cognate concept of speed is the more appropriate term with respect to understanding how movement specifically operates in certain action forms, and in particular, the speed scenario. First, the concept of movement is insufficient to differentiate an action scene from a more prosaic moment in a film. Dialogue scenes, for example, abound in films and normally entail shots of the movements of character's mouths and shifting expressions, yet it would be odd to countenance them as a type of action akin to the action scenarios outlined so far. Second, the type of movement that differentiates an action scene from the mere motion found in a dialogue scene is one that is defined by speed. As noted in the previous chapter, the principal factor that distinguishes the cat and mouse segment from the pursuit segment in the car chase in *Bullitt* (1968) is the contrasting differences in the speed of the vehicles and the resultant increase in risk that such differences entail.

Consider as well the pursuit sequence in *Death Proof* (Quentin Tarantino, 2007) in which Zoë Bell, a stuntperson who plays herself in the film, hangs onto the hood of a Dodge Challenger while being pursued by Stuntman Mike, a homicidal maniac, who tries to make her fall off the vehicle by repeatedly ramming it with his Dodge Charger. Clearly, what is critical to the pursuit's suspense is that the vehicles are travelling at speed, rather than at a slow pace, in which there would be far less danger posed to Bell if she were to slip off the hood. In a pursuit scenario, more generally, a pursuee must be swift if they seek to elude capture. Likewise, a pursuer must travel at speed if they want to overtake a pursuee taking flight. Similar observations can be drawn with respect to the role of speed in the fight scenario as well. In a fight scene, the power of a blow, be it from a fist or a sword, is often related to the speed at which it is delivered, and as noted in Chapter 5, speed is also integral to the dynamics of the fast draw duel. Rescues, as well, often must be undertaken under deadlines, so a rescuer must consequently make haste to free the captive. Speed, as a specific modality of movement, therefore is more prototypical to action than mere motion in and of itself.

Out of all the action scenarios covered so far, the event schema for the speed scenario prototype is the most elementary of action forms. If a projectile can be described as a speeding object moving with velocity, then its event schema consists of a vector of an object moving from point A to point B. However, for this event schema to be genuinely considered narrative in nature, some dimension of causality must also be present.

Consider, as an example, the speed sequence in *Batman* (Tim Burton, 1989). After rescuing Vicki Vale from a gas attack at the Gotham Museum of Art, and being pursued by the Joker's henchmen with the chase evolving into a fight, the film cuts to an autumnal night-time shot of a road in a forest from which the Batmobile emerges, moving fast enough to leave a trail of swirling leaves. The film then cuts to the interior of the vehicle, revealing Batman and Lane inside. After a moment, Lane asks, "Where are we going?", a question to which Batman does not verbally reply. But, as if in response to Lane's question, the spectator is shown a shot of Batman's foot pressing down on the accelerator, causing the vehicle to increase its speed. A series of five shots follow, all underscoring the vehicle's speed, as the Batmobile sends up a spray of water from the wet pavement, fires past the camera with its jet propulsion engaged, and crosses the frame of the remaining three shots from right to left at speed [*Figure* 8.1 and *Figure* 8.2].

The film returns back to the interior of the vehicle, with Lane scrutinizing Batman's masked face, to which he responds by switching on a bright light that turns Lane's gaze away to stare ahead at a rock wall toward which the Batmobile's hurtles. Lane shrieks with fright and covers her eyes, but when opened, she finds herself speeding through a darkened tunnel, and when she looks back, she spots the tunnel entrance closing through the camouflaged automated door. While shaking her head in disbelief, the Batmobile continues its trajectory through the tunnel until it stops inside the Batcave, which proves to be Batman's destination, as well as providing the answer to Lane's question earlier.

Figure 8.1 Representing speed in *Batman* (1989).

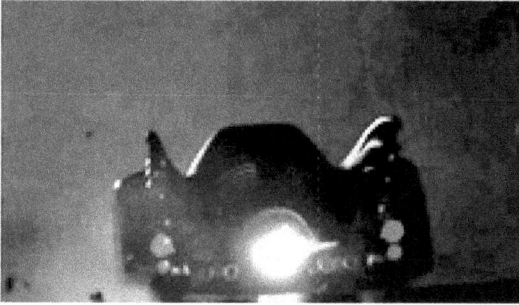

Figure 8.2 Representing speed in *Batman* (1989).

In this speed sequence, causality is manifested in primary and secondary forms. First, at the level of the event structure of the speed scenario, primary causality is exhibited in the sequence by presenting the mode of locomotion through which Batman is able to arrive at his destination. To the question of how Batman traversed from point A to point B, the sequence provides the explanatory answer - by means of his Batmobile. Such causality is particularly showcased when Batman presses down on the accelerator, and the Batmobile accelerates, with the subsequent series of shots revealing a cause-and-effect chain. Secondary causality, in contrast, consists of an additional layer that is presented through the series of events that are embedded into the event structure of the schema. In this scene, secondary causality is exhibited by Lane's and Batman's behaviour that is meant to be understood by viewers through reference to folk psychology in which psychological causality looms large[2] When Lane stares at Batman in an effort to ascertain his true identity behind the mask, her action motivates Batman to switch on the light as a means to redirect her gaze elsewhere. Further, Lane's shrieks and the closing of her eyes are intended to be understood as responses to the impending camouflaged entrance, with the fantastic events she experiences the source of her bewilderment.

Another significant element of this speed sequence that exemplifies the speed scenario prototype is how it is stripped of the character types found in the pursuit scenario. Batman is neither a pursuee nor a pursuer, and the speed exercised is neither motivated to escape or to facilitate capture, but to get to a destination in haste. As a result, the speed scenario departs from the dyadic character pairings that define the other action scenarios. In its purest form, the speed scenario prototype only exhibits one dramatic person-age – which I shall label the *speeder* - who speeds by recourse to their own bodily means, such as by running, or through the aid of a speeding projectile, such as the Batmobile, or any other mode of locomotion that is commonly associated with moving at velocity. As will be demonstrated later on in this chapter, the racing variant is one of the main variations of the speed scenario precisely because it reintroduces a dyadic pair, or a multitude of racers, who are rival competitors in some racing sport.

As a dramatic character in the speed scenario, the speeder also exhibits prototypical goals. One recurrent goal already discussed in relation to the speed sequence in *Batman* was the aim to get to a particular destination in haste. Another instance of such an aim is found in *Mad Max* (George Miller, 1979) after Max Rockatansky's wife Jessie and his son are brutally run down by

---

[2] For more on how folk psychology is used by film spectators to understand the motivations of character behavior in relation to mental states as causes, see: Per Persson. *Understanding Cinema: A Psychological Theory of Moving Imagery.* Cambridge: Cambridge University Press, 2003. pp. 159-220; Tico Romao. "The mark of the social: Stereotypes, folk psychology, and metonymy in mainstream film" in Johannes Riis and Aaron Taylor (eds.) *Screening Characters: Theories of Character in Film, Television, and Interactive Media.* New York: Routledge. 2019. pp. 93-109.

a savage motorcycle gang, who finds his son dead and his wife in critical condition on the road. Three shots then follow. The first consists of darkened clouds reinforcing the sombre turn in the story, as well as metaphorically expressing Max's internal storm brewing for a desire for vengeance. The next two shots then present an ambulance with its siren blaring as it zooms past the camera down a highway to its presumed destination of a hospital, a terminus confirmed in the next shot showing Jessie on life support in a patient room. In this instance, the aims of the ambulance driver, who is never shown, remain implicit, yet given the general knowledge that most spectators possess about the purposes of ambulances to transport the ill and injured to a hospital in an emergency, the shots are sufficient and narratively economical as they telegraph to the viewer the driver's intent and the vehicle's implicit destination.

Another recurrent aim of the speeder in the speed scenario prototype is not so much to arrive at a designated destination but to indulge in speed for its own sake as a means to experience the thrill of risk-taking that it offers. The 1950s hot rod cycle popularized the attendant dangers of youth, often portrayed as juvenile delinquents, who engaged in hot rod culture (Doherty 1988, 107-113). Such films would often manifest speed in their various forms, such as illegal street racing, sanctioned automobile racing on dedicated speedways, chicken runs, and pursuit sequences, with the aim to present it as a thrill ride.

An early instance of such a scene is found in *The Devil on Wheels* (Crane Wilbur, 1947), often cited as amongst the earliest hot rod films (Stanfield 2013, 38-39). A morality tale on the dangers of automotive speeding, the film centers upon Michael and Todd, two young teenagers who build a hot rod and compete in a street race. Michael's father, John, arrives in a new convertible and lectures the boys on the dangers of drag races after witnessing a fatal car accident. Despite this, John is keen to give his new car a test drive and convinces his wife to take the family out on "a little trip to Mountain Lake and back". The film then cuts to a busy two-lane highway with John passing multiple vehicles at once, revealing his own propensity for speed. His wife admonishes him for his careless driving, but John continues his reckless ways undeterred by passing vehicles on the right. A motorcycle policeman soon spots his speeding and follows after him in an implied pursuit. As expected, a minor collision occurs with another vehicle, the driver of which happens to be the judge who will preside over John's case of speeding infractions in the next scene. As this scene illustrates, the aim to head to Mountain Lake as a destination served as a pretext for John's underlying aim to experience speed in his new convertible. The A to B vector of the speed scenario's event schema remains implicit in the scene, but is no longer the narrative focus, which turns instead to depicting John's reckless speeding and the dangers it entails.

Unsurprisingly, such instances of the pursuit of speed for its own sake reappear in the *Fast and Furious* franchise, itself a reboot of the 1950s hot rod cycle. In the series' first installment, *The Fast and the Furious* (Rob Cohen, 2001), an instance occurs after Mia, the sister of Dominic Toretto — a renowned street racer, and Brian O'Conner, an undercover police officer investigating a series of hijackings, go on a date at a restaurant. After their attraction for one another has been established, Mia asks Brian if he wants to go for a drive. The story then cuts to an exterior shot of her souped-up Acura Integra, a Japanese sports car, shooting out onto a city street. The next shot reveals Mia at the wheel, giggling as she accelerates, with Brian as her passenger. She then expertly executes a U-turn at speed through oncoming traffic, laughing again as Brian looks on apprehensively. The scene appropriately ends with the Acura zooming off in the opposite direction.

What is notable about this instance of the speed scenario is that the narrative establishment of an A to B vector entailing a specific destination is atypically abandoned. What is presented instead is a brief destinationless journey that showcases Mia's driving prowess and her pleasure while driving at speed, which also serves the broader dramatic function of expressing her youthful sense of freedom that also characterises the racing subculture depicted in the film.

Another significant aspect of the speed scenario prototype is the relative nature of speed itself. The speed of a professional athlete sprinting on foot is best apprehended when contrasted with someone running who does not possess equal athletic ability. Conversely, the speed of a sprinter appears slight in comparison to the pace of an automobile or a locomotive, which in turn appear comparatively slower than the velocities obtained by a military jet or a rocket. Since speed does not possess a fixed value, its realization in film often occurs in a relational capacity as a result.

A good illustration of the relativity of speed is presented in the running scene in *Captain America: The Winter Soldier* (Anthony Russo and Joe Russo, 2014). The scene commences when Sam Wilson, a former pararescueman with the United States Air Force, jogs along the Tidal Basin in Washington, D.C., while dawn breaks. Suddenly Steve Rogers, Captain America's alter-ego, appears from the left of the screen and sprints past him, announcing "On your left" to avoid running into each other. The next shot shows Wilson jogging past the Thomas Jefferson Memorial at the same pace with Steve Rogers once again speeding past and alerting his presence with the same salutation, suggesting that he has lapped Wilson on his route. In the next shot, Wilson jogs past the Lincoln Memorial with Steve Rogers appearing once more, and as he is about to lap his slower competitor, Wilson orders "Don't say it!" in a comic banter that serves the foundation to their initial meeting and future camaraderie.

In this scene, Steve Roger's superhuman footpace is contrasted with Wilson's slower rate in multiple ways. First, Roger is shown to traverse the film frame quicker than Wilson. Second, Roger's bodily sprinting movements are swifter than Wilson's jogging motions. Third, Roger's multiple lapping of Wilson also implies he covered more ground due to his faster pace, which Wilson later estimates to be a total distance of thirteen miles achieved in only thirty minutes. As a result, the abstract notion of Steve Roger's speed derived from his superhuman ability is made more tangible in the scene through these contrasts. Further, such contrasts do not represent an isolated instance but are a basic strategy through which speed is depicted in films. As discussed earlier in relation to the car chase sequence in *Bullitt*, the speed of the vehicles involved in the pursuit component is apprehended as faster than in the preceding cat and mouse section. In addition, when the Charger and Mustang weave through city traffic, they also pass multiple vehicles whose comparatively slow pace serves to underscore the much faster speeds of the pursuer and pursuee.

Given speed's less tangible nature, filmmakers have used the soundtrack to signal its presence additionally. As previously noted, the speed of the vehicles in the car chase in *Bullitt* is not only expressed through contrastive strategies but also through sound design whereby the soundtrack shifts from Schifrin's jazz cue to the sounds of burning rubber, acceleration, gear changes, all of which are associated with vehicular speed.

One notable instance in which sound design and image track work in tandem to represent speed is found in *Unstoppable* (2010), in which a runaway freight train carrying tankers of molten phenol, a toxic compound. The train hurtles towards opposing rail traffic and is headed toward Stanton, a populated area, where it is likely to derail; the terminus to its projectile trajectory. Amongst the oncoming traffic is a passenger train conveying children on a rail safety trip. The scene commences with a shot of the runaway train hurtling down the track adjacent to a highway, but since it is unaccompanied by any other moving vehicles, the scene is unable to effect relative comparisons of speed. As a result, the soundtrack does most of the work by providing the freight train's roar and the screech of its wheels as it speeds along the rails. The next shot of the crewless locomotive cabin continues with the same sounds, but this is accompanied with the stronger visual cues as stationary trees blur past, once again underscoring speed's apprehension through relational comparisons.

The film then cuts to an interior shot of the railway carriage of the passenger train in which the children and their instructor are situated, who are oblivious of the mortal danger. The following shot presents a close-up of the passenger's train engineer apprehensive expression who is aware of the oncoming runaway train and had been instructed to divert his train into a railway siding. To underscore the speed of the passenger train, the film cuts to a point-of-view shot positioned at the front of its locomotive in which the track and surrounding vegetation rush past, as the soundtrack conveys an accelerated clickety-clack of the passage of the train. The film cuts back to a shot of the excited children, then returns to the oncoming runaway train, a shot which is additionally speed ramped to first accelerate the train's velocity to then abruptly slow its speed down for the spectator to take in its ominous power, as the soundtrack acoustically mirrors the latter half of the visual effect by conveying the sound of the train's rushed approach.[3]

The next shot presents the oncoming train again, but this time through an extreme wide-angle lens with the camera placed on the track to capture the runaway train speeding overhead, and it uses the same wall of sound in the previous shot. The film cuts back to the engineer who looks on with increasing alarm, as the passenger train's horns blare, a sound that continues through to the next shot that assumes the same optical point-of-view at the front of the passenger train that reveals the runaway train approaching around the bend. The film returns to the children who are now alerted to the runaway train's oncoming presence through the sounding of the horn, to then cut back to the engineer whose expression signals the danger of the situation.

The film then cuts to a shot of the runaway train and then to a shot of the passenger train to emphasize their intersecting trajectories that will lead to a probable collision, further heightened by the sounds of them rushing past the camera. The engineer is next shown in extreme-close-up, proceeded by a return to the optical point-of-view from the front of the passenger train revealing it switching to the siding, an image echoed by the sound of changing tracks, thereby averting a direct collision with the runaway train.

---

[3] Speed ramping is a visual effect achieved either in-camera or in post-production by altering the frame-rate of the film within the same shot. Increasing the frame-rate will slow motion down while decreasing the frame-rate will result in a sped-up effect.

As the passenger train screeches into the siding, the children rush to carriage windows to witness the runaway train roaring past. Its speed is communicated through a montage of shots consisting of blurred train images intercut with shots of the children gawking in awe, which itself is overlaid with a sound mix that combines the children's exclamations with the swoosh of the train speeding by, the screech of its wheels, and its clattering over the rails. The scene ends with another extreme wide-angle lens shot taken from the point-of-view of the track as the runaway train rockets past overhead in a speed ramped blur as it continues along its perilous trajectory. In such ways, the sound design not only participates with the image track in facilitating the spectator's apprehension of the runaway train's speed, but also anthropomorphizes it by imparting an acoustic impression of a colossal malevolent force.

Given that the speed scenario prototype in its pure form dispenses with the dyadic pairing found in other action scenarios, its dramatic structure and forms of ascendancy consequently take on quite different complexions. In the speed scenario, character aims retain their central role in shaping dramatic structure. However, instead of being set in relation to the aims of another character, they are primarily directed at the scenario's event schema and the forms of causality that arise within the scenario.

To illustrate, let's return to the *Batman* and *Mad Max* speed examples. In both instances, the event schema of an A to B vector predominates as the speeder's goal in both situations is to arrive at a destination through the causal means of their mode of locomotion. As a result, primary causality comes to the fore as the mode of locomotion factors into the success of the mission to arrive at the destination quickly. With respect to the *Batman* speed example, ascendency is achieved as a result of the speed of the Batmobile, as well as the fact that no substantive obstacles are placed in its path. Moreover, the secondary causality presented in the scene plays no tangible part in the success of the mission.

However, in the *Mad Max* speed example, both forms of causality are imbricated in the success of the mission. The ambulance driver, the implicit speeder in the scenario, does not merely want to arrive at the hospital in good time, but presumably also wants to save Jessie's life given her critical condition. In this instance, primary and secondary forms of causality coincide. The primary causality of arriving at the hospital in good time through the mode of locomotion of the ambulance becomes the means by which the ambulance driver seeks to achieve the goal of saving Jessie's life. The secondary form of causality again assumes a psychological form by providing the overriding motivation to speed. In such ways, the *Mad Max* speed example resembles the transport rescue variant discussed in Chapter 1. The ambulance driver is not merely a speeder but also a rescuer as well by transporting Jessie to a hospital. While the *Mad Max* speed example does not end with ascendancy since Jessie eventually succumbs to her injuries, the speeder remains a rescuer as well through their intent to rescue.

As the instances of speed in film discussed so far illustrate, the speed scenario prototype does not possess an inherent moral valence like most action scenarios. As a result, the speed scenario prototype accommodates a moral spectrum. For instance, the secondary causality expressed in the *Mad Max* speed example is laudable since the ambulance driver's broader aim is to rescue. In marked contrast, the A to B trajectory of the runaway train in *Unstoppable* causes the death of an engineer later on in the film when attempting to slow it down by stationing his locomotive at its front, and its potential derailment at its terminus is presented as a catastrophic outcome. Although the runaway train is technically inanimate, the film's sound design presents it however as an anthropomorphized malevolent force whose speeding trajectory causes death and destruction and puts innocent people at risk.

John's Mountain Lake drive in *The Devil on Wheels* involves notably less peril, but his desire to drive at speed for its own sake is portrayed as reckless, and worthy of social opprobrium, a theme taken up in the illegal street racing sequences manifested in 1950s hot rod films discussed later in this chapter. The speeding scene in *The Fast and the Furious* with Mia at the wheel bears some similarity with *The Devil on Wheels* since the dangers of speed for its own sake is implied when Mia's mid-street U-turn is executed in traffic, with her Acura almost coming in contact with another vehicle, underscoring the risk of the manoeuvre. Yet the film itself, and the *Fast and the Furious* franchise more broadly, does not adopt the moralizing tone exhibited toward street racing found in *The Devil on Wheels* and the hot rod films in which it is affiliated. Instead, Mia and the street racers that she associates with are presented as anti-heroes of sorts, youthful outlaws who value family and community, but indulgence in street-racing, and hijackings to support their income, placing them in a morally grey terrain compared to the Asian street-racing gang in the film who are more prone to resort to violence.

Batman's swift journey to the Batcave in *Batman* also sits within a morally grey territory. While no additional motivation to arrive at the Batcave is presented during the speed sequence, secondary causality is retrospectively introduced. After her visit to the Batcave, Lane finds herself sleeping in her apartment, to discover that Batman had rendered her unconscious by unspecified means in an aim to take film from her camera that revealed his identity as Bruce Wayne. Such an action retrospectively provides an additional reason why Batman was keen to arrive at the Batcave in haste, but the secretive means by which the film was obtained is more ethically questionable, a quality that suits the murkier superhero persona of the Dark Knight.

Like the heist scenario, the speed scenario prototype accommodates different levels of risk, be they implicitly present or explicitly manifest. In the *Batman*, *Mad Max*, and *The Fast and the Furious* speed examples, risk remains implicit given the dangers of travelling at speed and the ever-present possibilities of a mishap. Markedly increased levels of risk are obstacles that appear in the path of the speeding projectile. In the *Mad Max* speed example, no obstacles appear in the path of the ambulance, whereas the camouflaged entrance wall to the Batcave momentarily appears as a dangerous obstacle from Lane's perspective who responds to a perceived oncoming collision. In the *Fast and the Furious* speed example, the level of risk is heightened a notch to the point that they become tangible as a result of a near-miss with an oncoming car. *The Devil on Wheels* speed example ratches up the risk to a higher and explicit level by depicting a collision, but without fatalities or injuries result from the accident. The *Unstoppable* speed example manifests the greatest degree of explicit risk in the examples discussed so far, given the runaway train's near-collision with a passenger train conveying children, and its lethal encounter with another locomotive as the narrative progresses, to the point where its potential derailment would spell catastrophe for a populated community.

Speed Combinations

As noted in the previous chapter, the most evident combination with the speed scenario is that with the pursuit scenario, given that one of its defining features of the latter is speed itself. As an emergent combination with the pursuit scenario, the speed scenario's A to B vector is manifested in a pursuit situation as both the trajectory that the pursuee takes with the aim to elude capture, as well as the path that the pursuer takes to effect capture or to kill the pursuee. Such vectors are well illustrated in the desert landscape in which the first pursuit sequence in *Mad Max: Fury Road* (2015) is played out, when Furiosa steers the War Rig off the road leading to Gas Town to proceed instead along a trajectory that is defined by a desire to escape from the Citadel and Immortan Joe's hold over it.

With respect to combinations with other action scenarios where speed is less evidently a defining feature, it is necessary to first examine the ways in which particular combinatory instances conform to or deviate the action form in question. Let us first consider potential combinations of the speed scenario with the rescue scenario. While not all rescues necessitate speed in both these senses, ones that are undertaken under a deadline often do, and as a result, constitute emergent combinations since the necessity for speed arises inherently within those narrative contexts.

A clear instance of such an emergent combination occurs in *Barney Oldfield's Race for a Life* (Mack Sennett, 1913), a Keystone

Cops burlesque of the melodramatic action situations that D. W. Griffith popularized at the time. After Mabel, a young woman, spurns the amorous advances of the Villain, he orders his two henchmen to capture her and then chain her to a train track. Using a handcar, the villains head down the track to the nearest station to commandeer a steam engine and uncouple it from the train. In the ensuing melee with the engineer and his assistant, the Villain takes offence when one of his henchmen demands payment for his aid in the endeavour, so throttles him as well. The Villain and his remaining henchman climb into the engine and commence their trajectory toward Mabel with the sinister aim of running her over with the locomotive, which sets up the rescue premise as well as a deadline.

The railwaymen and the disgruntled henchman come to after their beating and decide to alert others of the Villain's heinous plan and the urgency to rescue Mabel. The henchman informs Mabel's Boyfriend, who discovers nearby a racing car owned by Barney Oldfield, the automotive racing legend, and beseeches him to rescue Mabel from her impending fate. They hop into the vehicle and speed off, initiating the rescue component of the sequence. The film then returns to the locomotive speeding down the track, with the Villain issuing orders to his henchman and then cuts to Mabel chained to the track, thereby establishing the rescuer, the captor and the captive — the principal figures of the rescue scenario — in quick succession.

Eventually, the railwaymen make it to a police station and inform the Keystone Cops of the situation, with several of the cops departing on a handcar to chase the Villain, vertically combining a pursuit element into the rescue sequence. Soon Oldfield catches up with the locomotive in his racing car, but the Villain retaliates by firing his pistol at them and hurls bombs at their vehicle. Oldfield accelerates, and soon the racing car speeds past the train, once again demonstrating the relative nature of speed.

Oldfield and Mabel's Boyfriend arrive first at the spot on the track where Mabel is chained and frantically file away at the chains while the locomotive bears down upon them. They release

Mabel and carry her off the track just before the locomotive speeds past. In anger, the Villain chokes the remaining henchman and attempts his escape from the locomotive, which is now at rest. The Keystone Cops finally arrive on the scene, but the Villain dispatches them all by firing at them with his pistol. As his crazed, murderous intent peaks, the Villain decides to shoot himself for good measure, but since no bullets are left in his pistol, he opts to strangle himself instead.

As this rescue sequence illustrates, speed is illustrated at both levels of causality. As a mode of locomotion, Oldfield's racing car traverses a trajectory at speed, while at the level of secondary causality, Oldfield's recognition that the rescue is to be conducted under a deadline further motivates travelling at speed in the form of arriving at the destination to free Mabel before the Villain arrives in the locomotive.

Questions pertaining to whether combinations are emergent or contingent are dependent upon which action scenario in the combination serves the context of emergence for the other scenario to arise. For instance, instead of posing the question whether speed is an emergent combination with the fight scenario, one asks whether the fight scenario is an emergent combination with the speed scenario. From this perspective, one examines what aspects of the speed situation in question necessarily derive from some aspect of the fight scenario prototype, instead of analyzing what aspects of the fight situation in question necessarily derive from some aspect of the speed scenario prototype.

In relation to the first question, if the instances of speed in question relate to the velocity of blows in a fight, then it would be appropriate to describe the combinatory relationship as emergent. In contrast, there is nothing in the speed scenario prototype that entails fighting, so any instance of combination of the two would be contingent. Combinations of the heist scenario with the speed scenario also exhibit distinctive contingent relations. Although heists are often undertaken under deadlines that bring urgency to proceedings, the sense of urgency normally translates into robbery efficiency rather than an A to B trajectory of speed. As a result, one can say that emergent action combinations exhibit developmental directionality that is dependent on the nature of the originating context of emergence.

Speed Scenario Variations

Variations on the speed scenario prototype assume three principal forms. The first pertains to variation of the modes of locomotion that are often connected with the genres in which they are situated. The second pertains to situations that involve falling, which involve a particular modality of locomotion. The third variation involves a deviation from the narrative focus upon the dramatic personage of the speeder, either through the reintroduction of the dyadic pair or situating the main dramatic figures external to the speeding projectile.

Generic Variation

Unsurprisingly, one of the main factors underpinning variation within the speed scenario prototype is the mode of locomotion through which the A to B vector is traversed at speed. Like the fight scenario, such variation is partially driven by the film genre in which the speed scenario is situated, as well as its historical setting.

In *Throne of Blood* (Akira Kurosawa, 1957), a samurai film based on William Shakespeare's Macbeth but set during feudal Japan, a number of speed scenes arise in the context of messengers on horseback delivering news. World War II films that involve aerial combat often present scenes of fighter planes travelling at speed, as illustrated in the *Flying Leathernecks* (Nicholas Ray, 1951), in which a squadron is depicted flying in formation in Grumman F6F Hellcats either undertaking a mission or returning to base. *Thunderball* (Terence Young, 1965) is an instance of the espionage film, as well as the fourth installment in the James Bond franchise, which is noted for its automotive pursuits. Given such generic expectations, the mode of locomotion of its speed sequence is an automobile as James Bond is picked up by Fiona Volpe, a

SPECTRE assassin, in her Ford Mustang, who travels to Nassau at an alarming rate. The speed sequence in *Iron Man* (Jon Favreau, 2008), true to the conventions of the comic book adaptation genre, showcases superhero powers, in this instance when Tony Stark first tries out a prototype of his jet-powered exoskeleton suit and attempts to break the altitude record set by an SR71 Blackbird.

The opening sequence to *Dodge City* (1939) can offer a more detailed instance of how modes of locomotion vary with respect to genre, as well as how they can disclose themes that are generically distinctive, in this instance, with respect to the western. The film opens with a steam locomotive powering through the plains on the first run to frontier town Dodge City. After passing the 23rd marker, Twitchell, the owner of the railway line, announces to his colleagues on the train, "Twenty-three miles in one hour and fourteen minutes. Gentlemen that is moving," underscoring the speed of the train at the outset.

Shortly they spot a stagecoach running parallel to the railway track that is delivering mail from Wichita. The scene then switches to the stagecoach driver, who informs his shotgun guard that the "snorting teapot" is already winded and whips his horses to gallop faster. Observing the speed of the stagecoach, Twitchell sends an order to the engineer to beat it to the end of the line, setting up a race between the two. The film then cuts to the wheels of the locomotive, and then a head-on shot of the horses, and continues to alternate between the two speeding trajectories, creating an explicit comparison between the two modes of locomotion [*Figure 8.3*]. A shot of the stagecoach reveals it gradually edging ahead of the train, but as the stoker on the locomotive throws more fuel into the fire that powers the steam boiler, the locomotive catches up and eventually overtakes the stagecoach, as the engineer waves goodbye to it and its occupants. As the passengers on the train celebrate their victory, Colonel Dodge, the founder of Dodge city, proclaims, "That's a symbol of America's future. Progress. Iron men and iron horses. You can't beat them."

Figure 8.3 Contrasting modes of locomotion in *Dodge City* (1939).

The speed sequence in *Dodge City* is notable in three important respects. First, it constitutes an instance of horizontal combination between the speed scenario in its pure form and one of its major variants, the racing scenario. Second, the sequence illustrates the relativity of speed as the perception of the velocities of the stagecoach and locomotive are heightened during the moments when they edge ahead of each other, implying one is moving faster than the other. Third, and most importantly, the sequence features two iconic modes of locomotion, namely a horse-drawn stagecoach and steam locomotive, both of which are notable features of the western's iconography. As notable icons of the western, they also metaphorically convey one of the major thematic oppositions of the genre, with the locomotive a metaphoric symbol of the advance of industrialization upon the west, and the horse-drawn stagecoach a symbol of the frontier's past, with the race itself a metaphor for the industrial progress that Colonel Dodge celebrates (Kitses 1969, 11).

The Falling Variant

The falling variant bears similarity with the daring leap variant discussed in Chapter 2 but need not involve an intentional fall or a leap executed as an attempt to escape. The variant also departs from the speed scenario prototype in two important respects. First, the falling variant presents a wholly distinctive mode of locomotion through the way in which the downward force of gravity acts on

263

the mass of a falling object. Gravity in this variant constitutes the motor of the free fall. Second, the falling variant diverges from the speed scenario prototype additionally with respect to the A to B trajectory traversed. Instead of the standard horizontal trajectory of a projectile along the x-axis, falling represents a vertical trajectory along the y-axis, an axis that Kristen Whissel observes has been increasingly employed in recent contemporary films in the staging of computer-generated action sequences to amplify the space in which the action occurs (2014, 21-58). As Whissel points out, utilization of the y-axis for the sake of action thrills has a long history, best illustrated in the ending of King Kong (1933), where the great ape plummets to his death off the Empire State Building.

One of the attractions of utilizing the y-axis in action sequences is the way it exploits a widespread fear of heights, with a fall to one's death representing the ultimate source of that fear. The fear of falling is also manifested in scenes involving extreme climbing and constitute the evident risks of such an activity, as illustrated by Ethan Hunt's free solo climb up a cliff face in the opening title sequence in *Mission: Impossible 2* (John Woo, 2000), as well as his climb up the exterior of the Burj Khalifa in *Mission: Impossible - Ghost Protocol* (Brad Bird, 2011).

As noted in the Introduction, the fear of falling also explains why action sequences are often staged at great heights, be they the mountainous cliffs in *Lust for Gold* (1949) or on a Harrier Jump Jet in *True Lies* (1994), given the additional risks that such settings entail. One film whose story is predicated on such risks is *Cliffhanger* (Renny Harlin, 1993), which is set in the Colorado Rockies and the protagonist Gabriel Walker, a former mountain climber and rescue ranger, becomes caught up with a criminal gang when their plane crashes into the mountains. Significantly, the film is bookended by spectacular falls. At the start of the film, Walker participates in the rescue of Hal and his girlfriend Sarah, stuck on top of a mountain peak. Walker runs a line from them to a rescue helicopter stationed on an adjacent peak, but when Sarah attempts to cross it, her harness breaks. Walker then scrambles over in an effort to save Sarah and is able to grab her wrist, but her hand slips out of her glove and falls to her death. The film's climactic ending mirrors this initial fall when Walker and Eric Qualen, the leader of the criminal gang, fight it out on top of an inverted helicopter hanging precariously from a winch cable affixed to a steel ladder on a cliff. Walker viciously kicks Qualen off the top of the helicopter, causing him to swing inside of it just when the ladder breaks free from the cliff. Walker leaps off just before the helicopter, with Qualen as its terrified occupant, makes its downward descent, exploding upon impact with the bottom of the gorge.

Qualen's death also manifests the well-worn convention of the antagonist villain coming to their sticky end through a fatal fall. Examples of such scenes from an even longer list include Mola Ram, a Thuggee high priest, who falls from a severed rope bridge dangling from a rock-face into the jaws of crocodiles in the river below in *Indiana Jones and the Temple of Doom* (Steven Spielberg, 1984); Hans Gruber, a master criminal, falls precipitously from a skyscraper when John McClane unclasps his wife's watch from which Gruber hangs, in *Die Hard* (John McTiernan, 1988); the Joker, a comic-book villain, is yanked off a ladder unfurled from an airborne helicopter by the weight of a stone gargoyle attached to his leg by a cable in *Batman* (1989); Alec Trevelyan, a rogue agent, is released from James Bond's grip from the top of an antennae into the concrete parabola of the radio telescope beneath; Ma-Ma, a drug lord, is shoved out of a window of a slum tower block by Judge Dredd in *Dredd* (Pete Travis, 2012); Koba, an embittered chimpanzee, hangs onto a girder of a destroyed tower, whose arm is grasped by Caesar, who Koba earlier betrayed, and is then released to plummet into the debris below in *Dawn of the Planet of the Apes* (Matt Reeves, 2014); and most famously Emperor Palpatine is tossed down a reactor shaft by Darth Vader after trying to kill his son Luke Skywalker in *Star Wars: Return of the Jedi* (Richard Marquand, 1983). As these cases illustrate, the convention is also used to effect narrative closure of both the action sequence as well as that of the film's broader story through the death of the antagonist.

265

A notable variation of the falling variant is the controlled fall. Instead of the state of helplessness that characterizes the speeder in a typical fatal descent, in the controlled fall variant, the speeder instead is able to exercise control over their vertical dive, often through the aid of a parachute. In the early 1990s, parachuting as action scenes was a minor cycle with *Point Break* (1991), *Drop Zone* (John Badham, 1994), and *Terminal Velocity* (Deran Sarafian, 1994) featuring notable skydiving sequences in which such controlled descents are showcased.

Controlled descents can assume alternate forms as well. The speed sequence in *Iron Man* (2008) discussed earlier, for instance, transitions from a y-axis vertical ascent as Tony Stark attempts to break the altitude record in his jet-powered exoskeleton suit to a downward fall when the suit freezes over with ice, causing its jet propulsion to shut down. Spinning in freefall, Stark tries to contact J.A.R.V.I.S., his computer interface system, in an effort to deploy the suit's flaps, but the communications link is also down. Stark then deploys the flaps manually, which breaks the ice on his suit and reboots its jet propulsion and navigation system just before making contact with a street to zoom through heavy traffic and head back to his mansion.

A more recent instance of the controlled fall is presented in the opening sequence of *Ad Astra* (James Gray, 2019), in which Roy McBride, a Major in U.S. Space Command, is stationed high up on the International Space Antenna, a colossal tower under construction to detect signs of intelligent life. A power surge emanating from the outer reaches of the solar system precipitates a series of explosions overhead as other workers and pieces of equipment plummet. Seeking a secure spot to take cover from the falling debris, McBride slips down to a high voltage switch and turns it off to avoid electrocution. Yet the explosions continue downward, eventually blasting McBride off the antenna.

In freefall, McBride spins as the vertical tower blurs by during his descent, highlighting the velocity of trajectory [*Figure* 8.4]. Tumbling wildly, McBride risks blacking out as he reaches terminal velocity speed. In an effort to stop the spin, McBride assumes a spread-eagle position long enough to deploy his parachute. However, debris from the antenna rains from above and pierce his parachute, setting up a deadline to reach the ground before the chute is no longer functional to slow his speed. Searching for a spot to land, McBride guides his parachute away from the trees to an open field, and as he safely touches the ground, a medical unit arrives.

Figure 8.4. The optical perception of falling in *Ad Astra* (2019).

These two controlled fall sequences are notable not only through their staging of action primarily along the y-axis but also by underscoring the agency of the speeders as they transition from an uncontrolled fall to a controlled descent, thereby saving their lives in the process. With respect to Tony Stark, such agency and mastery over technology are in keeping with his superhero status that prepares him for even more daring speed situations. With respect to Roy McBride, the controlled fall sequence from the antenna establishes his agency to extricate himself from dangerous situations and that he possesses the requisite level-headedness to carry out the risky space mission to which he is assigned.

Like other action scenarios, the falling variant exhibits a typically gradient, particularly in relation to risk. At the extreme end of the risk spectrum is the uncontrolled freefall whose danger is ultimate since they often result in death, as was the fate of treacherous villains listed earlier. Further down the typicality gradient are situated the controlled falls that do not necessarily result in death, but the risk of the speeder losing their life is presented either tacitly or explicitly, as illustrated in the *Iron Man* and the *Ad Astra* examples. In the mid-range are those falls that may prove injurious but are not necessarily fatal.

A good example of such occurs when Pike Bishop's gang crosses a sandy desert and descends down a steep dune in *The Wild Bunch* (1969). One of the gang members takes a tumble off his horse, causing other gang members to fall along with their horses. The scene involves risk to the gang members by falling off their horses and the danger of being crushed by them as they tumble down the dune as well. The horses themselves also risk injury. At the other end of the risk spectrum, posing the least amount of danger is the pratfall, perfected during silent era slapstick comedy, as illustrated in *By the Sea* (Charles Chaplin, 1915) when the Tramp, while eating a banana, carelessly discards its peel onto the sidewalk and then promptly slips on it, an act of poetic justice. While the pratfall gag is performed as comedy, the risk of potential injury is real for the comedian if not performed correctly.

The Racing Variant

Amongst all of the variants of the speed scenario prototype, the most recurrent and enduring is the racing variant. As indicated previously, the racing variant departs from the speed scenario prototype by narratively focusing upon a dyadic pair of rival racers, or upon a multitude of racers, instead of featuring a lone speeder on an A to B trajectory. Such dyadic pairs can be found in *Rush* (Ron Howard, 2013), a Formula 1 auto-racing film that depicts the rivalry between James Hunt and Niki Lauda. On occasion, a film will focus upon a lone speeder, such as Chuck Yeager attempting to break the sound barrier in *The Right Stuff* (Philip Kaufman, 1983) or Burt Munro, a New Zealander, who breaks the land speed record for a motorcycle in *The World's Fastest Indian* (Roger Donaldson, 2005), but these are the exceptions that prove the rule.

Another significant departure from the speed scenario prototype is the sports context in which the racing sequences are principally narratively situated. Such sports contexts can be informal, taken up on the spur of the moment, as illustrated by the drag race from a stoplight in *The Fast and the Furious* in which Brian O'Conner smokes' an arrogant driver in a Ferrari in his souped-up Toyota Supra. Sports contexts can be illegal street races as well that are more formalized in nature but are not formally sanctioned by a racing body, such as the drift race down a mountain in *The Fast and the Furious: Tokyo Drift* (Justin Lin, 2006). In their most recurrent form, the contexts are formally sanctioned competitions, such as the NASCAR races in *Days of Thunder* (Tony Scott, 1990).

Other key departure from the speed scenario prototype are the different types of goals that are exhibited by the speeder given the sports context, which at the local race level is the aim to travel faster than their competitors, with the larger aim usually to win the race, often accompanied with the overarching goal of winning a competition consisting of a series of racing events. Speeders in racing films are typically depicted as competitive in nature that motivates their desire to win. Given the sports context of the racing variant, the aim to get to a particular destination found in the speed scenario's A to B event schema is consequently transplanted in the racing context as the finish line. The A to B trajectories of the competing speeders normally assume parallel paths, be it the drag races on the street or the more formal contours of a racing track.

Another notable dimension of the racing variant is the polymorphous modes of locomotion that it exhibits. The variant has featured running in athletic competitions, as in *Chariots of Fire* (Hugh Hudson, 1981); swimming, as in *Pride* (Sunu Gonera, 2007) and *Nobeureshing* (Jo Yong-sun, 2013); bicycles, as in *Breaking Away* (Peter Yates, 1979) and *American Flyers* (John Badham, 1985); skis, as in *Better Off Dead...* (Savage Steve Holland, 1985); ostriches, as in *Prince of Persia: The Sands of Time* (Mike Newell, 2010); horses, as in *The Story of Seabiscuit* (David Butler, 1949), *Bite the Bullet* (Richard Brooks, 1975), *The Black Stallion* (Carroll Ballard, 1979), *Hidalgo* (Joe Johnston, 2004) and *Secretariat* (Randall Wallace, 2010); a camel amongst a set of horses, in *Ride the High Country* (Sam Peckinpah, 1962); chariots, as in *Ben-Hur: A Tale of the Christ* (Fred Niblo, 1925), *Ben-Hur* (William Wyler,

1959) and *The Fall of the Roman Empire* (Anthony Mann, 1964); boats, as in *Madison* (William Bindley, 2001) and *Speed Kills* (Jodi Scurfield, 2018); motorcycles, as in *Once a Jolly Swagman* (Jack Lee, 1949), *Tornado on Wheels* (Romolo Marcellini, 1957), *Little Fauss and Big Halsy* (Sidney J. Furie, 1970) and *Biker Boyz* (Reggie Rock Bythewood, 2003); aircraft, as in *Those Magnificent Men in Their Flying Machines* (Ken Annakin, 1965) and *Planes* (Klay Hall, 2013); futuristic podracers, in *Star Wars: Episode I - The Phantom Menace* (George Lucas, 1999); semi-trucks as featured in *Smokey and the Bandit II* (Hal Needham, 1980); and the various modes of locomotion featuring in virtual gaming worlds, such as the lightcycles in *TRON* (Steven Lisberger, 1982), *Tron: Legacy* (Joseph Kosinski, 2010), which also makes an appearance in the virtual automotive race in *Ready Player One* (Steven Spielberg, 2018).

Without a doubt, the most recurrent mode of locomotion is the racing car, with automobile racing constituting the mainstay of the racing variant with a history that extends to early silent cinema. Amongst the earliest appearances of an automobile in a race is *A Race for a Kiss* (Lewin Fitzhamon, 1904), in which two suitors, one on horseback, the other in a motorcar, race to win a kiss, and the hand in marriage, with a stylish young woman. From thereon, automobile racing films include *The Speed Kings* (Wilfred Lucas, 1913), *The Roaring Road* (James Cruze, 1919), *Excuse My Dust* (Sam Wood, 1920), *Burning Up* (A. Edward Sutherland, 1930), *The Crowd Roars* (Howard Hawks, 1932), *Blonde Comet* (William Beaudine, 1941), *The Big Wheel* (Edward Ludwig, 1949), *To Please a Lady* (Clarence Brown, 1950), *Checkpoint* (Ralph Thomas, 1956), *Viva Las Vegas* (George Sidney, 1964), *Grand Prix* (John Frankenheimer, 1966), *Le Mans* (Lee H. Katzin, 1971), *The Gumball Rally* (Charles Bail, 1976), *The Cannonball Run* (Hal Needham, 1981), *Safari 3000* (Harry Hurwitz, 1982), *Days of Thunder* (1990), *Thunderbolt* (Gordon Chan, 1995), *Driven* (Renny Harlin, 2001), *Michel Vaillant* (Louis-Pascal Couvelaire, 2003), *Rush* (2013), and most recently *Ford v Ferrari* (James Mangold, 2019).

A common theme in automobile racing films, be they of the illegal street racing kind or the formally sanctioned, is the risks that racers face by participating in the sport, which can result in fatalities, often derived from the recklessness of a driver. In the opening Monaco race in *Grand Prix*, for instance, Pete Aron and Scott Stoddard are teammates on the Jordan team. Shortly after the race has started, Stoddard overtakes Jean-Pierre Sarti, on the Ferrari team, in a manoeuvre that demonstrates his racing skills as well as the relativity of speed, as his car rushes past the Ferrari on the inside of a turn. Aron's gearbox, however, malfunctions, causing him to pitstop, but team manager Jeff Jordan orders him back onto the race.

Aron gets back on the track but ends up in front of Stoddard and is reluctant to let him pass. A blue flag is raised by a racing steward, but Aron again ignores that instruction to let Stoddard overtake despite being in a slower vehicle. Aron's gearbox then begins to stick, and he finally waves Stoddard to pass but abruptly brakes at that moment, causing the wheels of their vehicles to catch. The incident sends Aron's automobile into the railings to shunt off the track into the adjacent water, while Stoddard's car spins uncontrollably and careens along a rock face to crash onto the asphalt. A rescue crew then attends to Stoddard, alive but badly injured, as Aron emerges from the water, for the most part unscathed. Although both racers survive the crash, the sequence underscores the perils of automotive racing at speed.

The Chicken Variant

A variation on the speed scenario prototype, but one that is not as recurrent as the racing variant, is the 'game of chicken' that was most famously popularized in *Rebel Without a Cause* (Nicholas Ray, 1955), and as discussed in the last chapter, appears at the end of the concluding pursuit sequence in *The Driver* (1978). Instead of a contest of speed to win a race that defines the racing variant, the chicken variation is a test of nerve. In its usual form, the chicken variant consists of a dyadic pair of speeders who directly face each other in their respective automobiles and then drive at speed until one of the speeders yields way to avoid crashing into each other.

As noted, this format is used in *The Driver* to bring about an end to the pursuit sequence, and reappears in *Footloose* (Herbert Ross, 1984), except the duelling vehicles are two tractors with large diggers attached at their fronts, and while not speedy per se, manifest sufficient velocity and mass to be risky, as one tumbles down a slope after its driver bails out. The 'chickee run' in *Rebel Without a Cause* assumes a different format that is more consistent with the drag race except that both speeders, Jim Stark and Buzz Gunderson, head in the same direction toward a cliff in stolen automobiles. Stark leaps out of his vehicle before it reaches the cliff, but Gunderson's jacket sleeve gets caught on the door handle and plunges to his death, underscoring the inherent danger to the 'game'.

The Obstacle Variant

So far, the dramatic structure has been discussed in relation to a speeder, a dramatic figure, who is either the speeding projectile or is within a speeding projectile traversing an A to B trajectory. But there is another dramatic figure that arises in one of the speed scenario's significant variants, who is situated externally to the projectile but is in its path, who I shall label here as the *obstructor*, who assumes narrative focus. One simple reason for this switch is that speeding projectiles in the obstacle variant are either animal in nature, whose subjective states do not permit exploration as readily as human characters, or are inanimate objects where no such subjective states exist. Obstructors, in contrast, are normally sentient characters, but narratively function as obstacles in the path of a projectile. Amongst the most recurrent manifestations of the obstacle variant is the stampede in which a group of animals are running at speed and pose a danger to those characters who are in their path. The stampede is principally associated with the western with instances of it found in *The Thundering Herd* (Henry Hathaway, 1933), *Hollywood Cowboy* (Ewing Scott, 1937), *Dodge*

City (1939), and *How the West Was Won* (Henry Hathaway, John Ford, and George Marshall, 1962), but also reappear as dinosaurs in *Jurassic Park* (Steven Spielberg, 1993).

An example of the stampede that illustrates its prototypical features can be found in *Red River* (Howard Hawks, 1948). Thomas Dunson owns a cattle ranch in Texas, and in order to fetch the best price on his livestock, he organizes, along with his adopted son Matt Garth, a cattle drive to a railhead in Missouri. Along the drive, Dunson's men rest one evening, with the howling of the coyotes unsettling the cattle. Bunk Kenneally, a wrangler, appears and searches for sugar in the chuckwagon but causes a ruckus when pots begin to drop, which triggers the cattle to stampede. Dunson yells "stampede", an order to his men to round up the cattle, who then hastily leave the campfire and get on their horses.

The next shot shows the cattle speeding across the plain, with the action staged across the x-axis. The cattle then head toward the camp, demolishing one of the wagons in their path. The film then cuts to two successive low-angle shots taken from the perspective of the ground that presents the cattle thundering past with ominous power. Dan Latimer, another wrangler, attempts to round the cattle, but his horse stumbles, throwing him onto the ground where he gets crushed by the stampeding cattle. Dunson and his team continue to round up the cattle, and when another of his men tumbles off his horse, Garth and a wrangler bravely rescue him by lifting him off the ground and carrying him to safety through the rushing cattle. The cattle eventually approach a coulee, where they are successfully rounded up, ending the stampede. Dunson then takes stock of the damage and discovers that Latimer is missing, and organizes a search party. Amongst the carcasses of the cattle, they find his trampled body.

As dramatic personage, obstructors serve two narrative functions in this sequence. The first is to function as an obstacle in the path of the stampeding cattle, as did Latimer, who dies as a result, thereby illustrating the deadly potential of large animals collectively running at speed. Unlike inanimate obstacles, however, obstructors are human characters whose subjective states

273

evoke spectatorial sympathy for their plight, as illustrated by the close-up of Latimer screaming in fear, which is followed by his optical-point-of-view of the oncoming cattle [*Figure* 8.5 and 8.6]. The second way in which obstructors narratively function is to either redirect the trajectory of the speeding projectiles to minimize their destructive potential, as well as to bring their journey to a halt. Dunson and his men function in this capacity by rounding up the cattle and directing them to the coulee, which acts as a terminus to their stampede. Interestingly, the depiction of animals in stampedes is not presented as entirely directionless, but whose trajectory can be guided by obstructors. In the *Red River* example, the intervention of Dunson and his men provides greater directionality to their route.

Figure 8.5 Optical point-of-view of a stampede in *Red River* (1948).

Figure 8.6 Optical point-of-view of a stampede in *Red River* (1948).

As noted, projectiles can be inanimate objects whose A to B trajectories are similar to stampedes, but cause even greater levels of destruction. In *Gravity* (Alfonso Cuarón, 2013), debris emanating from the explosion of a Russian spy satellite begins to orbit the Earth at high velocity, becoming deadly projectiles for the astronauts working on the Hubble Space Telescope, obstacles in the path of high-speed debris. At an even greater magnitudes are the projectiles that are much larger in scale and mass, move at speed, and whose wake of destruction is catastrophic, which are hallmarks of the disaster film. Amongst these are tsunamis whose waves capsize ships, as illustrated in *The Poseidon Adventure* (1972) and its remake *Poseidon* (Wolfgang Petersen, 2006), and which generate instances of mass falling as the ocean liners flip over. In other instances, the obstructors are situated on land and who are either killed by the oncoming waves or must struggle to survive in the aftermath, such as in *The Day After Tomorrow* (Roland Emmerich, 2004), *Haeundae* (JK Youn, 2009), *2012* (2009), *The Impossible* (J.A. Bayona, 2012), *San Andreas* (Brad Peyton, 2015), and *Geostorm* (Dean Devlin, 2017). Strikingly, the flows of the animal stampedes resemble the flows of water when the tsunamis hit land, except that their paths of destruction are staged on a smaller scale.

In other disaster films, the high-speed projectiles originate from outer space, usually in the form of comets or asteroids, where the relevant obstacle is Earth itself, and the ensuing destruction is planetary. Examples of disaster films in this vein include: *When Worlds Collide* (Rudolph Maté, 1951), *Meteor* (Ronald Neame, 1979), *Armageddon* (1998), *Deep Impact* (Mimi Leder, 1998), and *Greenland* (Ric Roman Waugh, 2020). In such films, the A to B trajectory of the outer space objects sets them on a collision course with Earth with cataclysmic consequences. Obstructors in these films function in the same dual narrative capacities as in the *Red River* stampede example, as either unfortunate obstacles that are obliterated as a result of the impact of the projectiles or serve government agencies that seek to redirect or destroy the Earth-bound projectiles. In *Deep Impact*, the impact of the comet creates a tsunami as well, representing both forms of large-scale projectiles.

The obstacle variant offers an occasion to reflect upon the disaster film and its affiliations with the action scenarios discussed so far. As noted in the Introduction, a number of action theorists have included disaster films in their discussion of action without providing justification for their inclusion (Kendrick 2019; Lichtenfeld 2007). An action scenario approach, however, provides such a rationale by demonstrating that they are ensembles of action scenarios, which along with the obstacle variant, can consist of a mix of rescues, as illustrated by Superman's rescue of civilians affected by an earthquake in *Superman* (1978); escapes, especially the fleeing escape variant as manifested in *2012* and *Godzilla* (2014); destruction, as manifested in the destruction sub-variant, illustrated by the volcanic eruptions in *Dante's Peak* (1997). Disaster films, therefore, exhibit specific combinations of action scenarios.

Exemplar: *Ben-Hur* (1959)

While automobile racing films emphasize the dangers of the sport as a result of the speed of the vehicles, they hold no monopoly on racing risks, as the chariot race in *Ben-Hur* (1959) clearly attests. The chariot race is an exemplar not only on this score, but also due to its densely packed action contained in a sequence that is only slightly over eight minutes in duration. Notably, the film exhibits many of the conventions associated with auto-racing sequences, suggesting a broader range of the conventions operating across the racing variant. The sequence is also exemplary with respect to its narration that weaves moral valance, suspense, and dramatic structure to a satisfying resolution.

The celebrated racing sequence sets up the final confronta-tion between Judah Ben-Hur, a wealthy Jewish prince, and the protagonist of the film, and Messala, a Roman and Ben-Hur's former childhood friend. As antagonist, Messala betrays Ben-Hur by condemning him as a galley slave and sends his mother and sister to prison on trumped-up charges of intending to kill Valerius

Gratus, the Roman governor. After spending several years as a galley slave, Ben-Hur is assigned to Roman Consul Quintus Arrius and saves his life during a battle with a fleet of Macedonian pirates. Grateful for the rescue, Arrius successfully petitions Emperor Tiberius to permit Ben-Hur to become a free man and adopts him as his son. Ben-Hur becomes a champion charioteer but returns to Judea cursed with thoughts of vengeance. Along his journey, Ben-Hur befriends Sheik Ilderim, who urges him to compete in the Jerusalem chariot races, but Ben-Hur initially declines. After being misinformed that his mother and sister perished in prison, Ben-Hur agrees to take part in the chariot race with Messala amongst the competitors. Sheik Ilderim then approaches Messala, informs him of Ben-Hur's return, and, playing upon his pride, persuades him to engage in a high stakes wager, demonstrating Messala's underlying hubris.

On race day, the chariot competitors wait for Messala to appear, who eventually arrives on a Greek chariot that comes equipped with spinning blades upon its wheels, adding to the danger of the competition as well as emphasizing Messala's unscrupulous character who will stoop to underhanded means to win the race. After a grand opening ceremonial parade, Pontius Pilate, the Roman governor presiding over the race, announces the nationality of nine competitors in a roll call of Mediterranean antiquity. Pilate then drops of a white kerchief, a sign to two flag bearers on the start line to lower their flags to signal to the charioteers to start the race. At the first turn, Messala speeds past Ben-Hur. As the rest of the field negotiates the turn, one of the charioteers hits the curb, causing the chariot to overturn and dangerously toss out the charioteer onto the track.[4] Race attendants then rush out to remove the chariot and the injured charioteer, emphasizing the risks of the race early on. Messala is next shown to forcefully positions his chariot in front of the Alexandrian charioteer, causing him to slow down to avoid a collision. After passing the Alexandrian, Messala then manoeuvres his chariot towards that of the Cypriot charioteer in an effort to intimidate him with his spinning blades, whose chariot is nearly upended as it hits the racetrack's curb.

Through such underhanded tactics, Messala assumes an early lead over Ben-Hur as he completes the first lap. As they round a corner of the track, race attendants hurriedly remove the remnants of the first crash, a foreshadowing of pivotal encounters with obstacles later on in the race. Messala then speeds past the Corinthian charioteer to assume the lead of the race. Showing resolve, the Corinthian charioteer attempts to regain the lead by heading toward the inside of the track, but Messala uses the same dangerous blocking manoeuvre applied before. Undaunted, the Corinthian then passes Messala on the outside, thereby regaining the lead. In retaliation, Messala swerves towards the left wheel of the Corinthian chariot, with its blades making mincemeat of its wooden spokes. The wheel then flies off, sending the Corinthian out of the tumbling chariot, who is dragged along the track a short distance by his horses. He lets go of the reins and dodges an oncoming chariot, but is less successful with the next chariot that runs him over.

---

[4] Two continuity errors hinder the identification of the charioteers during the race. The first involves the charioteer who first crashes. The uniform of the charioteer, white with orange trim, does not wholly match those shown during the opening roll call. Although the uniform somewhat resembles the tunic worn by the Athenian charioteer, he appears later on in the race. The second error appears to erroneously imply that there are ten charioteers rather than the nine introduced at roll call, an implication arising when Ben-Hur makes his charge at the back of the field yet six charioteers are visible ahead, despite the fact that there were three previous crashes, which the viewer assumes would have taken those competitors out of the race. One unsatisfactory interpretive solution would be to contend that the first crash involved the Athenian who somehow returned to the race, but with his return not depicted on screen, creating a plot hole instead. Such confusions underscore the primary narrative focus placed upon Ben-Hur and Messala that directs the viewer's attention towards them, instead of keeping stock of the secondary charioteers.

As the crowd roars with horror, Ben-Hur quickly looks back at the accident to then forge his charge ahead for the lead. In a recurrent pattern, race attendants rush to remove the incapacitated Corinthian just before the arrival of the remaining chariots. After turning a corner, Ben-Hur makes his move to overtake Messala. Ben-Hur's attempt to pass is presented in a shot that showcases the relative speeds of the chariots as a means to emphasize Ben-Hur's superior pace [*Figure* 8.7-8.9]. In an effort to prevent the pass, Messala manoeuvres to attack Ben-Hur's chariot with the spinning blades and commences to whip him as well. Ben-Hur then veers into the path of the Phrygian's chariot to evade the blades, causing the Phrygian to crash into the wall, taking out another charioteer in the process, with the race attendants once again making their appearance on the track.

Figure 8.7 The relativity of speed in the chariot race in *Ben-Hur* (1959).

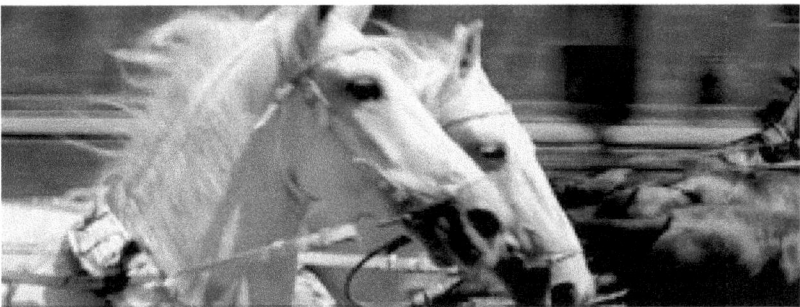

Figure 8.8 The relativity of speed in the chariot race in *Ben-Hur* (1959).

Figure 8.9 The relativity of speed in the chariot race in *Ben-Hur* (1959).

At the commencement of the third lap, Ben-Hur finds himself
behind the rest of the field as a result of the previous accident,
creating suspense whether he will be able to catch up to Messala,
who is in first place and is momentarily ascendant. Demonstrating
his charioteering skill, Ben-Hur speeds towards the charioteers
ahead and finds a line to weave past four chariots to place himself
in third, just behind the Alexandrian and Messala. Glancing back,
Messala sees Ben-Hur's advance as he speeds past the Alexandrian.
As Ben-Hur gains on Messala from the outside, the Athenian
and the Messenian charioteers make their charge on the inside.
Messala steers his bladed chariot towards the Athenian, who veers
out of the way but collides into the Messenian charioteer, taking
out both chariots as a result.

Past the next turn, Ben-Hur takes the inside line, unwittingly
setting himself on a collision course with the remnants of the
previous crash. Ben-Hur and Messala race neck and neck with
each other as the film cuts to the race attendants hurriedly removing the chariots and horses off the track. Ben-Hur and Messala
then turn the corner, with the film presenting a point-of-view shot
from the vantage of Ben-Hur's chariot, revealing the attendants
trying to remove the crashed chariots. Sensing an opportunity,
Messala steers his chariot into Ben-Hur's, thereby forcing him to
maintain his trajectory toward the crash ahead. Ben-Hur steers
closer to the curb in order to avoid colliding with Messala, but
in doing so takes out a Roman soldier stationed along the inside
curb, who falls to the ground and is run over by the Alexandrian
charioteer. The film returns to the point-of-view shot setting up an

imminent collision with the obstacles. As Messala veers clear of the wreckage, Ben-Hur's horses leap over them, sending him out of the chariot, yet Ben-Hur manages to hang on and miraculously climb back into the chariot.

As the sixth lap commences, Ben-Hur and Messala remain neck and neck, despite the near-collision and test of Ben-Hur's charioteering abilities. Unable to speed past, Messala resorts again to the dangerous tactic of taking out his competitors with the spinning blades. Positioning his chariot, Messala attempts to take out Ben-Hur's right wheel, who responds by veering out of the way. Messala tries again with the blades eating into the chariot itself, but Ben-Hur steers to the inside to avoid the blades.

At the seventh lap, Messala resorts to whipping Ben-Hur violently with his red lash. Defending himself, Ben-Hur blocks the blows with his arm as the wheels of the two chariots begin to interlock. Messala continues his assault, but Ben-Hur manages to wrap the whip around his arm, and in a tug of war, Ben-Hur yanks the whip out of Messala's grasp and beats him with it. To avoid the blows, Messala steers away from Ben-Hur's chariot, snapping his left wheel off in the process, the threshold moment of the race, which throws him to the ground. Holding onto the reins of his horses, Messala is dragged along the track and is soon trampled by the horses of the Carthaginian chariot racing behind. Messala then grasps at the shaft of the chariot as a means to lift himself out of danger but gets tangled up in horses' hooves and is violently spit out. Ben-Hur looks back at the accident and tosses Messala's whip away in disgust. The film cuts to Messala's bloodied body, who rolls over barely alive. The Judeans watching the race leap from stands onto the track in jubilation as Ben-Hur takes the last curve. Messala, near death, gazes on in defeat as Ben-Hur crosses the finish line, ascendant.

The chariot race in *Ben-Hur* is no mere competition for speed but a battle that exhibits the dichotomy between good and evil. From the outset, Messala is presented as the villain of the race, a narrative function stemming from his role as the antagonist within the film's broader story. When Messala arrives at the stadium, his chariot is revealed to be weaponized, which not only represents a means to win the race by unfair advantage but also reveals that he is willing to endanger the lives of others in doing so. In addition, Messala uses his whip as a weapon against Ben-Hur. That behaviour is sharply contrasted with Ben-Hur's, who exhibits charioteering skills and resolve and only engages in violence as a means to defend himself from Messala's attacks. Significantly, their horses are colour-coded as well. Ben-Hur's horses are white, while Messala's steeds are black, signifying the moral valence of the two competitors through the historical associations of these colours with good and evil.

Another significant feature about the race is the way it creates suspense by building upon this moral valence. As I have argued elsewhere (Romao 2004, 249), and following Noël Carroll's model (1996), for suspense to be produced in a film, a viewer must care for a character who is involved in a certain course of action that is perceived as the morally correct outcome, but is less likely to eventuate. As a result of the sympathy elicited towards Ben-Hur through Messala's previous treacherous actions, the viewer is cued to care for Ben-Hur's welfare during the race. In addition, Ben-Hur's win is not depicted as a given, but is hard-fought, as he contends with Messala's lead, the set-back that places him in the back of the field, as well as Messala's violent attempts to prevent him from overtaking his chariot. Ben-Hur's win is not only a moral victory but a moment of emotional relief.

The chariot race is also exemplary with respect to its use of conventions that are more commonly associated with the automotive racing film despite their different modes of locomotion and contrasting historical settings. Messala takes on the role of the reckless racer who puts at risk his competitors through his dangerous actions of blocking the path of other racers by veering into their line. The dolphin lap counter in the chariot race has its analogue with the pit board that serves similar functions in automotive racing films. Obstacles in the form of track wreckage that racers must negotiate and the benefits of taking the inside line are also shared traits.

The chariot race also includes instances of vertical combination with the fight scenario, particularly through Messala's bladed chariot, that bears similarities with the instances of vertical combination in auto-racing scenes in which vehicular ramming and shunting reveal fight situations. Such combinations are taken to a higher level in the gladiatorial combat featured in *Death Race 2000* (1975) and its rebooted franchise, commencing with *Death Race* (Paul W.S. Anderson, 2008), where the fight situations are showcased as much as the races themselves. Underlying these two different manifestations of the racing variant is speed itself that not only augments danger but the perception of action as well.

Chapter 8: Action Complexity and the Extended Action Sequence

O ne of the most notable developments in action sequences over the past few decades is their increased duration, particularly those found in the final act of a film. The concluding raid in *The Magnificent Seven* (Antoine Fuqua, 2016), for example, is a twenty-seven-minute affair, while the climactic battle sequence in *13 Assassins* (2010) runs close to forty-five minutes. Recent superhero films also abound with extended final act action set pieces. The battle of Sokovia in *Avengers: Age of Ultron* (2015) is close to twenty-five minutes in length, and the assault on Alcatraz in *X-Men: The Last Stand* (Brett Ratner, 2006) is twenty minutes in duration.

Although action scholar Lisa Purse (2015) has claimed that this development commenced in the 1990s, one can even go further back to the 1960s and observe notable increases in the duration of action sequences, often illustrated in James Bond films. For instance, Bond's escape from Dr. No's facility in *Dr. No* (1962) is over thirteen minutes in length, while the final underwater battle in *Thunderball* (1965) is a sixteen-minute plus action sequence. Nor are the decade's extended action sequences restricted to James Bond films. The train heist sequence in *The Wild Bunch* (1969) discussed in Chapter 4 runs just over fifteen minutes in length. Such extended action sequences manifested in 1960s films accord with Paul Monaco's description of the decade as the "cinema of sensation", and aesthetic that involved a change in shot and scene construction (2001, 2). Going back even further to the silent cinema, one must also note the twenty-eight-minute rescue in *The Birth of a Nation* (1915) as the progenitor of the extended action sequence.

Five Features of Action Complexity

One major question that arises when examining extended action sequences is how they are able to sustain viewer interest over such long stretches of screen time. I propose that such sustained interest is maintained as a result of action complexity, which manifests five essential features. The first feature of action complexity consists of multiple characters that feature in the sequence. *The Magnificent Seven* (John Sturges, 1960), for instance, features seven gunfighters that defend a Mexican village from a horde of bandits and follows the multi-character plot structure of *Seven Samurai* (Akira Kurosawa, 1954), the film upon which it was based. Significantly, some of the longest final act action sequences feature multiple protagonists, including *13 Assassins*, *The Avengers* (2012), *Avengers: Age of Ultron*, *The Magnificent Seven* (2016), *Guardians of the Galaxy Vol. 2* (James Gunn, 2017), *Avengers: Infinity War* (2018), *X-Men: The Last Stand*, and *X-Men* (2000). Such characters, in addition, possess individuating traits that are manifested in the sequence, as well as manifested in the overall film, and is increasingly the case, appear across a franchise.

Such multi-character sequences are to be distinguished from those scenes that merely feature multiple participants, what Kristen Whissel has labelled the "digital multitude" (2014, 68), characters, in other words, that are CGI created and do not manifest any individuating character traits. As noted in Chapter 5, the individuation of participants features especially in the fight scenario where one-on-one fight better facilitates such individuation, as illustrated by the Jason Bourne fight with Jarda in *The Bourne Supremacy* (2004), compared to the lack of individuation amongst the 'digital multitudes' featured in the multi-participant final battle in *The Hobbit: The Battle of the Five Armies* (2014).

The second feature of action complexity is the manifestation of multi-plotlines that are conveyed through parallel editing. It is one thing for a sequence to feature multiple individuated characters. It is a different order of complexity if the viewer is additionally tasked with following multiple characters in their own dedicated plotlines. At a minimum, parallel editing can alternate between the dramatic figures constituting the dyadic pairs that feature prominently in action scenarios. Parallel editing can cut from the narrative perspectives of the captive then switch to the rescuer, as manifested in *The Fatal Hour* (D.W. Griffith, 1908) that alternates between shots of a woman detective, bound and gagged facing a pistol set to fire when a clock strikes 12, and the police in a carriage, rushing to rescue her. Parallel editing has been used to switch between the escapee and the captor, as was the case in the scene in *Misery* (Rob Reiner, 1990) when Paul Sheldon, a famous author, attempts to escape on a wheelchair from the house of his captor, Annie Wilkes, who returns home and heads to the front door.

Switches in dyadic narrative perspective also recur in the capture scenario, as illustrated in the scene immediately after the train wreck in *The Fugitive* (1993), in which Deputy U.S. Marshal Samuel Gerard, the capturer, organizes a search and sweep for Dr. Richard Kimble, the target of the capture, who through parallel editing, is shown escaping from the vicinity of the crash. In a similar fashion, heist scenarios also employ parallel editing, as is the case in the extended heist sequence in *Rififi* (1955), in which the main plotline following a group of thieves breaking into a jewellery shop, to first cut to the exterior shots revealing the perspective of a guard making his rounds, and then later on, to return outside again revealing the narrational perspective of two police officers as potential capturers, thereby presenting all of the dramatic personages of the heist scenario prototype. Showdowns in westerns that involve fast draw duels are often presented through parallel editing patterns, such as the showdown between Paden, a former outlaw, and Sheriff Cobb in *Silverado* (Lawrence Kasdan, 1985).

Parallel editing is used routinely in pursuit sequences to alternate between the pursue and the pursued, as illustrated in many of the chases discussed in Chapter 6, a narrative structure that is already manifest in *The Runaway Match, or Marriage by Motor* (Alf Collins, 1903), the first film to feature a car chase, as an eloping couple are pursued by the fiancée's father. The racing variant of the speed scenario, particularly of the street racing kind, often take on a dyadic form between two racers, as the opening drag race does in *The Fast and the Furious: Tokyo Drift (2006)*, which also employs parallel editing to alternate between both of the racers to signal their respective positions during the race.

The relative complexity of such parallel editing depicting the dual story paths of dyadic pairs pales in comparison to the increased complexity of action sequences that offer a far greater number of plotlines. With respect to the rescue scenario, the final rescue sequence in *The Birth of a Nation* involved four separate plotlines, whereas the extended rescue sequence in *Superman* (1978) manifested ten different rescue situations possessing their own distinct storylines.

The escape scenario can also produce sequences possessing multi-plotlines, as illustrated in the second escape segment in *The Great Escape* (1963) that not only features eight individuated escapees, making the sequence multi-character but whose escape is depicted through six separate plotlines. The raid scene in *Point Break* (1991) presents a multi-plotline capture situation in which a team of five FBI agents assemble at the home of a surfer gang. Of the five agents, Johnny Utah and Angelo Pappas are granted their own plotlines throughout the raid, with the members of the surfer gang also granted their own narrational perspectives as they resist arrest and attempt to escape capture. In the heist sequence *Ocean's Eleven* (Steven Soderbergh, 2001), Danny Ocean, a con artist, leads a crew of ten accomplices to steal from a vault that holds the cash of three casinos owned by Terry Benedict, with each member of the team serving a function in the heist that is presented through multiple plotlines. The climactic heist sequence in *Fast Five* (2011) assumes a similar form to the heist sequence of *Ocean's Eleven* through its reliance upon multiple characters and multiple narrational perspectives, but in the context of an action combination of a multi-vehicle pursuit with a heist. Superhero films that feature multiple superheroes also provide multi-plotline opportunities. In the opening fight sequence in *Avengers: Age of Ultron*, six of the Avengers — Hawkeye, Black Widow, Iron

Man, Thor, Captain America, and the Hulk — are assembled together in a digitally seamed long take, after which they are narratively disassembled to assume their own plot perspectives as they combat enemy Hydra forces. The opening street race in *2 Fast 2 Furious* (John Singleton, 2003) doubles the number of participants in the opening drag race in *The Fast and the Furious: Tokyo Drift* and provides the narrational perspective of each of the four racers. As these cases illustrate, the inclusion of multiple characters possessing their own plotlines within extended action sequences prompts the viewer to attend to the different character experiences that the sequences provide, often possessing their own distinctive dramatic arcs.

The third feature of action complexity consists of those mechanisms that sustain viewer interest through narrative means, a feature that underscores the storytelling dimensions of action sequences through their dramatic structures and character goals. Two related narrative strategies come into play. The first is viewer interest, which media psychologist Ed Tan portrays as the investment in time and mental effort to follow a film, on the basis of the narrative expectations that a film sets up as to how its story will unfold (1996, 96-102). Such considerations also apply to extended action sequences that prompt viewer expectations as to how the sequence will narratively progress and resolve, expectations that have been discussed in this book under the rubric of dramatic structure, threshold events, and ascendancy. The second narrative strategy is suspense, which was defined in Chapter 7, and involves the viewer's emotional stake by caring for a character who is involved in a certain course of action that is perceived as the morally correct outcome but is less likely to eventuate.

An examination of the pursuit sequence in *Mission: Impossible - Ghost Protocol* (2011) can demonstrate how spectatorial interest and suspense are maintained throughout an action sequence. IMF agent Ethan Hunt is accused of bombing the Kremlin, heightening tensions between the United States and Russia. They discover the person responsible for the bombing is Kurt Hendricks, who used the attack as a diversion to steal a launch-control device to start a nuclear war. His right-hand man, Marius Wistrom, is due to meet Sabine Moreau, a contract killer who Hendricks hired to obtain the nuclear launch codes, at the Burj Khalifa in Dubai to exchange the launch codes for her payment in diamonds. Hunt and his crew - William Brandt, Benji Dunn and Jane Carter - come up with an elaborate plan to locate Hendricks by following Wistrom's trail. Carter will pretend to be Moreau as a means to identify Wistrom, while at the same time in a room just below, Hunt and Brandt will pretend to be Wistrom and his code verifying assistant to obtain the nuclear codes from Moreau. Brandt is to be fitted with a special contact lens that relays the codes to a briefcase that is in Carter's possession, from which the codes are to be printed but scrambled. In addition, the paper in which the codes are to be printed possesses isotopes that allow them to be tracked.

While preparing for the exchange, the IMF crew realize that Wistrom has brought along to the meeting Leonid Lisenker, a Polish cryptographer, who can verify if the codes are authentic, motivating the crew to instead provide Wistrom with the real codes instead of the fake ones, adding more risk to their mission. The exchange initially goes as planned, and when Lisenker confirms the authenticity of the codes, Wistrom snatches them and abruptly leaves, and after Lisenker exits as well with him into the hallway, Wistrom shoots him to cover his tracks.

Moreau in the other room then identifies Brandt as a spy when she spots Brandt's contact lens and orders her two assistants to kill him. While Hunt and Brant fight with Moreau's assistants, she flees the room in an attempted escape. Hunt orders Carter to stop her while he tracks down Wistrom. As Carter captures Moreau, Hunt follows Wistrom down the elevators, using his phone as a tracking device to lock onto the printed codes that Wistrom possesses. At the main lobby, Hunt spots Wistrom exiting a set of revolving doors, and as he tries to follow, a family enters the doors from the other side, blocking his path. Hunt detours to an alternative exit and heads to the escalator that Wistrom is beginning to descend, and just before he can continue with his tracking, he is held at gunpoint by Anatoly Sidorov and his assistant, Russian agents seeking to capture Hunt, still under the mistaken impression that he was responsible for the Kremlin bombing. Hunt asserts that it was a setup and attempts to escape from Sidorov, who discharges his gun, alerting Wistrom in the process. Hunt then slams the weapon into the faces of the two Russian agents, and tosses one down the escalator, while the other is thrown into the adjacent stairway. He then speeds down the steps to the hotel's drive-through to search for Wistrom, who he sees escaping on foot, and pursues after him.

Interest at this point in the sequence functions to answer viewer expectations with regard to Hunt's immediate goal not to lose Wistrom, which becomes the foreground viewer concern, while his broader goal of locating Hendricks shifts temporarily to the background. It is also at this point that suspense begins to peak as the viewer's emotional engagement with Hunt increases as a result of the fact that his ability to follow Wistrom is put into jeopardy by the obstacles put in his path, in the first instance in the form of a family blocking the revolving doors, in the second in the form of the Russian agents, suspense that is considerably heightened by the fact that Wistrom is escaping with codes that could start a nuclear war. The film cuts back to the interior of the Burj Khalifa as Brandt attends to the dying Lisenker, while Moreau attacks Dunn, causing Carter to fight it out with her and kick her through an open window to her death, a narrative tactic to delay story information concerning the pursuit.

The film returns to the foot chase below, and a large sandstorm arrives, making it more difficult for Hunt to keep track of Wistrom in the blinding sand. As Hunt catches up, Wistrom wheels around and fires at him with his pistol, but Hunt knocks the weapon out of his hand, and they briefly tussle, but Wistrom eludes Hunt's grasp. Wistrom runs through a market, but Hunt struggles to keep track of him through the aisles, and when he reaches an exit, he pulls out his phone to check the tracking device to search for Wistrom's location. The tracker shows Wistrom bearing down at Hunt at speed. Seeing the headlights of Wistrom's vehicle, Hunt leaps up and is able to cling onto the car and clambers to its roof. Hunt then punches and grabs Wistrom's head through the open driver's window, yet Wistrom steers the vehicle into a market canopy, forcing Hunt off the car and onto the street below. In Hunt's hands is a part of a rubber mask that he ripped off Wistrom's face, indicating that his pursuee is not Wistrom after all. The film cuts to Wistrom's impostor in the car, but the shattered windshield obscure's his facial feature, keeping his identity a mystery.

At this stage of the pursuit, interest and suspense manifest themselves at the micro-event level. The blinding sandstorm, Wistrom's attempt to shoot Hunt, and to run him down later, constitute salient micro-events that direct the viewer's attention onto them as foreground concerns, as attention to broader character goals shifts to the background. Interest consequently forges short-term expectations as to the outcome of these micro-events, whereas suspense becomes focused upon the immediate hazards that they pose to Hunt, risks that in these cases assume the form of attempts upon his life. Interest also peaks at the point when the viewer's understanding of the story is challenged when it is revealed that someone is masquerading as Wistrom, with expectations directed at whom this impostor will prove to be later in the story.

After falling off the vehicle, Hunt is able to establish that the impostor is still within range and absconds in a nearby vehicle, changing the mode of pursuit in the sequence, and consequently modulating the underlying narrative expectations and the conditions of suspense. Hunt then weaves through traffic along a freeway, with visibility reduced as a result of the sand storm, making his pursuit even more hazardous. Noticing on his tracker that the impostor is heading off the freeway at the next cloverleaf interchange, Hunt crosses into the opposing lane to also exit off the throughway as a means to intercept him on the bridge. Just before the two vehicles collide, Hunt leaps out, sending the other car spinning overhead, narrowly missing Hunt as it crashes. Checking the upturned vehicle and finding it empty, Hunt spots the impostor fleeing on foot and runs after him, and just before he can catch up, the impostor grabs onto a passing open truck and climbs aboard. Hunt runs after the vehicle, changing the mode of pursuit once again, but is not fast enough to keep up. The impostor peels off his mask revealing himself to be Hendricks all along, Hunt's primary target, yet watches him slip out of reach, ending his chase. Although the pursuit sequence does not approach the length of longer final act set pieces, the chase is still representative of the mechanisms of interest and suspense that are used in longer action sequences where background and foreground expectations are mobilized through a chain of micro-events and suspense is maintained by placing characters in evolving contexts of jeopardy.

The fourth feature of action complexity is the significant turning points that are manifested in the plot of an extended action sequence, which also constitute narrative mechanisms that drive viewer interest. Such plot points are normally understood as moments in a narrative where the story is taken in a new direction, often resulting in a change of goals for the main character (Colman et al. 2013; Thompson 1999). For instance, in the *Mission: Impossible - Ghost Protocol* pursuit sequence, a major plot turn occurred with Hunt's discovery that someone was masquerading as Wistrom, which is later revealed to be Hendricks, who was able to elude capture. Such plot points are usually identified as the turning points that divide the overarching story into acts. However, plot points can also be manifested at the local level of a sequence or scene.

As has been noted, action scenarios possess event structure, with the segmentation of that structure often falling on the plot points that represent a turn in the action. As illustrated in the *Mission: Impossible - Ghost Protocol* pursuit sequence, such micro-plot turning points would coincide when the impostor's change mode of locomotion from foot to automobile, changing the complexion of the chase, as well as Hunt's change in locomotion from foot to automobile, facilitating his effort to intercept the impostor on the overpass. Another significant benefit of introducing turning points in extended action sequences is to facilitate viewer comprehension. Thompson has claimed that one of the main reasons why a film's story is broken into smaller parts is to assist in its comprehension

(1999, 22). Given the prolonged durations of extended action sequences, such logic in breaking down its plotline into smaller digestible chunks equally applies as a means to assist the viewer in following its narrative development.

So far, the four features discussed have been those that are not distinctive to action sequences. Many films possess multiple individuated characters who also possess their own distinct plotlines but do not feature significant levels of action, as the films of Robert Altman attest (Azcona, 2010). Similarly, interest and suspense are basic features of engaging with narrative film, as well as non-fiction. Their use in the design of action sequences attests then to the narrative dimensions of action and the ability of these features to help craft extended action sequences. Plot points, in addition, are universal features of mainstream narrative film.

However, the fifth feature of action complexity is distinctive to action sequences since it relates to the phenomenon of action scenario combination. Such combinations can be manifested at the level of typicality gradient, in which the sequence explores different variants of a particular action scenario, as was the case with the extended rescue sequence in *Superman*, or that a sequence runs the gamut of action scenario combinations, whether vertical or horizontal in nature, as initially illustrated in the climactic action sequence in *Lethal Weapon* (1987) that features instances of the escape, rescue, fight, and the pursuit scenarios, and ends with the destruction variant.

The contribution of action combinations to sustaining extended action sequences is twofold. First, variations on action situations over the course of a sequence itself renews interest at the level of action form. A twenty-minute pursuit sequence may exhaust viewer engagement, but an action sequence that horizontally mutates into other action forms, as well as vertically combines with other scenarios, can sustain interest as a continually evolving narrative context. Second, as shown in *Mission: Impossible – Ghost Protocol* chase, interest and suspense do not remain static throughout a sequence containing combinations and changes in modes of pursuit, but instead modulate in relation to the specific action contexts in which the characters are situated. The sequence, for instance, commences with an initial fight situation with Moreau's assistants, then enters into another fight situation with the Russian agents, then transforms into a foot pursuit, and then changes its mode of pursuit to an automotive chase, to revert back to a foot chase. In each of these phases of the action sequence, interest and suspense modulated to the contours of the action context, at both the micro and macro event level, thereby refreshing the spectator's expectations and modifying the nature of the suspense generated.

While these five features are also manifested in shorter action sequences, they go a long way to explain how action sequences can be sustained for much longer stretches without necessarily sacrificing spectatorial engagement. While extended action sequences will differ with regard to the degree that they deploy these five features in tandem, a general pattern emerges as to their overall form. Extended action scenes frequently exhibit parallel plots that fit into a broader plot structure, especially in cases in which individuated characters work together toward a coordinated goal. Individuated characters pursue their sub-goals in dedicated plotlines consisting of micro-events. Interest and suspense are also expressed at the local and global level, with respect to the immediate character goals along a specific plotline, and are also directed at the fate of the broader mission, which are further modulated by the evolving action forms in which the characters are situated. The extended action sequence exhibits an overarching structure of peril consisting of micro and macro events, in which character goals are manifested at the local and global level, situated in action forms that come in the form of vertical and horizontal combinations, all of which sustain an evolving flow of interest and suspense. The extended action sequence is, therefore, the prototype of action complexity.

Exemplar: The Avengers (2012)

To illustrate how these five features of action complexity are manifested in an extended action sequence, the thirty-one-minute final act sequence in *The Avengers* (2012), often referred to as the Battle of New York, will be analyzed. The film itself is a pivotal entry in the Marvel Cinematic Universe, which concludes the first phase of the series by bringing together the superhero characters introduced in earlier MCU installments, namely, Iron Man, the Hulk, Black Widow, Hawkeye, Thor, and Captain America, setting up a multi-protagonist framework for the film's narrative structure. A key theme of the film is how superheroes overcome their egos and divisions to work together as a unified team, a recurrent convention common to other films in a variety of genres that feature characters working together in a collective capacity (Strong, 2006). As we shall shortly see, this theme of team unison is stylistically expressed in the sequence as moments of interconnecting sub-plots as well as shots that connect the narrative spaces of such plotlines. Hence the notion of assemblage that is invoked in the film's release title - *Avengers Assemble* – which exhibits three interrelated senses: a franchise marketing strategy that promotes the assemblage of superheroes in the film; a narrative strategy centring upon multiple protagonists assembled together as a working team; and a stylistic strategy that metaphorically expresses the theme of assembled unity through interconnecting subplots and linked narrative spaces.

Narrative Set Up and Unity Theme

Given the degree to which the final action sequence interlinks with the themes of team unity in *The Avengers*, it necessary to first outline its story in detail. The narrative context of the final action sequence is initially established at the start of the film in a brief scene set in some distant corner of outer space in which a robed figure, named The Other, informs an unseen ruler, later revealed to be Thanos, of a plan to obtain the Tesseract, a cube with boundless energy. The plan entails securing the service of Loki, a disgraced Asgardian and Thor's adopted brother, who agrees to obtain the Tesseract from Earth in exchange for a powerful scepter that permits him to control the Chitauri army, an alien race, as a means to conquer the planet and subjugate Earth's people. At a desert facility in New Mexico, the Tesseract energizes and creates a wormhole portal, through which Loki appears and uses his scepter to control the minds of Erik Selvig, an astrophysicist, and Clint Barton (also known as Hawkeye, a superhero with superior archery skills) to do his bidding. Nick Fury, the director of S.H.I.E.L.D., a secret government agency, attempts to sneak away with the Tesseract but is stopped by Loki, who intimates his aim to conquer humankind. Barton then shoots Fury, and as Loki's party leaves with the Tesseract, the facility begins to collapse as a result of the portal destabilizing.

Fury survives the attack and initiates the Avengers Initiative, a plan to mobilize individuals with exceptional power to defend the world from global threats, through which Natasha Romanoff, Dr. Bruce Banner, Tony Stark, and Steve Rogers (the civilian aliases for the Black Widow, the Hulk, Iron Man, and Captain America) are recruited.[1] Meanwhile, at Loki's hideout, Selvig requires iridium to stabilize the Tesseract to open the portal again. Barton and Loki head to Stuttgart, where a scientist has a reserve. However, Loki is detected by S.H.I.E.L.D. in Stuttgart, prompting Fury to send Captain America and Black Window to capture him. Loki and Captain America soon battle it out, but Iron Man arrives, and with his unsolicited assistance, are able to persuade Loki to surrender.

As the three Avengers escort Loki back to S.H.I.E.L.D.'s Helicarrier in a quinjet, Thor appears and seizes Loki from the jet and takes him to a nearby forest and demands that he hand over the Tesseract and abandon his mad project. Before Thor can proceed any further, Iron Man arrives and engages in battle with Thor, underscoring the need for unity amongst the team. Captain America attempts to intervene in their fight, but Thor strikes his vibranium shield with his hammer, sending a shock wave through

---

[1] Given that these characters are designated by both their civilian and superhero names in the film, switches in reference in this discussion will be based whether their appearance in a scene is in a superhero or civilian mode.

the forest, knocking all three down. Sensing the destruction they could wreak in conflict with one another, Thor acquiesces to Captain America's common sense to stop the fight and joins the team as they transport Loki to the Helicarrier. While there, Loki is imprisoned on the Helicarrier in a glass cell designed originally for the Hulk in the event Banner would not be able to contain his rage.

It is at this point in the story that the Avengers appear at their most disunited and distrustful. While Stark and Banner try to locate the Tesseract in a laboratory through its gamma radiation signature, Rogers joins them. As Stark and Rogers' personalities clash, Stark informs him that he had secretly planted a decryption device on the Helicarrier's bridge to discover what Fury is hiding. Banner also shares his suspicions with Rogers that Fury has not been entirely open about the Tesseract and its use by S.H.I.E.L.D. With those seeds of doubt planted, Rogers leaves the laboratory to search the ship and discovers weaponry used by Hydra, a terrorist organization that he fought during World War II in *Captain America: The First Avenger* (Joe Johnston, 2011). At the same time, Romanoff is engaged in conversation with Loki and erroneously infers that he plans to unleash the Hulk to create chaos, which in turn makes her wary of Banner. Fury then enters the lab, suspecting that Stark was behind the hack. Stark's decryption device then discovers secret files in S.H.I.E.L.D.'s mainframe, prompting Stark to ask Fury, "What is Phase 2?". Rogers then bursts in and slams a Hydra weapon on a table and states with evident anger directed at Fury that Phase 2 is S.H.I.E.L.D. using the cube to make weapons. Fury tries to deflect Roger's discovery, but Stark presents a diagram revealing a missile using the Tesseract's energy source as a payload.

Just as suspicions come out in the open, Thor and Romanoff then enter the lab, with Banner pointedly asking Romanoff if she was aware of the covert program, who responds with equal distrust that Loki is manipulating him. Breaking off from the sniping match, Banner turns to Fury and poses the question as to the reason why S.H.I.E.L.D. is using the Tesseract to build weapons of mass destruction. Fury then points accusatorily at Thor, stating that "It was because of him". Fury goes onto explain that Thor's previous visit to Earth resulted in the destruction of a town when he battled the Destroyer, an automaton sent by Loki to kill Thor, as depicted in the earlier installment *Thor* (Kenneth Branagh, 2011), bringing about an awareness of potential threats from outside of the solar system, as well as that on Earth, necessitating a defensive system. But most of the Avengers remain unconvinced. Rogers points out that Fury was unable to control the cube, while Thor blames his tampering with the Tesseract as what attracted Loki and his allies to it in the first place. The argument degenerates as the characters taking petty swipes at each other, to the point they become unintelligible through overlapping dialogue and remain oblivious to the fact that the blue gem in Loki's scepter begins to glow. The film captures this moment by rotating the camera upside down, presenting an inverted image of unity as the team are presented at their most divisive, where interlinkages amongst them do not signal solidarity but distrust for one another [*Figure* 9.1].

Figure 9.1 Inversion of team unity in
The Avengers (2012).

The film then cuts to the interior cockpit of a transport jet, which locks into the signal from Loki's energized scepter as a means to guide it to the Helicarrier. Aboard are Barton and a crew of rogue agents assisting him, who prepare to attack the Helicarrier and rescue Loki, to whom Barton still serves. Barton's actions further underscore the theme of disunity by presenting a member of the Avengers but who is under the spell of their enemy. The film then cuts back to the lab as the heated argument continues, with Banner offering a darker metaphor of their disunity by asserting, "I mean, what are we, a team? No, we're a chemical mixture that makes chaos. We're a time bomb". As if to illustrate Banner's point, Rogers accuses Stark that he is no hero and is unable to make a 'sacrifice play', and before they come to blows, the film cuts back to Barton on the transport jet, as he fires an arrow at the Helicarrier's hull, attached with a timed explosive.

Back at the lab, tensions continue to boil, but two events occur at the precise narrative mid-point of the film. The first consists of the tracking device locating the Tesseract in the vicinity of New York, preparing the viewer for the battle to come, with the second presenting Barton triggering an explosion that takes out one of the turbine engines of the Helicarrier. The explosion also sets in motion a seventeen-minute extended action sequence that manifests multi-protagonists, features multiple narrative threads, and develops along a path of action combinations that imbue interest and suspense. From that moment onward, the first plotline of teamwork and unison begins to emerge.

Instead of Stark suiting up to fight Rogers, he puts on his Iron Man armour to work in unison with Rogers and Fury to get the craft back in working order. However, the blast sent Romanoff and Banner crashing down to another level, pinning Romanoff in the debris as she watches with alarm Banner turning into the Hulk, a chemical time bomb and agent of chaos not dissimilar to the description of the team he had earlier described. As Romanoff frees herself, she tries to escape from the enraged Hulk pursuing her, leaving a trail of destruction. Just when the Hulk has Romanoff cornered, Thor blasts through a wall, taking the Hulk with him into the aircraft hangar, affecting an embedded rescue.

Thor and the Hulk commence to brawl, prompting Agent Maria Hill to alert Fury of the danger that the rampaging Hulk can do to the ship if unchecked. Fury advises creating a 'distraction', which Hill does by ordering a jet to fire upon the Hulk. Enraged, the Hulk leaps upon the jet and rips it to pieces as the pilot jettisons. The plane explodes, causing the Hulk to fall to Earth, with his danger to the Helicarrier neutralized.

As Iron Man and Captain America continue to fix the Helicarrier, the narrative then shifts to resolving the two remaining plotlines, both of which are cross-cut with each other, in ways that lay the foundations for the unity that the Avengers team requires to halt the invasion threat in the final action sequence. The first consists of responding to Barton's attack on the ship, as Fury hails over the radio for assistance to stop him. Romanoff, still shaken by her encounter with the Hulk, acknowledges the call and leaves to locate Barton. She finds him, and they engage in hand-to-hand combat. Romanoff slams his head against a railing and slugs him, knocking Barton out and releasing him from Loki's spell.

The second plotline concerns Thor and any remaining familial allegiance with Loki holding him back from fully joining the Avengers team. This second narrative thread is picked up when Loki creates a holographic illusion of himself leaving the glass chamber, tricking Thor to rush in an effort to prevent his escape. The glass door soon shuts behind, trapping Thor in the cell, with Loki gazing upon his trapped brother, along with one of Barton's rogue agents who presumably had freed him earlier from the chamber. As Loki is about to jettison the cell, he hears the sound of the assisting rogue agent hitting the grilled floor as S.H.I.E.L.D. agent Phil Coulson appears, brandishing a large weapon who orders Loki to move away from the control panel to the cell. But Loki performs his hologram trick again and materializes behind Coulson and gore's him with the blade of his scepter. Pointing at the bloodied blade with a smirk, Loki reveals his monstrous self and presses the button that releases the cell, and Thor within it, to plummet to his presumed death. As the cell tumbles, the approaching land sets a deadline for Thor to escape, which he does by finally smashing through the glass just before the cell collides with the ground. Iron Man and Captain America finally get the turbine engine to function again, saving the Helicarrier and its crew from an imminent crash, yet Loki manages to escape on the transport jet, which concludes the seventeen-minute action sequence and sets up the final confrontation to come.

The film, therefore, places the unity of the Avengers team as one of its central dramatic concerns. Although the first Avenger mission in Stuttgart was successful, Iron Man's arrival was unplanned and he behaved like a maverick, heralding future friction through his lack of ability to conform. On the way back to the Helicarrier, Thor next intervenes in the team's plans to take Loki as a prisoner, thereby provoking a fight between him and Iron Man, which offered a glimpse of the potentially destructive force of their disunity.

Their antagonisms and mistrust towards one another come to a head just before the narrative mid-point of the film, with Barton's attack on the Helicarrier instigating the commencement of narrative threads of unity, starting with Iron Man and Captain America's teamwork, a rescue effort to save the craft from crashing to the Earth. Barton's concussion finally frees him from Loki's grip, which returns him to the team with the pointed aim of defeating his previous master. The Hulk who was initially portrayed as an agent of disruption through his uncontrolled rage directed at Romanoff and later Thor, but when he re-joins the team in the concluding battle, that anger is redirected at Loki and his Chitauri army, implying that in the intervening period, Banner was able to gain greater control over his monstrous green alter-ego, thereby becoming a reliable team member. Thor's antipathy toward Loki is also solidified by witnessing him murder Coulson, as well as through his attempt at fratricide by dropping him out of the sky, actions that push Thor to work in greater unison with the other Avengers to resist the alien invasion. Coulson's death, in addition, takes on a sacrificial dimension to the cause of team unity, a sacrifice that Fury later uses to manipulate Rogers and Stark to overcome their differences and work together, by presenting them with Coulson's Captain America card set, seemingly blood-stained through his death, but later revealed to be bloodied by Fury to pretend the cards were with Coulson when he died.

The Battle of New York: Linked Narrative Spaces and Interconnecting Plotlines

It is notable that Coulson's card set, appropriately symbolic of a belief in superheroes, features in the first shot of the Battle of New York sequence. When Fury is confronted by Agent Hill at the bridge of the Helicarrier about his lie to Rogers and Stark, Fury sighs and explains, "They needed the push". As he gazes meditatively at the cards, Iron Man can be seen rocketing past in the distant background with the quinjet following at speed, conveying Hawkeye, Black Widow and Captain America [*Figure 9.2*].

Figure 9.2 Linked narrative spaces in
The Avengers (2012).

Not only does the shot confirm the belief in superheroes as they hurry to confront Loki and his army through an opening speed scenario, but it also initiates a stylistic motif that runs through the action sequence of linked narrative spaces that are expressive of unity. Through an over-the-shoulder shot that approximates Fury's optical point-of-view, a line of vision links his narrative space with that of the space that Iron Man and the quinjet traverse, expressively connecting the two branching plotlines and their shared mission to defeat Loki and thwart his plans to conquer. With this initiating image, the plotlines in the action sequence start to multiply, as illustrated in Table 4, in relation to the major participants in the action that represent shifts in narrative perspective as the action sequence unfolds.

303

Table 4: Battle of New York Plot Structure*

Subplots	Characters and Key Narrative Events
1st Subplot	Bartlett MacDonald Ashley-Pitt Hendley Blythe Nick Fury and Agent Hill: monitor events on Helicarrier, deal with Council, and attempt to stop pilot's tack-off.
2nd Subplot	Iron Man: confronts Loki, counters Chitauri attacks, and redirects nuclear missile through the portal to the mothership.
3rd Subplot	Chitauri Army: descends through the portal, attacks citizens and battles Avengers.
4th Subplot	Citizens and police: citizens flee and take cover from attack. Police fire at Chitauri and heed Captain America's directions.
5th Subplot	Thor: fights with Loki and assists other Avengers in battle.
6th Subplot	Hawkeye, Black Widow, and Captain America: arrive in quinjet, engage with Chitauri, shot down by Loki, crash landing on the street, battle Chitauri, rescue civilians, eventually disassemble after the defeat of the first Leviathan to pursue different story functions.
7th Subplot	Loki: escapes Thor's wrath, calls in Chitauri reinforcements, pursues Black Widow, and is captured.
8th Subplot	The Hulk: defeats the first Leviathan, assists Avengers battling Chitauri, and rescues Iron Man.
9th Subplot	Captain America: rescues boxed-in citizens, directs police, battles Chitauri, rescues more citizens.
10th Subplot	Hawkeye: assists Iron Man and Black Widow from the top of a building.
11th Subplot	Black Widow: formulates a plan to shut the portal, commandeers Chitauri chariot, shuts down the portal.
12th Subplot	Selvig: awakens from the blast and assists Black Widow in shutting down the portal.
13th Subplot	Pilot: takes-off from Helicarrier and releases nuclear missile.

*The thirteen subplots in the battle sequence are listed in rows in order of appearance. New spin-off subplots are also listed when a character departs from a subplot to generate a new one.

Iron Man is then shown flying to the Stark Tower, with his armoured suit occasionally short-circuiting, due to it being severely damaged when fixing the turbine engine, motivating the need to change armour, thus making Stark temporarily vulnerable. Arriving at the Tower, Iron Man finds the Tesseract portal device set up by Selvig. Iron Man orders him to shut it down, and blasts the device with his gauntlet repulsors, but it sends him flying back, along with Selvig, as a result of the device's energy shield. Descending into the Tower's penthouse, and after removing his armour, he confronts Loki, who awaits the opening of the portal and the arrival of the Chitauri. Stark then pours himself a drink, an act that diverts Loki's attention, while he puts on a pair of bracelets that can activate the Mark VII armour, a new suit yet to be deployed.

After threatening Loki that all of the Avengers will be after him, Loki places the tip of his scepter on Stark's chest in an effort to control his mind, but his metallic chest piece makes Stark invulnerable to its power. In anger, Loki grabs Stark and throws him to the ground and picks him up again for a more lethal toss. Stark orders J.A.R.V.I.S., his computer interface system, to deploy the Mark VII armour. Loki smashes him through a window to tumble to the ground, invoking the falling variant of the speed scenario. The Mark VII fires out of a closet like a rocket pod that speeds after Stark on his downward trajectory, setting up a deadline to attach onto him before he hits the ground. The suit attaches onto Stark, and he deploys its jets and fires up vertically to the top of the Tower. Reminding Loki of Coulson's murder, Iron Man aims his right gauntlet repulsor at Loki, firing just before he can raise his scepter in defence, and blasts him to the floor.

The film cuts to the Tesseract powered device that shoots a vertical beam of energy opening a wormhole portal above the Stark Tower, and more ominously, over New York City. The Chitauri fleet of space chariots then makes their downward descent through the portal, with an optical point-of-view shot presenting the view from a Chitauri invader, which links the space of the invading force, presumably somewhere in a different part of the universe, with that of the space above New York's skyline, a linking of two intergalactic spaces upon which the invasion is predicated. Iron Man fires upward to engage with the oncoming enemy, staging a fight scenario firmly along the y-axis. A Chitauri invader fires first with his blaster, which Iron Man easily dodges, who then returns fire with his gauntlet repulsors, exploding one of the Chitauri's chariots. Iron Man next deploys miniature missiles from his suit and takes out a number of the invading chariots, but the Chitauri continue to pour out from the portal. Citizens watch in alarm from the streets below, who soon become targets of the invaders as they destructively blast at them, causing them to flee and take cover, vertically combining the fight scenario with the fleeing escape variant.

The film cuts to the Stark Tower as Loki surveys the devastation from the ongoing attack from above. Thor then lands on a balcony just below and orders Loki to turn off the Tesseract. Loki asserts that there is no stopping it; there is just the war, and when Thor responds, "So be it" Loki leaps down to attack. The two engage in combat using their specialized weapons, as Thor wards off the blasts from Loki's scepter with his hammer. A deflected blast sends one of the Stark Tower letters crashing downward, which motivates a cut to the streets below as citizens continue to flee. The police then arrive as the panicked pandemonium continues. An officer exits his car to gaze upward, providing a cue to an optical point-of-view shot of his visual perspective as Iron Man zooms past, pursued by several Chitauri chariots, linking the narrative space of the panicked streets with that of space of aerial combat-pursuits. The extended action sequence, therefore, proceeds along three axes of action. The first is played out along the y-axis of the vertical portal beam. The second is played out along the horizontal x-axis of the streets, while the third exploits both the x and y-axes through weaving aerial combat-pursuits.

The quinjet finally arrives, introducing a 6th subplot, as Black Widow informs Iron Man that they are headed Northeast and on the trail of the Chitauri pursuing him. Remarking about their lateness, Stark jibes if they had stopped at a drive-thru, but more importantly, instructs Black Widow to fly up Park Avenue while he leads the pursuing Chitauri to cross their path, a coordinated act underscoring their team effort. The composition of next shot depicts Loki and Thor still locked in battle in the foreground, while Iron Man and the pursuing Chitauri zoom past the Stark Tower in the background, thereby linking their two narrative spaces momentarily.

Iron Man executes a sharp bank causing one of the Chitauri chariots to crash into a building and leading the rest in front of the path of the quinjet. Black Widow is next shown deploying the quinjet's Gatling gun, quickly followed by an interior shot of its cockpit revealing Iron Man flying past horizontally, another linking of narrative spaces, just before Black Widow lights up the pursuing Chitauri with a spray of bullets. Iron Man is informed by J.A.R.V.I.S. of more incoming Chitauri, with the next shot presenting the quinjet amidst a swarm of Chitauri, while shooting down several of their chariots.

The film then returns to the fight atop Stark Tower, as Loki slams Thor's head into a glass panel. Hawkeye and Black Widow are shown observing their fight below, with the next shot depicting their perspective from the cockpit, linking their narrative space with that of Thor and Loki's location [*Figure* 9.3]. Hawkeye notifies Black Widow of Loki's presence and positions the quinjet so she can take a shot at him. The film cuts back to the Stark Tower fight, with Loki getting the upper hand by knocking Thor down with his scepter, with the next shot a reversal of the previous linking shot by presenting Loki's narrative perspective, who is fired at by the quinjet and responds by blasting it with his scepter, destroying one of its turbines [*Figure* 9.4]. The shot not only links the two narrative spaces but also offers the sequence's first subplot intersection through their causal interconnection. The two plotlines are then rapidly intercut, a cross-cutting that ends with the crash landing of the quinjet onto a street below. Despite the crash, Hawkeye, Black Widow, and Captain America emerge from the craft unscathed and enter into a boulevard filled with New Yorkers fleeing in fear as the Chitauri swarm overhead.

Figure 9.3 Linked narrative spaces in
The Avengers (2012).

Figure 9.4 Causal interconnections in
The Avengers (2012).

As the three head toward Grand Central Station, they pause, staring upward after hearing a metallic groan from above. Emerging from the portal amongst another wave of Chitauri invaders is a Leviathan, a colossal entity resembling a gigantic sea creature that is cybernetically enhanced and which additionally serves as a transport vehicle for the invading Chitauri army. The shot of its entry through the portal underscores the link narrative spaces that the wormhole permits, and its downward descent to fly just above the boulevard in full view of the three Avengers also connects the different levels and axes of action in which the extended sequence is staged. As the Leviathan passes along the boulevard, Chitauri invaders are ejected from its body and attach themselves along the sides of adjacent buildings, while others are fired directing into buildings where they commence attacking civilians.

Given this pivotal plot turn, it would be useful to note how viewer interest and suspense have been mobilized so far in the sequence. The broader expectations concerning the outcome of the battle initially triggered when Iron Man and the quinjet departed from the Helicarrier are relegated to background concerns with the sequence's major plot turns generating interest at the foreground level. Such major plot turns consist of events relating to the invasion itself and the gradual addition of Avengers to combat them. The first major plot turn of the sequence consists of the portal opening allowing the Chitauri invaders to pour in, with expectations directed as to how Iron Man will confront the initial wave. The second major plot turn pertained to the arrival of the Leviathan, constituting a significant escalation in the attack, with expectations turning to how the Avengers will combat the creature as well as the additional Chitauri invaders it transports.

The gradual arrival of the Avengers also constitutes moments of spiked interest, setting up expectations as to their individual contributions in the battle. Suspense is also tied to the major plot turns of the invasion, to the degree they impinge upon the broader project of the Avengers to defeat the invading forces. The significant number of the Chitauri invaders that initially swarm out of the portal is alarming, especially in relation to the fact that Iron Man is the sole Avenger present to counter-attack. Similarly, the arrival of the Leviathan constitutes an ominous turn in the overall battle, testing the ability of the Avengers to respond in kind.

Suspense is also triggered at the micro-event level during intense moments of peril and vulnerability for the Avengers. For instance, when Stark is tossed out of the window by Loki, suspense is generated whether the Mark VII armour will attach to Stark in time. The moment when Loki blasts the quinjet offers another micro-event, triggering suspense as to whether the Avengers inside the craft will survive the crash without significant injury. However, suspense is not generated in relation to the fleeing citizens despite the fact they are the targets of lethal attack from the Chitauri invaders, given that they are not sufficiently individuated as characters to provoke sustained sympathy, nor are they offered the same degrees of screen time as the Avengers. The only citizen who receives a slightly greater degree of individuation is Beth, a young waitress, who is shown twice in the sequence: first fleeing from the first wave of the Chitauri attack, then later rounded up with other citizens by the Chitauri. She appears later in the denouement in a news item defending the actions of the Avengers and thanks Captain America for saving her life. In such ways, the narrative function of civilians is primarily to highlight the rescue heroics of the Avengers rather than function as targets of narrative interest or sympathy for spectators.

The narrative switches to Iron Man's narrative perspective, as he processes how to take on the Leviathan, and queries Captain American if Banner has arrived, providing a clue how Iron Man plans to defeat the creature. As Iron Man flies parallel with it, he tries to locate a weak spot, as the Leviathan slices through a building with one of its fins. The film returns to Stark Tower, with Thor trying to appeal to reason to convince Loki to call off the invasion, as well as provide sibling support while doing so, but Loki treacherously uses the opportunity to stab him in his abdomen. Thor temporarily collapses, holding himself up with his right hand, then charges at Loki in a rage, kicking him into a glass panel, to then pick him up and throw him forcibly onto the balcony floor. Before Thor has an opportunity to attack again, Loki rolls off the edge of the Tower and onto a passing Chitauri chariot. Flying amongst a swarm of Chitauri, the chariots weave their way through the streets, with a brief cut back to Thor removing the blade away and tossing it aside in anger.

The film returns to the action on the streets, with the three Avengers taking cover behind a taxi abandoned on a bridge, just when Loki and a pack of Chitauri zip past, constituting a connecting thread of action from the previous fight atop the Stark Tower. The film then assumes the narrative perspective of the speeding Chitauri, who fire at the fleeing civilians below, cutting to a quick frontal shot of Loki leading the pack, to return to shots of their attack on the civilians. The film cuts back to the three Avengers, revealing Captain America's view of the beleaguered civilians, who observes that "They're a fish in a barrel down there". Black Widow gets up and fires a couple of rounds at the advancing

Chitauri infantry unit as Hawkeye hurries to obtain a better position. Black Widow and Hawkeye assure Captain America that they can hold off the Chitauri unit on their own. Hawkeye then gets up and quickly fires off two arrows into the heads of a couple of Chitauri, with Black Widow firing further rounds at them as a means to provide cover for Captain America, who he leaps from the bridge onto a bus below in an effort to rescue the trapped civilians, all the while avoiding the blasts from surrounding Chitauri. This temporary split from Black Widow and Hawkeye represents a minor sub-plotline, but a form of separation that is not based upon disunity but instead upon coordinated action.

The film cuts back to Black Widow keeping the Chitauri at bay while Hawkeye rescues civilians trapped in a bus and directs them to safety. Black Widow continues with her fire, with the film cutting to a Chitauri receiving a shot to its head, and cuts back to reveal Hawkeye joining Black Widow and engaging with the Chitauri with his trademark archery. The film returns to Captain America running at speed and leaping over obstacles with ease. Panicked citizens are again shown, further motivating Captain America's need to rescue them, followed by shots of the police firing at the overhead flying Chitauri chariots. A young NYPD officer is shown pleading to a Police Sergeant to call in the National Guard, revealing in the process how the police are wholly unequipped to deal with the attack.

Captain America then arrives, intersecting his sub-plotline with that of the citizens and police on the street, and gives them a series of orders to take the exposed civilians to safety and to set up a perimeter to keep them out of the battle area. The Police Sergeant queries why he should take orders from him, and as if in response, Captain America wards off a Chitauri attack before the eyes of the police officers. Convinced of Captain America's fighting credentials, the Police Sergeant parrots his orders to the police in the area through his two-way radio, thereby instituting Captain America's rescue plan.

The film returns to the narrative perspective of Iron Man zooming around a building to confront the Leviathan and fires miniature missiles into the creature. Annoyed, the Leviathan spins round to pursue after Iron Man, shattering the corner of an adjacent building, causing the debris to fall to the street, with a shot of fleeing citizens taking refuge, indicating that they are additionally imperilled by the destruction wrought by the battle. A cut returns to Iron Man, who rhetorically poses the question to J.A.R.V.I.S. what is the next step in dealing with the Leviathan, cueing viewer's interest in relation to what shape that step will take, a question the film will shortly emphatically answer, and then leads the pursuing Leviathan down an avenue. The story then cuts back to Black Widow and Hawkeye engaged in close combat with the Chitauri infantry unit, as Captain America returns to join them in their fight, having completed his rescue mission. As more Chitauri infantry enter into the skirmish, bolts of lightning rain down upon them as Thor descends from the heavens, slaying the last members of the unit, and by joining with the three Avengers, his sub-plotline intersect with theirs, underscoring the theme of unity.

The assembled Avengers then debrief on the status of the battle, with Thor stating he has unfinished business with Loki. Captain America tells him to save it, to instead focus on the immediate task at hand contending with the Chitauri. Just as Captain America is about to give orders, Banner arrives on a beat-up motorcycle, adding to the forces of the Avenger team. Captain America informs Iron Man that Banner has arrived, providing the opportunity to implement his plan to defeat the Leviathan, namely in the shape of something equally as monstrous as the alien creature, in the form of the Hulk. Iron Man tells Captain America to get Banner suited up and that he's bringing 'the party' to them as a means to prepare for their coordinated strategy. The next shot reveals Iron Man speeding around a building with the Leviathan emerging behind him, with its fins again ripping apart a building, and then cuts back to the other Avengers who look on in apprehension.

The film cuts back to Iron Man as he leads the gigantic creature towards them on street level, with the creature leaving a path of destruction. The shot shifts to Banner's narrative perspective as the creature approaches in the distance, as Captain America urges him to get angry, aware of the imminent deadline of creature's arrival. Yet Banner calmly retorts, "That's my secret, Cap. I'm always angry" and transforms at the last moment into the Hulk who slugs the creature with a mighty blow. The Hulk then slows its advance with his enormous strength, causing the creature to flip over, exposing its flesh behind its armour, allowing Iron Man to fire a missile into a soft spot. The Avengers on the street take cover as the Leviathan explodes, with its massive skull crashing to the ground. The film cuts to a shot of the Chitauri screeching in horror in response to the creature's death, and returns back to the Avengers with the Hulk releasing a tremendous roar, and Iron Man joins the group. The camera circles around them, creating a key moment in the sequence, as well as in the film, when all the Avenger sub-plotlines intersect in a show of iconic unity [*Figure 9.5*].

Figure 9.5 Intersecting plotlines and iconic unity in
The Avengers (2012).

The film then shifts to an aerial shot looking down at the creature's exploded carcass, a shot that is revealed to be Loki's optical point-of-view of the scene, who orders the rest of the Chitauri forces to be mobilized. More Leviathans descend from the portal, and as the Avengers gaze upward, Captain America gives a series of directives for each of the Avengers to fulfil to combat the incoming Chitauri wave, orders that entail the disassemblage of the Avengers but in a manner informed by a unity of purpose. The Hulk is given the directive to 'smash', a task he undertakes with relish as he leaps from building to building, pulverizing the Chitauri clinging onto them, and takes out a Chitauri chariot speeding by. Thor is next seen flying to the top of the Chrysler Building, and using his hammer, summons lightning from the sky, which he directs at the portal, taking out several Chitauri chariots along with the Leviathans emerging through the wormhole. The film then briefly returns to the Fury on the Helicarrier, who is notified by Agent Hill that The World Security Council, the international body that oversees S.H.I.E.L.D., wish to communicate with him, a future discussion that is intended to trigger viewer interest as to what the conversation concerns.

The film returns to Hawkeye, now on top of a building, to better fire with his bow at the passing Chitauri chariots and coordinate with Iron Man during his flybys. Noting the long string of Chitauri chariots pursuing Iron Man, Hawkeye informs him that the Chitauri are poor at banking along curves. Iron Man takes note and then flies past Hawkeye, allowing him to fire an arrow at a Chitauri chariot, which breaks it in two, with its parts colliding with the trailing chariots. Iron Man then banks sharply, heeding Hawkeye's instruction, which takes out one of the remaining pursuing crafts, and zooms through a tunnel to bank sharply upon exit taking out the remaining pursuers.

The film then switches to show a Leviathan about to smash into a building and cuts to the interior, revealing its approach through the perspective of alarmed office workers, who then clear out of the path of a rampaging Hulk who leaps out of the window to latch onto the jaw of the Leviathan, in an effort to bring it down. The story returns to Black Widow in mid-fight with a Chitauri invader and uses its energy rifle to dispatch it. She spins around, anticipating another attack to discover Captain America leaping in to join her. With evident weariness, Black Widow asserts that the battle will be meaningless until they are able to close the portal, formulating a plan to get up to the Stark Tower. Running toward Captain America, she leaps onto his shield, who fires her upward so that she can latch onto a passing Chitauri chariot, setting in motion the plotline to close the portal as a means to terminate the invasion.

Precariously clambering aboard the speeding craft, Black Widow slices the chain attaching a Chitauri to the chariot and sends the invader flying off with a kick. She then leaps onto the Chitauri steering the craft, impaling it with two blades as a means to direct the chariot in the desired direction. Another Chitauri chariot commences to pursue Black Widow and fires at her with an energy rifle, initiating a digitally seamed long take, similar to the one discussed earlier manifested in *Avengers: Age of Ultron*, but Iron Man speeds into the frame and blasts the pursuing chariot with his repulsor gauntlets, affecting an embedded rescue, that is vertically combined with a pursuit situation, which itself is vertically combined with the broader fight scenario of the battle.

The long take continues by following the Iron Man's path who flies down toward the street cluttered with Chitauri infantry, knocking out several of them as he rockets past, and then pauses to assist Captain America by directing his repulsors at his shield, the beams of which Captain America redirects toward the surrounding Chitauri. Iron Man then rockets upward alongside a building, taking out several Chitauri, and passes Hawkeye, busy shooting at a Chitauri with his bow. The virtual camera then momentarily stays with Hawkeye, who then fires an arrow at a passing Chitauri chariot, with the camera following the projectile's flight. The arrow pierces the head of the driver of the Chitauri chariot, sending it tumbling into the Leviathan upon which the Hulk is perched, who busies himself by tossing Chitauri to their death.

As the camera reverse tracks, Thor lands on the creature and joins in the battle. The Hulk then hoists up a large piece of Leviathan armour, which he plunges into the creature like a giant blade, which Thor thrusts further downward with an electrified blow from his hammer. The long take ends with that blow, but the action continues as the Leviathan is shown crashing into Grand Central Station. Although the segment ends with the gag of the Hulk sending Thor offscreen through a powerful punch, its function is to underscore team unity, especially through the digitally seamed long take that combines the stylistic logic of interconnected subplots as the narration intersects with each of the Avenger's narrative paths, while at the same time linking narrative spaces through the connecting vision of the virtual camera.

Back at the Stark Tower, Selvig awakes from the concussion received from the Tesseract blast, ridding him from Loki's spell, a component of the plot development of the closure of the portal, initiated by Black Widow. Back on the streets, the National Guard makes their appearance and engage in fire with the Chitauri but plays no further narrative role in defeating the invasion. The film then returns to Captain America in hand-to-hand combat with a Chitauri; Captain America is notified by Hawkeye through radio that the invading forces have rounded up civilians at a bank.

The film then cuts to the bank, in which the civilians have been herded, along with Beth, with the Chitauri aiming their energy rifles at them from an upper balcony. A Chitauri then activates a timed grenade, setting up a deadline as to when it will explode, and presumably armed with the intention of using it against the civilians. Captain America suddenly summersaults through a window in and throws his shield at the Chitauri, knocking the helmet off its head. Two other Chitauri fire at him, but Captain America leaps out of the way and kicks an overturned table at them. He then picks up one of the Chitauri and tosses him to the floor a level below. He is then grabbed by another Chitauri, but again Captain America displays his athleticism by executing a backward flip, spinning the invader around to block the blast from the helmetless Chitauri. The Chitauri then scrambles for the bomb as its beeps become more incessant, and then tosses it at Captain America, who blocks the blast with his shield, sending him flying out the window, landing forcefully onto a car in the street. Barely surviving the blast, Captain America dismounts from the vehicle as the battle begins to take its toll upon him. Police and firefighters are then shown escorting the civilians out, with Beth looking upon him with concern.

The film returns back to Fury and his ongoing conversation with the Security Council, allowing the viewer to discover they are pressing him to launch a nuclear missile at Manhattan, an order

Fury refuses to execute. The story cuts back to Black Widow still aboard the Chitauri craft but now pursued by Loki in his chariot, who fires at her. Black Widow asks Hawkeye for some help, which he obliges by shooting an arrow at Loki, which he manages to grab just before being impaled, but its armed tip explodes, sending Loki tumbling back down onto the Stark Tower, with the sequence offering another embedded rescue. Black Widow then dismounts from her chariot through an impressive summersault that lands her close to the portal device.

The film cuts back to Loki, and while getting his bearings, he is suddenly charged by the Hulk, who slams him inside Stark's penthouse. Getting up, Loki orders him to stop, announcing that he is a god, but before he can finish his speech, the Hulk grabs him by his legs and smashes him repeatedly into the floor like a rag doll. Outside, Black Widow discovers the portal device along with Selvig, who informs her that despite Loki's mind control, he built in a shutdown mechanism involving the scepter, which Loki abandoned on the balcony below when attempting to escape from Thor's ire.

The film then briefly cuts to Thor knocking a couple of Chitauri off of a chariot before it collides with a Leviathan emerging from a collapsing building. Iron Man then speeds by trying to penetrate the Leviathan's with his lasers but with no effect. He then speeds forward to loop back to directly face the Leviathan and speeds into its mouth, firing multiple miniature missiles inside the creature. Through the blast of the explosions, Iron Man is thrown onto the street below, smashing through a phone booth and into a parked taxi. Before he has a chance to recover, several Chitauri approach, blasting their energy rifles at him.

Despite the momentary victory of destroying another Leviathan, the Avengers are shown to become increasingly overwhelmed by the sheer number of the invading Chitauri. The film cuts to Hawkeye, who shoots his last arrow into a Chitauri, and defends himself from another by using his bow as a club, and kicks it off the building. Looking up, Hawkeye sees a swarm of Chitauri chariots descending upon him. Retrieving his last arrow from the impaled Chitauri, Hawkeye makes his escape with a daring leap off the building, and while falling, spins around to fire his last arrow, now equipped with a grappling hook and attached cord, which fastens to the side of the building, from which he uses his downward momentum to swing into a window, painfully landing on the floor amongst the broken glass. The Hulk is next shown, also engulfed by a swarm of Chitauri chariots who fire their energy beams at him relentlessly, presenting the Chitauri gaining ascendency.

The film then cuts back to the Helicarrier from which a pilot is about to take off who is instructed by the Council that Nick Fury has been relieved of his command and is ordered to execute the launch of a nuclear missile at Manhattan. Agent Hill alerts the crew as Fury rushes to the flight deck armed with a rocket-propelled grenade and takes out a jet during take-off. But another jet takes off carrying the nuclear payload, provoking Fury to urgently warn Iron Man of the deployed missile. While under sustained attack from the Chitauri surrounding him, Iron Man orders J.A.R.V.I.S. to direct all powers to his thrusters, allowing him to escape from the Chitauri unit. The film returns to the narrative perspective of the pilot as he triggers the release of the missile, relaying to the Council that impact will be in two minutes and thirty seconds, setting up a deadline for Iron Man to intervene. Captain America and Thor are briefly shown battling the Chitauri on the streets, again emphasizing the successive attrition of the Chitauri onslaughts upon the Avengers.

The story then returns to Black Widow brandishing Loki's scepter as Selvig directs her to penetrate the Tesseract's spherical forcefield. Black Widow announces over the radio that she can close the portal, and Captain America urges her to do so, but Iron Man countermands the order by informing the Avengers of the incoming missile and its impending explosion. The film then cuts to Iron Man's optical point-of-view, revealing the missile in the distance. Iron Man pursues after the missile and clasps onto it to redirect its trajectory toward the Stark Tower, enacting the pursuit-rescue sub-variant. Captain America warns that his mission constitutes a one-way trip, motivating Iron Man to instruct J.A.R.V.I.S. to save some fuel for his return journey. However, J.A.R.V.I.S. prudently asks if he should call Pepper Potts, Stark's assistant and love interest, implying that his return is not guaranteed. Iron Man agrees, but Potts is absorbed with the news coverage on television and does not see the call. Iron Man's rescue effort, therefore, recalls his earlier confrontation with Captain America, who had suggested he did not possess the spirit to be a hero since he was unable to make the "sacrifice play", but precisely demonstrates his heroic status by attempting to save the citizens of Manhattan while risking his own life.

With the nuclear explosion looming, Iron Man speeds towards the Stark Tower, still clenching the missile and as he reaches it, and redirects his trajectory along the y-axis in an upward ascent toward the portal as the Avengers below look on in apprehension. Upon Iron Man's entry through the portal, the crew of the Helicarrier erupts in jubilation. As his armour suit systems begin to fail, Iron Man releases the missile that speeds towards the Chitauri mothership, detonating upon impact and engulfing it in a ball of expanding nuclear heat, which disables the invading forces on Earth as a result, who now lie inert.

Slipping out of consciousness, Iron Man commences his return journey through an extended freefall. As the blast of the nuclear explosion nears the portal, Captain America orders Black Widow to close the portal, setting up another deadline that Iron Man must meet. Black Widow thrusts the scepter into the Tesseract device, terminating its beam and causing the portal to shrink. Iron Man falls through it just before it closes but still continues his uncontrolled freefall. As Thor prepares to fly up, the Hulk makes a tremendous leap, catching Iron Man in his descent, and grasps the side of a building in an effort to slow them down. Cradling Iron Man in his arms, the Hulk lets go of the building to crash onto a car and slide through the rubble, taking the brunt of the impact. His efforts not only constitute an embedded rescue but also reflect his change into a full-blown team member, from one who once threatened other Avengers to one who saves their lives.

After a moment of suspense in which it is uncertain if Iron Man survived the ordeal, the Hulk lets loose an enormous roar that awakens him. Coming to, Iron Man is informed that the Avengers won the battle, and before celebrating their victory by collectively going to a shawarma joint, the Avengers assemble one last time to apprehend Loki, ending the action sequence with the capture scenario in victorious unity [*Figure* 9.6].

Figure 9.6 Intersecting plotlines and victorious unity in *The Avengers* (2012).

Through its duration, multiple intersecting subplots, and linked narrative spaces, the Battle of New York sequence provides insights into how extended action sequences are narratively constructed. Given its extended duration, it is not surprising that the sequence features six major plot points that segment it into shorter sections, making it easier for the viewer to parse. The six major plot points are: the firing up of the Tesseract that opens the portal; the arrival of the first Leviathan; the defeat of the first Leviathan; Loki initiating the second wave of the invasion; the releasing of the nuclear missile by the pilot; the explosion of the missile; and the closure of the portal. Each of these plot turns set forth a series of causal events that significantly shape the narrative course of the sequence.

The firing up of the Tesseract causes the portal to open, which in turn facilitates the Chitauri invasion. The arrival of the first Leviathan changes the complexion of the battle, with its subsequent defeat at the hands of the Avengers, not only a moment of ascendancy but the catalyst that motivates Loki to initiate the second wave of attack. The firing of the nuclear missile is a major turning point in the sequence as well in that its launch brings about the end of the sequence through its explosion that disables the Chitauri invaders and causes their defeat. The closure of the portal shuts the opening between the two intergalactic narrative spaces that facilitated the invasion and marks the return to some level of time-space normality, with Iron Man's rescue and Loki's capture acting as action denouements to the preceding battle sequence as a whole.

These plot points also affect narrative unity through the way they mirror each other. While the opening and the closing of the portal do not demarcate the start and end of the extended action sequence, they offer bookends that contain its essential element – the battle. The arrival of the first Leviathan and its eventual defeat also mirror each other in ways that segment that particular plot development through its figurative 'birth' from the portal to its ultimate death. The shots of the second wave of the Chitauri invasion are answered by the shots of them crashing to the ground and lying inert, a conclusion to that plotline that dovetails into the storyline of the nuclear missile where its explosion brings to conclusion both narrative developments. Through such mirroring devices, the sequence exhibits a broader narrative unity despite its multi-character and multi-plot complexity.

From an action scenario perspective, the sequence is an action combination superstructure composed of a range of action forms that combine both vertically and horizontally. At the global level of the sequence, its overarching structure is itself a combination of the fight scenario, drawing upon the conventions of the battle and the military unit manifested in war films, along with the western rescue variant, as detailed in Chapter 1. The sequence can be rightfully viewed as an elaboration upon the rescue variant found in the classical western, in which the Avengers function in the role of rescuers, with the New York citizens functioning in the role of captives who do not possess the agency to resist the Chitauri invasion and are as a result at their mercy. As heroes, the Avengers possess the exceptional abilities to defeat the villains in battle, with the aim of saving the city and keeping its citizens safe, all the while risking their lives in the process, thereby vindicating their hero status. The Battle of New York, as an instance of the fight scenario, therefore represents an embedded plot function that manifests itself with a broader rescue project.

At the local level, the sequence consists of a compendium of action scenarios, featuring all of the major action scenarios covered in this book, with the exception of the heist scenario. The rescue scenario, for instance, not only structures the overall sequence but also underscores the Avengers hero function in the multiple scenes where they are actively rescuing citizens from the Chitauri attack. Iron Man's 'sacrifice play' additionally conveys thematic resonance on what constitutes the heroic, as does the Hulk's rescue of Iron Man by additionally signalling team unity. The escape scenario principally features in the sequence in the form of the fleeing variant as citizens take shelter from the destruction ensuing after waves of attack, in ways that are reminiscent of the scenes of fleeing and destruction that typify the disaster film. Loki's escape from Thor's rage, however, conveys a different symbolic weight, one that is cowardly and designed to fit in with his wider set of disreputable character attributes. The capture scenario is manifested twice in the sequence, briefly in the scene when the Chitauri invaders round up the citizens at a bank, requiring Captain America's rescue efforts, but more strikingly reappears as the closing image of the sequence when the Avengers apprehend Loki.

The fight scenario is amongst the most pervasive action forms in the sequence, as one would expect from a depiction of a large-scale battle. Fights manifest themselves at the local level as ongoing skirmishes between the Avengers and the Chitauri, as well as in the form of the unidirectional variant when the Chitauri attack citizens. Loki, as the principal antagonist, is also the site of a number of fight situations involving all of the Avengers, most notably with Thor, in which their protracted tussle highlights their fraternal divide. Loki also behaves as an aggressor when he directs unidirectional violence at Tony Stark during their confrontation at the Stark Tower penthouse, blasts the quinjet with his scepter, and fires at Black Widow while pursuing after her in a Chitauri chariot. Loki is also the recipient of unidirectional attacks when Hawkeye fires an explosive tipped arrow at him and is slammed repeatedly on the ground by the Hulk. The sequence also abounds with the destruction variant, be it the destruction of property that the Chitauri wage against the city, the explosions of the Chitauri chariot when blasted out of the sky by the Avengers or blow up when careening into a building. The obliteration of the Chitauri mothership through the detonation of the nuclear missile represents the culmination of this fight variant.

The pursuit scenario also features in the sequence, namely in the form of Chitauri chariots chasing after Iron Man or pursuing Black Widow when she commandeers a Chitauri chariot. Such instances of speed are not restricted to pursuits that appear in the sequence but also are manifested with respect to the modes of locomotion of characters. The speed scenario is particularly recurrent with respect to Iron Man, who is shown to rocket through the air along the y and x-axes in most of the scenes in which he is depicted. The Chitauri chariots as a mode of locomotion are also characterized by their speed, be they involved in pursuits or depicted simply zipping past. The quinjet is also presented flying at speed, as is the F-35 jet that transports the nuclear payload, with the shot of the firing of the missile presenting an instance of the relativity of speed as it zooms quickly beyond the range of the jet.

Speed is also expressed in manifestations of the falling variant, most evident when Tony Stark plummets off of the Stark Tower and when Iron Man freefalls through the portal. By making use of a full range of action scenarios, the sequence is able to maintain interest by diversifying the forms of action that appear, either by manifesting themselves in pure form or by appearing in combination with other action forms. In addition, such evolving situations of peril modulate viewer interest and suspense over the sequence's duration, creating troughs and peaks of dramatic engagement rather than a static flow. The Battle for New York is not only an exemplar of the extended action sequence by exhibiting the five features of action complexity but also a model of action scenario combination.

Glossary

Aftermath shot: A shot, or set of shots, which depict the consequences of acts of violence, and destruction, which usually comes at the end of a scene or sequence as a form of punctuation that marks closure.

Agency: The ability of a character to exhibit free will, and the possession of skills and knowledge to pursue their immediate and long-term goals in an action context, be it to defend themselves from attack or extricate themselves from danger.

Antagonist: One of the two main combatants in the fight scenario who engages in physical conflict with the **protagonist**. The protagonist-antagonist structure of the action scene or sequence often but not on all occasions replicates the broader story's protagonist-antagonist structure.

Ascendency: An aspect of the dramatic structure of an action scenario through which one of the participants, or set of participants, gains an advantage over their adversary or adversaries in relation to their opposed goals.

Captive: A character in the rescue scenario who is typically unable to extricate themselves out of a constraining or dangerous situation by recourse to their own abilities.

Captor: A character in the rescue and escape scenarios whose chief narrative functions are to keep the **captive** confined, resist rescue attempts, and prevent the **escapee** from escaping. In some cases, the captor can be nature itself.

Capturer: A character in the capture and heist scenarios whose primary narrative function is to apprehend the target, often by creating a trapping situation.

Contingent combinations: Forms of action scenario combination in which one scenario does not naturally arise from another scenario.

Deadline: A narrative strategy to generate suspense in which characters must undertake an endeavour within a prescribed time that is either narratively implicit or explicit. It is often associated with last-minute rescues.

Dramatic structure: The overall organization of the events in an action scenario, in which a participant, or set of participants, compete with their adversary, or adversaries, in a conflict that eventually reaches a decisive turning point, the threshold moment, where one participant usually emerges victorious over the other. In instances of the speed scenario that do not possess a dyadic character pairing, dramatic structure arises from the **obstacles** a **speeder** faces while undertaking a mission.

Emergent combinations: Forms of action scenario combination in which one scenario naturally arises from another scenario.

Escapee: A character in the escape scenario who possesses the agency to extricate themselves out of a constraining or dangerous situation by recourse to their own abilities, and in some cases, with the assistance of helpers.

Event schema: The knowledge a viewer or a filmmaker possesses that describes the sequence of events of a particular action scenario, setting up expectations on how the scenario will unfold.

Exemplar: A specific and memorable instance of an action scenario, or action scenario combination, manifested in a film that is stored in the long-term memory of a viewer or a filmmaker.

Folk psychology: A model of the human mind that viewers possess through which characters in films are understood to possess mental states that include beliefs, intentions, goals, thoughts and emotions, and that such mental states are understood to motivate a character's actions.

Guard: A character in the heist scenario whose chief narrative function is to prevent the theft of objects of value located in a secured space and often acts as an obstacle to the **thief**.

Horizontal combination: A type of action scenario combination in which different action forms link up sequentially as a sequence that unfolds over time.

Mode of locomotion: The means of locomotion by which a character in an action sequence moves, typically at speed.

Mode of pursuit: The composition of a pursuit sequence with respect to the modes of locomotion that it exhibits.

Moral valence: The moral framework that governs a particular instance of an action scenario that is determined by the morality of character actions within the scenario as well as shaped by the morality of character actions expressed within a film's broader story.

Obstacle: A character or inanimate object that functions to impede another character's progress in a particular instance of an action scenario and contributes to its dramatic structure.

Obstructor: A character in the obstacle speed variant who narratively functions as an obstacle in the path of a speeding projectile or set of projectiles.

Parallel editing: An editing technique by which two or more lines of concurrent action occurring in different locations are intercut with each other.

Primary causality: The causal means propelling the mode of locomotion by which the **speeder** traverses an A to B trajectory.

Protagonist: One of the two main combatants in the fight scenario who engages in physical conflict with the **antagonist**. The protagonist-antagonist structure of the action scene or sequence often but not on all occasions replicates the broader story's protagonist-antagonist structure.

Prototype: A member of an action scenario category that is more recurrent in films and more representative of that category by possessing a greater number of its defining features than other members in that category.

Pursuee: A character in the pursuit scenario whose narrative function is to escape at speed from a scene and elude capture or attack from the **pursuer**.

Pursuer: A character in the pursuit scenario whose narrative function is to intercept the **pursuee** with the ultimate aim to either capture or kill them.

Rescuer: A character in the rescue scenario who attempts to rescue the **captive** from a constraining or dangerous situation and encounters physical risks in the process.

Risk: The threat of physical harm or death that a character experiences directly or is an inherent potential in a specific instance of an action scenario.

Secondary causality: The causal effects of character actions manifested at the event level of a particular instance of the speed scenario, which may or may not be imbricated in the **primary causality** of a **mode of locomotion**.

Speeder: A character in the speed scenario who speeds by recourse to their own bodily means, or through the aid of any other mode of locomotion, along an A to B trajectory.

Stunt: The undertaking of an action that is perceived to involve physical risk for both the character and the actor, or the stunt double, performing the action.

Target: A character in the capture scenario whose primary narrative functions are to resist and elude the **capturer** or a team of capturers.

Thief: A character in the heist scenario whose narrative function is to attempt to steal objects of value in a secured location and avoid detection.

Typicality gradient: A spectrum that defines an action form category in which instances are ranked in relation to the greatest degree of typicality to the least degree of typicality.

Typicality perception: The viewer's ability to perceive accordances between a specific narrative situation with the features of a prototype of an action scenario.

Vertical combination: A type of action scenario combination in which different action forms combine concurrently.

Bibliography

Introduction

Bateson, Gregory. 1972. *Steps to an Ecology of Mind: Collected Essays in Anthropology, Psychiatry, Evolution, and Epistemology*. New York: Ballantine Books.

Bordwell, David and Kristin Thompson. 2003. *Film Art: An Introduction*. New York: McGraw-Hill.

Box Office Mojo. "Top Lifetime Grosses". https://www.boxofficemojo.com/chart/ww_top_lifetime_gross/?area=XWW&ref_=bo_cso_ac, last accessed 25/03/2021.

Buckland, Warren. 1998. "A Close Encounter with *Raiders of the Lost Ark*: Notes on Narrative Aspects of the New Hollywood Blockbuster" in Steve Neale and Murray Smith (eds.) *Contemporary Hollywood Cinema*. London: Routledge. pp. 166-177.

Friedkin, William. 1977. "Anatomy of a Chase" in Richard Koszarski (ed.) *Hollywood Directors* 1941-1976. New York: Oxford University Press. pp. 391-403.

Gunning, Tom. 1990. "The Cinema of Attractions: Early Film, Its Spectator and the Avant-Garde", *Wide Angle*. 8 (3/4). pp. 63-70.

Hibberd, James. 2019. "Game of Thrones director discusses the super-sized Battle of Winterfell", *Entertainment Weekly*. April 26th. https://ew.com/tv/2019/04/26/game-of-thrones-director-battle-of-winterfell/

Higgins, Scott. 2008. "Suspenseful Situations: Melodramatic Narrative and the Contemporary Action Film", *Cinema Journal*. 47 (2). pp. 74-96.

Jacobs, Lea and Ben Brewster. (1997). *Theatre to Cinema: Stage Pictorialism and the Early Feature Film*. Oxford: Oxford University Press.

Jeffords, Susan. 1994. *Hard Bodies: Hollywood Masculinity in the Reagan Era*. New Brunswick, NJ: Rutgers University Press.

King, Geoff. 2002. *New Hollywood Cinema: An Introduction*. London: I.B. Tauris.

Kendrick, James. 2019. "A Genre of Its Own: From Westerns, to Vigilantes, to Pure Action" in James Kendrick (ed.) *A Companion to the Action Film*. Chichester: Wiley Blackwell. pp. 35-54.

Lichtenfeld, Eric. 2007. *Action Speaks Louder: Violence, Spectacle, and the American Action Movie*. Revised and Expanded Edition. Middletown, CT: Wesleyan University Press.

Livingston, Paisley. 2012. "Spectatorship and Risk" in Mette Hjort (ed.) *Film and Risk*. Detroit: Wayne State University Press. pp. 73-95.

Murphy, Gregory L. 2016. "Is there an Exemplar Theory of Concepts?", *Psychonomic Bulletin & Review*. 23 (4). pp. 1035–1042.

Neale, Steve. 2000. *Genre and Hollywood*. London: Routledge.

Polti, Georges. 1916. *The Thirty-Six Dramatic Situations*. Franklin, Ohio: James Knapp Reeve. [First publish in French in 1895].

Purse, Lisa. 2011. *Contemporary Action Cinema*. Edinburgh: Edinburgh University Press.

Schubart, Rikke. 2019. "'I am Become Death': Managing Massacres and Constructing the Female Teen Leader in The 100" in James Kendrick (ed.) *A Companion to the Action Film*. Chichester: Wiley Blackwell. pp. 417-438.

Smith, Murray. 1998. "Theses on the Philosophy of Hollywood History" in Steve Neale and Murray Smith (eds.) *Contemporary Hollywood Cinema*. London: Routledge. pp. 3-20.

Romao, Tico. 2003. "Engines of Transformation: An Analytical History of the 1970s Car Chase Cycle", *New Review of Film and Television Studies*. 1 (1). November. pp. 31-54.

Romao, Tico. 2004. "Guns and Gas: Investigating the 1970s Car Chase Film" in Yvonne Tasker (ed.) *Action and Adventure Cinema*. London: Routledge. pp. 130-152.

Rosch, Eleanor. 1973. "Natural categories", *Cognitive Psychology*. 4 (3). pp. 328–350.

Tasker, Yvonne. 1993. *Spectacular Bodies: Gender, Genre and the Action cinema*. London: Routledge.

Tasker, Yvonne. 2015. T*he Hollywood Action and Adventure Film*. Oxford: Wiley Blackwell.

Taves, Brian. 1993. *The Romance of Adventure: The Genre of Historical Adventure Movies*. Jackson: University Press of Mississippi.

Chapter 1

Bordwell, David. 1985. "Time in the Classical Film" in David Bordwell, Janet Staiger and Kristin Thompson. *The Classical Hollywood Cinema: Film Style & Mode of Production to 1960*. London: Routledge. pp. 42-49.

Bordwell, David. 2007. "Anatomy of the Action Picture", *Observations on Film Art*. http://www.davidbordwell.net/essays/anatomy.php, last accessed 26/03/2021.

Carroll, Noël Carroll. 1996. "Towards a Theory of Film Suspense" in *Theorizing the Moving Image*. Cambridge: Cambridge University Press. pp. 94-117.

Dixon Jr., Thomas. 1905. *The Clansman: A Historical Romance of the Ku Klux Klan*. New York: Doubleday.

Franklin, John Hope. 1979. "Birth of a Nation: Propaganda as History", *The Massachusetts Review*. 20 (3). Autumn. pp. 417-434.

Grey, Frank. 2019. *The Brighton School and the Birth of British Film*. London: Palgrave Macmillan.

Gunning, Tom. 1991. *D. W. Griffith and the Origins of American Film Narrative: The Early Years at Biograph*. Urbana: University of Illinois Press.

Kinney, Alison. 2016. "How the Klan Got Its Hood", *The New Republic*. 8th January. https://newrepublic.com/article/127242/klan-got-hood, last accessed 25/03/2021.

Musser, Charles. 1991. *Before the Nickelodeon: Edwin S. Porter and the Edison Manufacturing Company*. Berkeley: University of California Press.

O'Connor, Tom. 2018. 'Stan Lee Quotes: Legendary Comic Book Creator Dies at 95', *Newsweek*. 12th November. https://www.newsweek.com/stan-lee-quotes-legendary-comic-book-creator-dies-1212430, last accessed 25/03/2021.

Stokes, Melvin. 2007. *D.W. Griffith's The Birth of a Nation: A History of "The Most Controversial Motion Picture of All Time"*. Oxford: Oxford University Press.

Wright, Will. 1975. *Sixguns and Society: A Structural Study of the Western*. Berkeley: University of California Press.

Chapter 2

Keane, Stephen. 2001. *Disaster Movies: The Cinema of Catastrophe*. New York: Columbia University Press.

Lichtenfeld, Eric. 2007. *Action Speaks Louder: Violence, Spectacle, and the American Action Movie*. Revised and Expanded Edition. Middletown, CT: Wesleyan University Press.

Chapter 3

Anderson, Michael J. "Hatari! and the Hollywood Safari Picture", *Senses of Cinema*. September, 52. http://sensesofcinema.com/2009/feature-articles/hatari-and-the-hollywood-safari-picture/#44, last accessed 25/03/2021.

Friedman, Lester D. 2000. *Bonnie and Clyde*. London: British Film Institute.

Player, Ian. 1967. "Translocation of White Rhinoceros in South Africa", *Oryx*. 9 (2). pp. 137-150.

Smith, Murray. 1995. *Engaging characters: Fiction, emotion, and the cinema*. Oxford: Oxford University Press.

Smith, Steven. 1997. "In 'The Lost World', Bits of Old Movies", *Los Angeles Times*. May 29th. https://www.latimes.com/archives/la-xpm-1997-05-29-ca-63567-story.html, last accessed 25/03/2021.

Thompson, Kristin. 1999. *Storytelling in the New Hollywood: Understanding classical narrative technique*. Cambridge, Massachusetts: Harvard University Press.

Wollen, Peter. 1972. *Signs and meaning in the cinema*. Bloomington: Indiana University Press.

Chapter 4

Bordwell, David. 2017. "One Last Big Job: How Heist Movies Tell Their Stories", *Observations on Film Art*. 12th October. http://www.davidbordwell.net/blog/2017/10/12/one-last-big-job-how-heist-movies-tell-their-stories/, last accessed 19/06/2021.

Fink, Nikki. 2011. "'Fast Five' Will Transition Franchise from Street Racing to Future Full of Heist Action", *Deadline*. 25th April. https://deadline.com/2011/04/fast-five-will-transition-franchise-from-street-racing-to-heist-action-125552/, last accessed 25/03/2021.

Lee, Daryl. 2014. *The Heist Film: Stealing with Style*. New York: Columbia University Press.

Chapter 5

Bordwell, David. 2001. "Aesthetics in Action: Kungfu, Gunplay, and Cinematic Expressivity" in Esther C. M. Yau (ed.) *At Full Speed: Hong Kong Cinema in a Borderless World*. Minneapolis: University of Minnesota Press. pp. 73-93.

Buscombe, Edward (ed). 1988. *The BFI Companion to the Western*. London: British Film Institute.

Cooper, Pat and Ken Dancyger. 2005. *Writing the Short Film*. Burlington: Focal Press.

Desser, David. 2000. "The Martial Arts Film in the 1990s" in Wheeler Winston Dixon (ed.) *Film Genre 2000: New Critical Essays*. Albany: SUNY Press.

Duncan, Stephan V. 2006. *A Guide to Screenwriting Success: Writing for Film and Television*. Oxford: Rowman and Littlefield Publishers.

Gallagher, Mark. 2019. "Around the World in Action" in James Kendrick (ed.) *A Companion to the Action Film*. Chichester: Wiley Blackwell. pp. 74-77.

Tasker, Yvonne. 2015. *The Hollywood Action and Adventure Film*. Oxford: Wiley Blackwell.

Taves, Brian. 1993. *The Romance of Adventure: The Genre of Historical Adventure Movies*. Jackson: University Press of Mississippi.

Teo, Stephen. 2016. *Chinese Martial Arts Cinema: The Wuxia Tradition*. 2nd Edition. Edinburgh: Edinburgh University Press.

Chapter 6

Abrams, Bryan. 2015. "Here's How They Built the Beastly Machines for *Mad Max: Fury Road*", *Motion Picture Association*. 14th May. https://www.motionpictures.org/2015/05/heres-how-they-built-the-beastly-machines-for-mad-max-fury-road/, last accessed 25/03/2021.

Barrett, Kyle. 2017. "Mad Max: Fury Road: Challenging narrative and gender representation in the action genre", *Media Education Journal*. 3 (17-18). Winter. pp. 3-6.

Buscombe, Edward. 1992. *Stagecoach*. London: British Film Institute.

Du Plooy, Belinda. 2019. "'Hope is a mistake, if you can't fix what's broken you go insane': a reading of gender, (s)heroism and redemption in *Mad Max: Fury Road*", *Journal of Gender Studies*. 28 (4). pp. 414-434.

Canutt, Yakima and Oliver Drake. 1979. *Stunt Man: The Autobiography of Yakima Canutt with Oliver Drake*. New York: Walker and Company.

Leitch, Thomas. 2002. *Crime Films*. Cambridge: Cambridge University Press.

Chapter 7

Anderson, Aaron. 1998. "Kinesthesia in martial arts films: Action in motion", *Jump Cut*. 24. December. pp. 1-11.

Carroll, Noël. 1996. "Toward a Theory of Film Suspense" in *Theorizing the Moving Image*. Cambridge: Cambridge University Press. pp. 100-109.

Doherty, Thomas. 1988. *Teenagers and Teenpics: The Juvenilization of American Movies in the 1950s*. Boston: Unwin Hyman.

Kendrick, James. 2019. "A Genre of Its Own: From Westerns, to Vigilantes, to Pure Action" in James Kendrick (ed.) *A Companion to the Action Film*. Chichester: Wiley Blackwell. pp. 35-54.

Kitses, Jim. 1969. *Horizons west; Anthony Man, Budd Boetticher, Sam Peckinpah: Studies of Authorship within the Western*. London: Thames and Hudson.

Lichtenfeld, Eric. 2007. *Action Speaks Louder: Violence, Spectacle, and the American Action Movie*. Revised and Expanded Edition. Middletown, CT: Wesleyan University Press.

Romao, Tico. 2004. "Guns and Gas: Investigating the 1970s Car Chase Film" in Yvonne Tasker (ed.) *Action and Adventure Cinema*. London: Routledge. pp. 130-152.

Schivelbusch, Wolfgang. 1986. *The Railway Journey: The Industrialization of Time and Space in the Nineteenth Century*. Oakland: University of California Press.

Stanfield, Peter. 2013. "Intent to speed: cyclical production, topicality, and the 1950s hot rod movie", *New Review of Film and Television Studies*. 11 (1). pp. 34-55.

Tasker, Yvonne. 2015. *The Hollywood Action and Adventure Film*. Oxford: Wiley Blackwell.

Whissel, Kristen. 2014. *Spectacular Digital Effects: CGI and Contemporary Cinema*. Durham: Duke University Press.

Chapter 8

Azcona, María del Mar. 2010. *The Multi-Protagonist Film*. Oxford: Wiley-Blackwell.

Coleman, David, Tico Romao, Cedric Villamin, Scott Sinnett, Tania Jakobsen, and Alan Kingstone. 2013. "Finding Meaning in All the Right Places: A Novel Measurement of Dramatic Structure in Film and Television Narratives", *Projections*. 7 (2). pp. 92–110.

Monaco, Paul. 2001. *The Sixties: 1960-1969*. Berkeley: University of California Press.

Purse, Lisa. 2015. "Rotational Aesthetics: Michael Bay and Contemporary Cinema's Machine Movement", *Senses of Cinema*. 75. June.

Strong, Jeremy. 2006. "The team film genre", *Kinema*. Fall. pp. 1-9.

Tan, Ed S. 1996. *Emotion and the Structure of Narrative Film: Film as Emotion Machine*. Mahwah, New Jersey: Lawrence Erlbaum Associates.

Thompson, Kristin. 1999. *Storytelling in the New Hollywood: Understanding Classical Narrative Technique*. Harvard: Harvard University Press.

Whissel, Kristen. 2014. *Spectacular Digital Effects: CGI and Contemporary Cinema*. Durham: Duke University Press.

Index

Acknowledgments

Much of the writing of this book coincided with the outbreak of the COVID-19 pandemic. Going to the cinema, one of my favourite social activities, was now off-limits as cinemas shut down. As a result, film viewing, the central basis for this book's research, was no longer social but instead was done in isolation via streaming services or dvd/blu-rays.

My family came to the rescue and made movie nights social and fun again while accommodating my desire for action. My partner and kids dedicated themselves to watching the entire *Fast and Furious* series, the *Mission: Impossible* franchise, and many others. They offered insight and acted as sounding boards as I mused about the films afterwards. Some of these films excelled in entertainment and suspense, while others were eye-roll-inducing duds. Nevertheless, I am grateful to them for accommodating my film choices and enduring the lesser films while I mentally noted their action scenarios.

I would especially like to thank Amir Said, my publisher, for the opportunity to realize this book. He immediately understood the value of the work, its contribution to film studies, and, more specifically, the study of action in movies. He also provided invaluable feedback on its shape and form and helped steer a course that was both academically rigorous and equally of interest to all the film connoisseurs who love a well-staged action sequence, as I do.

About the Author

Tico Romao is an Assistant Lecturer for the Department of English and Film Studies at the University of Alberta. He has a Ph.D. from the University of East Anglia, with expertise in action cinema. He has authored several publications and his research interests include cognitive film theory, social cognition, and title sequences.

Milton Keynes UK
Ingram Content Group UK Ltd.
UKHW020706050923
428087UK00018B/1582